From SOE Hero to
Dressing the Queen

From SOE Hero to Dressing the Queen

The Amazing Life of Sir Hardy Amies

Lynda Rowland

Pen & Sword
MILITARY
AN IMPRINT OF PEN & SWORD BOOKS LTD.
YORKSHIRE – PHILADELPHIA

First published in Great Britain in 2023 by
Pen and Sword Transport
An imprint of
Pen & Sword Books Ltd.
Yorkshire - Philadelphia

ISBN 9781399049948

Typeset in INDIA by IMPEC eSolutions
Printed and bound in England by CPI Group (UK) Ltd, Croydon CR0 4YY.

Pen & Sword Books Ltd incorporates the imprints of Pen & Sword Books
Archaeology, Atlas, Aviation, Battleground, Discovery, Family History, History,
Maritime, Military, Naval, Politics, Railways, Select, Transport, True Crime,
Fiction, Frontline Books, Leo Cooper, Praetorian Press, Seaforth Publishing,
Wharncliffe and White Owl.

For a complete list of Pen & Sword titles please contact

PEN & SWORD BOOKS LIMITED
47 Church Street, Barnsley, South Yorkshire, S70 2AS, England
E-mail: enquiries@pen-and-sword.co.uk
Website: www.pen-and-sword.co.uk

or

PEN AND SWORD BOOKS
1950 Lawrence Rd, Havertown, PA 19083, USA
E-mail: Uspen-and-sword@casematepublishers.com
Website: www.penandswordbooks.com

For my husband John, who is my rock, and my children Bruce and Natalie who inspire me every day.

Contents

Disclaimer

Acknowledgements

I would like to thank everyone who has helped me bring this book to publication.

Firstly, to all those who have kindly given interviews, photographs and memories, in particular, David Freeman, whose generosity, patience, and hospitality have been invaluable. Many thanks also to Mr Roy Allen for his memories and insight into life in the House of Hardy Amies. In addition, Jon Moore, Bill Howat, Derek Granger, Marilyn Jones, Sir Roy Strong, Richard Martin, Chris Stratmann, Nicholas Worth, Susanne Smart, Jenny Palmer, Jonathan Loe of J P Hackett, Savile Row, and Denise Kemp of St Matthew's, Langford. I would also like to mention Chris McClements and Gareth Williams for their technical and creative input, as well as John Bedford and Carol McKendrick for all their kind advice. I hope I have not forgotten anyone!

Thanks also to The National Archives, in particular Marcus Wheatley, for his friendship and professional help, Nick Mays, News UK Archives, The Imperial War Museum, The Fashion Museum in Bath, Cheltenham Libraries, and *The Lady* magazine. I am also very grateful to my Commissioning Editors, Jon Wright and Charlotte Mitchell at Pen and Sword Books, as well as Harriet Fielding and Olivia Camozzi.

Finally, to my friends and family, especially John for his constant support, patience, and technical assistance, without which I would not have got this far, and also to Bruce for his idea and Natalie for her creative eye.

Foreword

Sir Edwin Hardy Amies was one of the leading English fashion designers of the twentieth century. His fame centred not just on his creative skills but also on his relationship with Britain's post-war high society. The enthusiasm of Princess Elizabeth for the outfits he made for her tour of Canada in 1950 led to the award of the Royal Warrant five years later. All this is fascinating enough, but there is a great deal more to say about Hardy Amies. The way in which he balanced stylish theatricality with acute skills in sales promotion is particularly notable. He was also a natural linguist, picking up German, and possibly also German men, in the late 1920s. Yet his war service, in which he proved himself through his courage as a member of the Special Operations Executive challenged stereotypes that depicted homosexuals as effete and potentially treacherous. It was fully merited that he was awarded the *Ordre de la Couronne* for his services to Belgium. He brought his customary attention to detail to the service of his country, discovering that subtle alterations might be made to utilitarian British uniforms in order to render them more becoming and less uncomfortable. He is described in this book, most fittingly, as having fought the war with 'pride and panache'.

Seen from a contemporary perspective he lacked training in design and business. As was often the case in those times success was a matter of upbringing, connections and luck. The role of his mother, who worked both before and during her marriage as a respected 'vendeuse' (saleswoman) at a highly-regarded court dressmaker, was crucial. The wife of her former employer was, quite by chance, the recipient of a letter passed on by a friend of Hardy Amies in which he had described a particularly lovely gown. That passing impression, made at Christmas party in the fateful year of 1933, led to an invitation to try his hand as a designer for the 'Lachasse' brand. He fit right in, although his strongest work was not to be realised until after the war.

The grand era of Hardy Amies, like that of Norman Hartnell and Edward Molyneux, was the mid-twentieth century. This was a period when the glamour of the monarchy was widely accepted as a national exception in a nation otherwise wedded to austerity and socialist planning. It was still the age of the 'season' and of steady demand on the part of mothers for suitable outfits for themselves and their daughters to wear at court. Amies brought a touch of masculine dandyism to his designs for women, in so far as he focussed on refinement, precision in detail and the structure of his garments. He realised that this venerable tradition was fading through the 1960s and was able, at least to some extent, to reinvent his image for the new populist age. He was responsible, for example, for the pop modernism of the costumes used in Stanley Kubrick's film *2001: A Space Odyssey* (1968).

Hardy Amies continued his work interests until almost the very end of his life. His sexuality, once the subject of great discretion, became more widely known as social mores relaxed. He was therefore, in life and legacy, very much a period piece in the positive sense that he was an exemplary product of his times. He was, let us not forget it, a highly successful and creative man despite prevailing snobbery and homophobia. The full details of his life deserve to be better known and appreciated. This book will help to ensure that that happens.

Dominic Janes
Professor of Modern History
Faculty of Humanities and Social Sciences
Keele University, UK.

Preface

When I set out to write this book Sir Hardy Amies was simply a name I had heard of in connection with the queen's clothing and perhaps, menswear. As a person with a good deal of interest in both the royal family and the world of fashion, I was aware of him but had never really learned a lot about him. In fact, I primarily thought of Norman Hartnell as the queen's couturier, as he had designed both Her Majesty's wedding and coronation dresses. Also, since I am more interested in womenswear than menswear, Hardy Amies was not at the top of my list of revered fashion designers, despite my great interest in vintage clothing.

It was only when I discovered that Hardy had had a notable wartime career in the intriguing undercover world of intelligence, while simultaneously establishing himself in women's fashion during the Golden Age of Couture, that I decided here was a man whose story did not seem hitherto, to have been given the attention it deserved.

Researching his life has made me appreciate him as an immense talent, a strong, highly intelligent, engaging, and curious character, a man very much of his time, and a popular and treasured friend to people of all ages, education, and character, and from all strata of society.

He had something of a reputation as acerbic and snobbish, but that was a feature that most of his friends regarded as just part of the persona of *Hardy Amies*, which was of course the name of both the man and the business. He created a character that he believed embodied the *Living Label*. It would show itself in brief, dramatic vignettes, staged for effect, rather than manifesting itself as an intrinsic part of his personality.

The juxtaposition of his wartime service with the establishment of his glittering couture career makes for a fascinating story. He was a fully committed and enthusiastic military man, living almost covertly as a homosexual while in the army. Indeed, this is what he would have had to do in his ordinary, everyday life too. Like all gay men in the early part of the twentieth century, he would have lived a double life up to, and even probably after, the decriminalisation of homosexuality in 1967, despite all the modernisation and advancement which was going on in other sectors of society around them.

Hardy's was a joyous life and he seems to have welcomed new experiences throughout his 93 years. He leaves a legacy which shines a light on many changes and developments in both the world of business and society in general. Having had a life almost as long as that of our late queen, his wealth of experience and embrace of progress and people represented a comprehensive vision of the twentieth century and all of its various phases.

Her Majesty the Queen's death as I was just completing this book, brought into focus many of the qualities, accomplishments, and ethics which she embodied, and which to some of us seem to be disappearing from today's society. She was the epitome of grace, diligence, duty, and service, qualities held in high regard, and indeed also, for all his little peculiarities, largely embodied by Sir Hardy Amies.

Introduction

The darkness that settles over a quiet Oxfordshire village in the English countryside has a depth and intensity quite different from night-time in a city. To those who had ever experienced such a thing, it would be comparable to a Second World War blackout. The pretty honey-coloured Cotswold stone buildings seem to slumber almost invisibly among the trees, and the tower of the beautiful eleventh-century church of St Matthew watches over the community as it sleeps.

Behind the heavy brocade curtains of a large upstairs window in the picturesque Old School House in Langford, an elderly man lies awake with, coincidentally, thoughts of the early 1940s running through his mind like scenes from a wartime movie. These visions would often be interspersed with feelings of remorse and regret. Recollections of his role in the Second World War would occasionally preoccupy the gentleman as he made his way so successfully through his life afterwards, eventually reaching the grand age of 93, with many accomplishments to his name.

The only clue to the identity of the restless elderly man was the pair of exquisitely tailored pyjamas he wore to sleep in. Dressing appropriately at all times was an overriding principle throughout his life and he was not about to drop his standards, even in private and during the twilight of his years, for the gentleman tossing and turning in his bed there that night was Sir Hardy Amies. Sir Hardy had risen to become one of the most internationally famous British couturiers of the Golden Age of Glamour, which shone so brightly in the 1950s.

However, being officially recognised for his military service never quite outweighed his unjustified feelings of inadequacy and ineptitude, most specifically over his part in sending other young men – and perhaps some women – into the mouth of danger, and sometimes to their deaths, during the Second World War. Was he also subconsciously reliving his own secret struggle, never outwardly acknowledged, with being a gay man in the highly censorious and ultimately homophobic world of the military in the first half of the twentieth century? Looking at his service record, held at Britain's National Archives, it is not obvious that he encountered any overt hostility or prejudice, despite being part of what could be perceived as a persecuted minority at the time. However, in those days, indirect discrimination and prevailing disapproval were undoubtedly endemic in society.

'Don't ask, don't tell', was certainly the approach taken by the British military at the time.

There appear to have been many reasons why Sir Hardy later revealed that his wartime service, 'was in some ways one of the most difficult and unhappy periods of my life'.[1] Although he never actually 'came out' during his lifetime, Sir Hardy Amies was a flamboyant, self-styled 'Old Queen', whenever circumstances permitted it. However, such occasions would probably not have included the many times when he visited Buckingham Palace to oversee fittings for the royal wardrobe of an actual 'queen', Her Majesty, Queen Elizabeth II. Actually, it is highly unlikely that the monarch would have batted an eyelid at the revelation of her couturier's sexuality and nor did she appear to do so in the case of her other royal dressmaker, Sir Norman Hartnell, affectionately described by Sir Hardy as another 'Old Queen'.

Whether openly acknowledged or not, gay staff have been a feature of the royal household for many decades, so the duo of dressmakers was unlikely to have encountered any discrimination at court. However, an anecdote from Bill Howat, Sir Hardy's long-term chauffeur should, perhaps, be taken with a pinch of salt. When asked what Her Majesty said to him during his investiture, Sir Hardy apparently replied, 'As a matter of fact she said, "Well, it's the first time I have knighted a queen!"'

Sir Hardy Amies' preoccupations as he drifted in and out of sleep that night were more likely to have been focused on his time as an intelligence officer in the highly secretive Special Operations Executive (SOE) during the Second World War, than the subsequent years he spent in the glamorous world of fashion and high society.

As he reminisced in his first autobiography, *Just So Far*, published in 1954, he frequently pondered on the fate of the young Belgian agents he was tasked to train and direct to undertake often potentially fatal missions. Rising to the rank of major during a period as temporary head of the SOE's

Belgian unit, he was deeply involved in the strategy and planning behind many operations between 1941 and 1945, when the war in Europe ended. As he also said himself, one of the worst things about the conclusion of his wartime duties was not being able to talk about any of it because, as he said, 'I rather like talking.'[2]

Sir Hardy seems to have had the feeling throughout the war that he was having a 'soft' time running the Belgian arm of the SOE from London, training agents and saboteurs from the Allied forces to further the resistance movement. He talked about this in an interview with the businessman and writer Naim Attallah in 1992 (reproduced in Attallah's book *of a Certain Age* (*sic*)) and revealed how his attitude to the activities of the SOE developed, saying, 'I didn't think the idea of dropping parachutists into occupied countries was working; I suspected always that we were so infiltrated that we dropped people straight into enemy hands.'

His feelings of guilt combined with the secretive nature of his work and the repressive attitude towards homosexuality in the military cannot have made for a particularly comfortable or satisfying period in his life, although he was praised for his achievements, personality, and attitude in his service record. The fact that he was also able to continue to run his burgeoning design business throughout those years as part of the British Board of Trade's wartime clothing initiative, would perhaps have lightened his mood. He also greatly enjoyed the comradeship involved in serving his country and, although he was pleased to get back to civilian life, as a patriot he always regarded his wartime service as great experience and a firm foundation for what lay ahead.

However, in the interview with Naim Attallah, he explained: 'I considered myself lucky to have spent the major part of the war in a branch of the War Office in London. I still suffer from a bad conscience from that time … I didn't believe in what I was doing.' he concluded rather desperately. This feeling of responsibility and shame about operations he found cynical and 'amateurish' would stay with him throughout his life. Nicholas Worth, who worked as a fitter and the only male *vendeur* at the premises of Hardy Amies Ltd in Savile Row in the late 1990s said that, even then, 'He didn't ever want to talk about the war.'

Amies' early years were a fascinating combination of the physical, academic, and artistic, as perhaps was not that unusual among civilians called up as military personnel in wartime. It was only at such momentous times that people from all sectors of society were suddenly thrust into occupations and environments that they would most likely never have encountered during peacetime. For Hardy Amies, it appears to have been an introduction to a new and enriching set of opportunities, which, despite their sometimes traumatising after-effects, were overwhelmingly valuable, character-forming, and influential throughout the course of his life.

Hardy had already set himself a firm foundation with his experience of European travel, varied career moves, and social interaction on a very extensive level. By his mid-thirties, he had all that, plus a pretty accomplished military service record to his credit, and was ready to finally launch himself fully into the working role he had long seemed destined for.

Part One

The Early Years

Chapter 1

The Making of a Maverick

Hardy Amies always said that he was 'almost born on the steps of the dress shop where my mother worked' in central London. His only sister was a girl who grew up with absolutely no interest in clothes, so he became the child who took on his mother's traits and talents, ultimately following her into the glittering world of high fashion.

Sadly, his mother did not live to see her son appointed to the position of couturier to the queen, but he always felt that his life-long familiarity with the world of clothing through Mary Hardy's influence compensated for the fact that he was not technically trained as a designer and helped in no small way with his rise to the top of the profession. Hardy eventually took his mother's maiden name – which had been his middle name – as his forename, dropping his given name of Edwin, after his grandfather. He felt that 'Hardy Amies' rolled off the tongue beautifully and it was easy to simply drop his original forename without too much confusion.

His grandfather, the elder Edwin Amies, was considered quite a successful businessman, being the proprietor of a factory producing 'dandy rolls' from which the watermarks in paper and banknotes were printed. Edwin had been widowed at a fairly young age and subsequently developed something of a reputation as a man-about-town both in London and Paris. He appears to have lived rather beyond his means, however, as there was less money than expected in the family after his death. This perhaps explains his son's and grandson's subsequent urge to strive for upward mobility, status, and, to some extent, wealth, during their lifetimes.

Hardy's father Herbert was a tall, handsome, yet modest man who had taken up what was then referred to as a 'salaried position' with the London County Council before marrying Mary Hardy. In the interview with Naim Attallah, given when Hardy was 83 years old, he describes his parents in a pragmatic way: 'I actually got on better with her than I did with my father,' he says, 'though he was a most affectionate man and we didn't get on badly by any means.'

Comparing his parents he continues, perhaps a little indiscreetly: 'in the long run he wasn't very bright, and she was brighter. My mother had what is laughingly called taste – of course it was restricted to suburban taste, her life being very circumscribed.' He goes on to describe Mary as 'a village girl', but one who could recognise the behaviours and characteristics of a lady as a result of being exposed to the periphery of high society during her career with a prestigious court dressmaker.

Edwin Hardy Amies was born on 17 July 1909 and began life in a flat in Maida Vale, London. Maida Vale is part of the City of Westminster and is now a desirable residential area in the heart of central London. In the early twentieth century, many of the red-brick Edwardian mansion blocks which are a feature of Maida Vale now were just being built, creating an abundance of flats and apartments.

After two years in Maida Vale, the Amies family moved out to the village-like environment of Alperton in Middlesex. A daughter, Rosemary, was born in October 1915, shortly after Herbert Amies had joined up for service in the First World War.

Hardy remembered leaving London with his mother and sister to take refuge with various relatives in the rural idyll of Kent while his father was away serving his country. This was quite common among young London mothers, who rented out their homes and took their children to stay with older family members for support. As the war raged on, however, the family returned to Alperton, seemingly to facilitate the continuation of the young Hardy's education, and he attended The Upper Latymer School in Hammersmith, in the playground of which he remembers cheering the Armistice in November 1918.

On Herbert's return from the army, emboldened by his status as a Captain in his regiment, he was sent out into the wilds of Essex by the London County Council, which was, at that time, forging ahead with great plans for new housing estates in the area. Hardy's father was to negotiate the purchase of a huge swathe of land on which the pioneering Becontree estate would be established.

As a result of his new appointment, Mr and Mrs Amies moved their growing family out to Barking in Essex, which was then practically in the countryside and not a part of the urban sprawl which makes up outer

London today. Hardy enrolled at a new school, Brentwood Grammar, just north of London which, at the time, was evolving into 'a full-fledged public school'.[1] It was here that his confidence began to grow and he developed a lasting characteristic which was a combination of conceit and self-delusion, but which was usually presented with his tongue slightly in his cheek.

Richard Martin is Director of the Cotswold Woollen Weavers in Oxfordshire, near Hardy's later country home, and from which Hardy would often buy cloth for the business and his own personal use. Richard recalled how Hardy had the knack of taking the credit and the glory for events that were probably nothing to do with his actual endeavours:

> Hardy was almost allowed to get away with things which other people probably wouldn't be. He did it as if he was making a joke, so he was never really pompous.
>
> He told me, 'I went to Brentwood School, which afterwards became quite a famous public school', as if somehow his going there had had a really positive effect! I think he said these things quite consciously but always with a hint of mischievousness, as if he didn't really expect you to take it completely seriously.

Hardy's innate sense of drama and theatricality seem to have underpinned many of his unique characteristics. At Brentwood, he was by no means sporty and eschewed the football, rugby, and cricket fields for the lure of the stage, particularly loving the autumn term as there was always a school play in which to become involved. That is not to say that Hardy avoided sport throughout his life, as he played tennis avidly from his 20s right up until what would be considered his twilight years, and did not shy away from physical challenges of various kinds.

Hardy revelled in his roles in school productions, rather effeminately describing his characterisation of Jessica in *The Merchant of Venice* as looking 'ravishing in a long black wig'.[2] He was already showing signs of flamboyance in both action and language, a quality he would maintain all his life. He later managed to 'deviously' obtain the role of Mrs Malaprop in Richard Brinsley Sheridan's comedy *The Rivals*. With his growing love of the stage and the arts generally, it was to be a source of great pleasure to him in later life that Sheridan once occupied the Savile Row house which would become the premises of Hardy Amies Ltd.

As far as academic subjects went, Hardy claims he did not particularly excel. He looked back with reproach on the history master whom he implies was more interested in promoting school football while making his nominated subject of history duller than Hardy thought possible. The fact that he went on to have a life-long interest in history, gave Hardy a feeling of some remorse that he had not been able to learn at school what he later had to 'toil over'.

Neither was he inspired by the modern languages tuition on offer, despite discovering just a few years later that he had quite a propensity for them. At school he fared better at English, both Literature and Language, but at art and drawing he describes his talent as being a little below the average, which would disappoint him in his later career. However, he describes his affection for the wife of his housemaster, who appeared to take on the role of moral and spiritual guide to the pupils as well as organising entertainment and social gatherings for them. At one such Christmas party Hardy recalls with some significance, 'she asked us to wear fancy dress which we were to make ourselves. I do not think I was surprised at winning the first prize: it seemed to me so natural that I should be the best at that sort of thing.'[3]

Despite his apparent lack of great academic achievements, Hardy was put into higher streams than he felt he had attained the requisite skills for, and was recommended for a Cambridge scholarship in the mid-1920s. As he stated himself, he may easily have given the impression of being more mature than he was. He considered himself backward in Latin and all forms of mathematics and any other subject where any sort of accuracy was essential. Hardy ultimately failed the entrance exam for the Cambridge scholarship, concluding that he was recommended for it before he was ready.

The question of what the young Hardy was going to do with his life soon became a regular topic of discussion at the Amies family home near the Becontree estate, of which Mr Amies senior was now the Principal Resident Agent for the London County Council. Hardy himself acknowledged that when participating in these discussions he could be 'tiresome and petulant'.

Somewhat fortuitously, a new English master by the name of Howard Hayden had arrived at Brentwood School. As well as inspiring his pupils in his subject, he also threw himself into even more ambitious and plentiful theatrical productions and Hardy, by then in the Upper Sixth form, admits in his 'professional autobiography' *Just So Far*, which he began writing in 1952, that he wanted this man's admiration or, at the very least, approval.

Taking into account his confidence and his aptitude for English, Howard Hayden decided that Hardy had the qualities which might suggest he would make a successful journalist and, with the help of the local MP, a meeting was duly arranged between Hardy, his father, and R.D. Blumenfeld, the editor of the *London Daily Express*. This meeting marked a turning point in the young Hardy's life.

It turned out that Blumenfeld did not greatly admire or value an elite Oxbridge education among his writers, preferring them to have had experience out in the real world, especially if that experience was gained through travel.

'Send him to both France and Germany for a year each and then come and see me again', he told Mr Amies. So, with the prospect of Hardy taking up a career as a journalist, plans were soon put into place for his horizons to be broadened by overseas travel. Fortunately, his much-admired English master had a contact who ran an English school in Antibes in the South of France, and he invited Hardy to go over and work as a teacher, with the planned departure date set at Easter 1927.

Chapter 2

Parental Influences

Hardy admired both his parents. His father was what was then considered lower middle class, and possessed of a good nature alongside his appealing looks. He was also very hard-working. His mother was pretty, intelligent, and probably more ambitious than her husband, despite being from a less financially stable background. During his interview with Naim Attallah, it is suggested to Hardy that 'one has the impression that yours was not a happy childhood'. Hardy's reply is succinct and appears to refute that view: 'It was certainly pursued by a lack of money, but although that imposed huge restrictions, we were not on the poverty line. Overall, I think we were happy.'

Mr Amies senior rose to a fairly well-paid job at the London County Council and managed to provide both his children with a private education. The reference to money in the answer to the question posed by Naim Attallah seems to refer to the family's financial position in a slightly negative light. Perhaps the level of lifestyle to which Hardy had become accustomed by the 1990s somewhat clouded his judgement over what constituted a modest upbringing back in the days before and between the two world wars.

With his sister Rosemary having no interest in clothes or fashion, the path was clear for the more artistic Hardy to become his mother's favourite, although this did not mean she was overly protective of her son in any way. Both his parents, as well as Hardy himself, were keen for him to fly and to find his own fortune, and at no time does he appear to have been held back or limited in his aspirations by a lack of parental encouragement or sense of adventure.

However, in Hardy's autobiographies, he acknowledges the huge role his mother, in particular, played in his life choices and career. He describes her as having elevated herself from modest beginnings to a successful business career and also a rewarding and advantageous marriage. Despite what he considered a totally unjustified inferiority complex, he describes her as having an independent spirit, intelligence, sensitivity and 'above average good looks and figure'.

Having been born with an eye defect which a painful childhood operation could not correct, Mary Hardy was shy and self-conscious. However, this did not prevent her from becoming an accomplished and effective 'vendeuse', or saleswoman, at one of the highly regarded court dressmakers of the time. These were businesses which provided high-quality clothing to people who were to be at court in the presence of the sovereign. Such enterprises obviously operated with the utmost discretion and demanded extremely high standards from their staff and in their working practices.

Mary began her career as a junior in the showroom but quickly rose to become one of the senior saleswomen, continuing her career after her marriage and the birth of her first child, which was most unusual in those days. Hardy's father, Herbert, was from a rather more middle-class family and certain, mostly female, relatives of his referred to Mary rather disparagingly as a 'shopgirl' in their snobbish, Victorian way.

The couple had met when Herbert spotted Mary looking into the window of Chappell's music shop in Bond Street and supposedly followed her to where she was to catch the bus home to her lodgings in Bayswater. His impulsive pursuit paid off and the two began 'courting', as it was then rather quaintly known. They married in 1906 and lived in the flat in Maida Vale, where Hardy was born. The subsequent move to Alperton, Middlesex, was to provide Hardy with many happy childhood memories.

The manager of the court dressmakers at which Mary worked, Machinka & May and later Madame Durant, was a Miss Gray, who was later to become a significant figure in Hardy's career. Miss Gray left her post at Madame Durant in Bond Street and took Mary Hardy with her as a senior vendeuse when she launched a new establishment of her own in Brook Street, Mayfair.

Mary was such an indispensable part of the business that she did not start her maternity leave until very close to the birth of her first child, hence Hardy's assertion that he 'was almost born on the steps of a Court dressmaker'. Once Mary resumed work, Hardy recalled being taken into Miss Gray's establishment by his mother, particularly on Saturdays, where he was spoiled by the female workforce who gave him pieces of material to play with in the stockroom 'to keep me quiet'.

This tranquil and cosy period was curtailed in 1915 when the twin events of his father joining up during the First World War and the birth of Hardy's sister Rosemary, necessitated his mother finally giving up her beloved work completely. On Captain Amies' return from the front at the end of the War in 1918, the children did not recognise him when he appeared at the door of the house. Like many wartime families, the mother and children had developed an extremely close unit during the hardship of the war years, and it was difficult for them to adapt to having a man about the house again.

In 1918 Hardy's mother gave birth to another child, Wilfred, who had Down's Syndrome. Wilfred was rarely publicly acknowledged by Hardy or Rosemary, although it is believed that they both contributed towards his care throughout his life and, in the interview with Naim Attallah, Hardy states that he 'inherited responsibility for him' when his parents died, although Wilfred was living in a residential home by that time. Wilfred was briefly mentioned by Hardy in *Still Here*, his second autobiographical volume which was published in 1984, and then as '… a mongol – lodged away from home most of the time'. This detachment should not be taken as neglect or cruelty on the part of Hardy or his family, it merely represents the common treatment of children with such a condition back in the early twentieth century. Although in common usage at the time, the term 'mongol' is considered offensive today and would never be used. Wilfred would rightly only ever be referred to as having Down's Syndrome.

In the Naim Attallah interview, Hardy was asked if he felt any resentment about the amount of care and attention the younger boy required, but Hardy compassionately replied: 'Not in any way whatsoever. It's only looking back that I realise that it must have been a tremendous strain on my mother and the resources of my father. But I wasn't conscious of that at the time and I never had any feelings of disappointment.'

Once Herbert Amies was assigned the job of managing the development of the Becontree estate, the family moved to a nearby farmhouse while the building was taking place. Captain Amies received great recognition as the Resident Agent of what was then one of the largest public housing schemes in the world.

Mary, meanwhile, threw herself into volunteering at the local hospital, as well as for other charities and the church, and her life was very much home based. As a family, the Hardys had not been abroad for holidays or any other purpose. So, when the question came up about Hardy's future, the prospect of him leaving to travel to Europe in the pursuit of education and experience was quite a momentous one for both the young man and his mother.

The decision to follow the *Daily Express* editor's advice about travel would launch him into a future that would eventually both reflect and honour his heritage, while at the same time opening doors into a whole world of new experiences.

Chapter 3

Hardy Spreads His Wings

With Hardy now nearing the end of his time at Brentwood School and preparing to take up the suggestion of travelling in order to further his education, plans were set in motion. It was decided that he would accept the offer of a job at the language school in Antibes and things seem to have fallen into place quite easily.

In the south of France an 'adopted aunt' whom Hardy had known when both she and the Amies family had lived in Maida Vale, was to keep an eye on him while he became established in his teaching role. Mademoiselle Louise Probet-Piolat was a glamorous French woman who had become acquainted with Mary through her work as a fitter in the couture business. By this time she had moved back from London to Nice, which is approximately sixteen miles from Antibes. Hardy set out to stay with her in order to begin the next stage of his life's journey in April 1927.

In *Just So Far*, he recalls that his parents felt a sense of safety and security knowing he was going to Antibes where his 'Aunt Louise' could keep a watchful eye on him. Once installed in his new role, the young Hardy found that his day-to-day routine did not quite live up to his expectations. He was required to teach simple arithmetic and spelling to the young children of wealthy American and English parents who left them behind while they took lengthy grand tours of the rest of France and Italy.

Hardy did not find this work particularly stimulating, and was also disappointed by his lack of access to any of the other potential attractions of spending time in Europe. He was not impressed by the unexciting cuisine on offer to staff at the school, and felt the social life available to him was far too restrictive for a curious and energetic teenager.

Realising quite quickly that Hardy was becoming disillusioned with the monotonous routine of teaching schoolchildren, Mlle Louise recommended he actually move to Nice to teach English privately to the three sons of some friends of hers. This role was much less formal and offered a great deal more variety of opportunities for the adventurous young man. Hardy described this period of his adolescence in affectionately glowing terms. 'Here I spent three wonderfully happy months,' he wrote. 'The boys had no more intention of learning English than I had of teaching them.'[1]

The location of this new post was a property in a small, rural village in the hills, called Vieux Cannet. It proved an exceedingly happy move for Hardy, and one that seemed to involve more recreation than actual teaching duties. Long rambles, outdoor swimming, and a great deal of reading seemed to occupy his time there, but it was not long before he was feeling tempted by the bright lights of Paris.

Fortunately, his youthful, restless nature was satisfied by another timely turn of events. Significantly, a contact of his mother's last employer, Miss Gray, had found Hardy a job in a postal company and he was thrilled at the prospect of moving again. It says much for the young man's resourcefulness and amiable nature that he was able to make these moves with confidence and the support of those around him.

Hardy embraced the opportunities that being in the city of culture provided, often putting his modest earnings towards theatre tickets and gaining access to other cultural pursuits. The primary achievement of his time in Paris was becoming fluent in the French language but, by 1928, he was restless once again and after about a year, felt ready to move on to Germany, to a small village between Coblenz and Bonne on the Rhine.

He quickly picked up the German language and was soon comfortable enough to make a substantial career change and take on a job as a tile salesman for a small firm, although a role actually designing the tiles would have interested him more. Hardy also became firm friends with the owner of the business, a 'bright-eyed and lively' thirty-something German by the name of Johann Witte, but known to all as 'Jonny'. This slightly older man was to be possibly the first of many influential male figures in Hardy's personal life, his career, and his burgeoning artistic and cultural persona.

In *Just So Far*, Hardy writes with a high level of insight into the political atmosphere of Germany between the wars. Whether this is enhanced by hindsight, or represented a highly intelligent understanding of the mood of a country that was still trying to re-establish its strength of character after the First World War, is hard to say.

He refers to the population generally as 'ingenious, industrious and ambitious', and noted how the older generation still held fast to their high standards of character, formality, and culture. Hardy found that many of the younger Germans he met, and indeed Jonny Witte himself, were passionately interested in the international scene and he detected a sense of wishing to become 'good Europeans' in Germany, an altruistic trait which he felt the French did not have.

In the late 1920s and early 1930s with the changes in the political environment in Germany, many wealthy and socially elevated citizens welcomed the views and aims of Adolph Hitler. Hitler was gaining power and support and would soon find himself leading a growing movement against the existing democracy.

Hardy elaborates on this in the Naim Attallah interview and addresses the question of whether, at that point, he was himself 'an enthusiast for Hitler'. Many aristocratic and aspirational British people admired the elitist aims of the up-and-coming German politician, who was at that time the leader of the National Socialist German Workers' Party. This was an extreme nationalist movement with very strong anti-Semitic leanings. The party was heavily anti-Marxist and opposed to the democratic government of the Weimar Republic, and was later, of course, known as the Nazi Party.

'The family with whom I stayed welcomed Hitler as a saviour of the middle classes and the aristocracy,' he recalled, 'and I simply went along with them and didn't question their judgement.'

Referring to Jonny Witte he said, 'He was an intelligent and clear-thinking man, who favoured the Nazis to begin with, but changed in the course of events and, by the time I left, he was very disillusioned.'

Jonny was more than happy to offer Hardy a job, as he was aware that he needed someone to help him sell his company's wall tiles to English- and French-speaking countries. Hardy's penchant for learning languages meant that Jonny could quickly entrust him with tasks such as dealing with business inspectors, managing the accounts, and making sure that the factory's operations always fell within federal regulations. Despite being given more and more responsibility in the business, Hardy would really rather have been put into a creative role designing the tiles. However, after being given a chance to try his hand at that, he notes in *Just So Far* that 'the results of some of my experiments were not only hideous but unsaleable',[2] so he quickly reverted to his administrative duties! He need not have thought that this was the end of his foray into the world of tile design, however, for later in his career, he did design a range of wall tiles and these were to be a feature of his own country home many years later.

In Germany Hardy quickly rose to the position of second in command to Jonny Witte, and his satisfaction in his job was equalled by the appeal of the social and cultural life in the nearby town of Coblenz, which was at the time still under French occupation after the First World War. It was at the Municipal Theatre and Opera House that his knowledge and appreciation of classical music really established itself and he would also frequently make trips to nearby Cologne or Dusseldorf to broaden the scope of his musical understanding.

He writes of an abundance of physical and outdoor activity too. When hiking or taking excursions to castles on the Rhine and the Moselle he often became acquainted with the regions' wines en route. In fact, he learned much about wine and also a good deal about how to drink it during his time in Germany. 'If it is essential – and I think it is,' he says in *Still Here*, 'that any man should learn how to get gloriously and rapturously drunk, there is surely no better place to go than Germany. An evening's drinking of one sort of wine made from one particular grape means that you will have to pay very lightly for your follies.' A useful lesson learned!

Much of this ribaldry and revelry took place in the company of Johnny Witte, whom Hardy acknowledged later in his interview with Naim Attallah, 'was very attracted to me'. It is highly likely that the two enjoyed a close and possibly intimate relationship during Hardy's time in the country. Witte's name appears several times in the visitors' books from Hardy's London residences between 1953 and 1970 and the two men appear to have maintained contact throughout their lives.

No doubt Hardy's sensibly restrained approach to 'entertainment' meant that he was usually able to rise bright and early to enjoy activities such as deer-hunting, swimming, and boating, as well as venturing further to climb in the Alps in Switzerland, throughout this time. He also intriguingly refers to the 'curious nightlife of Berlin and the more virile and vigorous junketing in the dives off the *Reperbahn* in Hamburg'. This area has been a notorious entertainment focus for hundreds of years, and houses the city's red-light district. The young Hardy would undoubtedly have found some of the sights quite shocking initially, but quickly came to acknowledge that he learned a lot during his early foray into Europe, rather enigmatically concluding that 'it is difficult to define in what direction'.[3] There were certainly very diverse and alternative forms of entertainment on offer at the time, particularly in the cities of France and Germany. The writer and horticulturist Vita Sackville-West, who was married to the politician and writer Harold Nicholson, said, 'There are certainly very queer things to be seen in Berlin', and this was in a letter to her own same-sex lover Virginia Woolf![4] She went on to say she thought her husband would have fun out there; the couple obviously enjoyed an unconventional and open relationship and, presumably, were not easily shocked.

Between 1919 and 1933 Germany had become known as the Weimar Republic following the abdication of Kaiser Wilhelm II. As its political structure became more volatile and its people more poverty stricken and constrained, a subculture was emerging. Berlin in particular was the home to many avant-garde nightclubs, some of which were openly welcoming to gay patrons. As Chris Bryant says in his book *The Glamour Boys*:

> True, Paragraph 175 of the German Reich's Criminal Code still pro-
> hibited homosexuality, but Berlin enjoyed a carnival of emancipation,
> as its Social Democratic Prussian government instructed the police
> to turn a blind eye and give homosexual venues official licences ... to
> cater for virtually every sexual taste – and every pocket.[5]

The writer Christopher Isherwood documented these times in his autobiographical novel, *Goodbye to Berlin,* which was later adapted into a play and a musical which ultimately led to the award-winning 1972 film *Cabaret.* In something of a parallel with Hardy, Isherwood had left the stuffy and restricting confines of England during the time between the two world wars and discovered a very different world for young men such as himself. With the advancement of the Nazi Party however, the nightclubs and cabaret bars of the capital became targets, and from the mid-1930s anti-homosexuality laws meant that patronising such establishments could almost certainly lead to arrest, with many of the venues being forced to close down completely.

Hardy became aware of the political dynamics and the portent of change throughout German society at this turbulent time so, although travel, culture, and his work served him well during his two-and-a-half years in the country, soon the question of his future, at the tender age of just 21, raised its head once again – not least via his father.

Chapter 4

Rumblings of War and a Foot in Couture

Herbert Amies had become aware that Hardy was very happy in Germany and did not seem to be keen to leave in order to follow the path that had been projected for him at the time of his meeting with the London newspaper editor. As Hardy recalled, he had returned home each Christmas but had no desire to renew his acquaintanceship with R.D. Blumenfeld at the *Express*. He was anxious to get back to Germany.

The reasons for this included the prospect of parties and cultural events, but also 'because Jonny was expecting me to meet him in Paris'. He was obviously enjoying himself and was in no hurry to leave Germany. As mentioned earlier, the younger Hardy appears to have established a relationship with Jonny Witte which was more than just professional. Jonny was 30 years old and the intense friendship between the two men had probably reached its peak by this time. Important as it must have been, Hardy could see that he had probably gained all he could from the association and for him, at least, it was time to move on. A compromise with his father needed to be reached, and it was one which involved Hardy staying in Germany but moving to a British firm which had a branch over there.

In 1930 the changing political landscape of Germany was becoming apparent as Hardy started a new role with British company W & T Avery which had a factory in Karlsruhe, a large city near the French and German border. Troubling social and political rumours were circulating however, and consequently it was decided that it would be sensible for him to return to the UK, despite his command of the language and knowledge of the country enabling him to feel increasingly at home there.

His two-and-a-half years in Germany was over; he left the day after attending a festival in Coblenz, organised to celebrate the departure of the last French soldier of the occupying French Army. He observed afterwards that no one at that time could have foreseen that another war and a further period of occupation were to follow so soon afterwards.

When Hardy reflected on his time in Germany it seems that he felt its impact on a personal level, but also with a clear understanding of the national and international situation it found itself in during those turbulent years. He keenly felt the sense of national competition between the two countries of France and Germany and gave a great deal of thought to the benefits of both nations' cultures and achievements and their claims to high status within Europe.

However, his heart was still in Germany and he obviously hoped that his connection to the country where he had lived for a substantial length of time would continue with his next career move. Thus, he began working for the weighing machine company W & T Avery in Birmingham. He found the British midlands in the 1930s rather bleak but, due to his language skills, he quickly found himself in the continental department of the company with the promise of European travel in the future.

Disappointment was to follow however, and, on completing the training in the workings of Avery's revolutionary new weighing machine, Hardy was more than a little crestfallen to find that he was an executive salesman with a target territory of two square miles in East London. He persevered and made a success of the role, eventually graduating to a more salubrious and lucrative patch between Oxford and Reading, which at least opened up the opportunity of touring the countryside in his own open-top sports car in order to sell his wares.

His success at the job was rewarded with membership of the 'Hundred Per Cent Club' for high sales figures, for which he was given a beautiful silver cigarette case, which was still among the cherished possessions left when he died. Such items were popular as gifts at the time, and the fact that this one was made by Hermes, was perhaps instrumental in Hardy keeping it for the rest of his life, such was his admiration for prestigious things. The beautifully crafted object was passed on with the rest of his estate at the time of his death in 2003.

Nonetheless, with no foreign travel materialising, his dislike of the job was growing and he later said in relation to that time, 'If a new door is opened for you and the promised adventure looks good – leap in unhesitatingly.'[1]

By a twist of fate this new adventure once again was to materialise, indirectly, courtesy of Hardy's mother, Mary. It would be folly to underestimate the overwhelming and in many ways serendipitous effect she was to have on her son and his future career. The unexpected catalyst for the life-changing moment which would advance Hardy's future pathway, was a letter he wrote describing a dress he had seen being worn at a Christmas party in 1933. The recipient forwarded the glowingly descriptive note to the wearer of the dress, Mrs Shingleton, who just happened to be the wife of the owner of the fashion houses his mother had worked for when Hardy was a boy. 'Mrs Shingleton' was none other than the Miss Gray who had previously employed Hardy's mother as a 'vendeuse'.

Mr Shingleton had amalgamated Miss Gray's eponymous business with his: 'Paulette', as well as 'Lachasse', a younger, sportier brand, whose Design Director, Digby Morton, just happened to be about to leave his post to set up on his own. As a result of their connection, and Hardy's obvious interest in, and insight into, fashion, Mrs Shingleton strongly suggested the young man to her husband as a replacement for the departing male designer. With Digby Morton having been influenced heavily by the likes of Coco Chanel and Edward Molyneux, two of the biggest names in continental fashion at the time, Hardy knew immediately that he wanted the job and the chance of following in Morton's footsteps. This was despite being offered 'less than half of what I was then earning' as an illustrious and successful weighing machine salesman. The value of the residual goodwill and enviable reputation that Digby Morton had built up at Lachasse was certainly not lost on Hardy when considering taking up the new role.

So it was that in February 1934, aged 24 and with no previous experience, Hardy Amies took on his first job in fashion at Lachasse, a company he describes in his book *The Englishman's Suit*[2] as a 'ladies' bespoke tailoring establishment'. In the preface to *Still Here*, Hardy recounts his mother asking how his first day had gone on his arrival back. 'It was just like going home', he replied. Due to the times he had spent with his mother from his early years, he was so familiar with the surroundings and operations of a couture house that it seemed to override any feelings of under-confidence or lack of technical knowledge. 'Without any formal training or indeed experience, I took to my work like the proverbial duck to water,' he declared. He also described his mother's work colleagues as having been his 'first adult friends'.

Although his original role at the company was more managerial than design-based, Hardy was soon tasked with designing the entire collection the following August. Lachasse was a relatively new design house, having been established in 1928 in Mayfair. After just a year in the post he was officially rewarded with the title of Managing Designer. It was at this point that Hardy encountered two of his most loyal lieutenants: Mr Todd and Mr Ernest, head tailors who were to move with him and stay within his employ for the entirety of their future careers.

Hardy fully admits that, at that stage he was learning on the hoof and modestly describes some of his early output as 'hideous', but, alongside the designing, he was also honing his management and business skills, which stood him in good stead in the future when establishing his own couture house. Digby Morton had specialised in elegant women's suits, much favoured by the sophisticated London ladies who were the customer base for Lachasse, Miss Gray, and Paulette, the two other businesses in the Shingleton group.

Hardy gives several insights into his Lachasse days in his 1994 work *The Englishman's Suit*, a small yet comprehensive sartorial manual for the discerning gentleman. Many aspects of this guide to male dressing transferred very neatly into women's wardrobes too. He immediately found himself working with wool and tailoring, two aspects of clothing which were to become synonymous with Hardy Amies for the rest of his career across both men's and women's collections. Hardy's natural eye for tailoring made him a perfect choice for the job at Lachasse, and helped him to structure the staple women's suit around what he saw as befitting a more active lifestyle for the modern customer. In *The Englishman's Suit*, he says, 'The clientele at Lachasse was truly "county": ladies wanted suits for racing, but a good suit would have to be smart enough to wear in London for lunch.'

It was his emphasis on the technical side of the design process and his self-confessed love of 'working in tweed' that saw Hardy touring the tweed mills in Cumberland in the north of England. It was here that he discovered a plum-coloured, soft, tweed fabric which he described as 'glowing'. The resulting two-piece outfit he subsequently created was named '*Panic*' and was shown in the Hardy Amies spring 1937 collection for Lachasse. It was a sensation.

Panic seems a rather contentious name for a ladies suit, or 'coat and skirt' as they were apparently called 'by the gentry',[3] but there was a reason behind the choice of such seemingly inappropriate titles. Hardy explained the rather esoteric naming of the outfits, or 'models', in *Just So Far*, saying: 'We always rather enjoyed naming the models. The names must never be eulogistic: if you call a model, as the French used to, *Mon favori* or *Irresistible* the customer would always be on her guard.' He prudently saw the folly in raising expectations too highly at the time when he was still establishing his reputation.

It is fascinating to read the simple yet beautifully presented manilla fashion show catalogues from the early days of Hardy Amies Ltd, which reveal the imaginative names some of the outfits were given. For instance, *Pope Joan* was a red, silk satin party dress, and *Silage* a reversible green and brown suit paired with a shirt in black and yellow silk shantung. Both very evocative names for garments listed in the 1952 showroom catalogue.

Hardy was particularly happy to replace Digby Morton at Lachasse as he recognised the way the house favoured structured designs rather than the soft and flowing styles which those couturiers who had taken on more of a French influence were producing. His interest lay heavily in the architectural styling and planning of a ladies' – or indeed gentlemen's – suit, rather than the closely form-fitting, natural lines of evening dresses of the time, which were often created on the live model or the dressmaker's dummy.

According to Hardy, 1937 was the year that many Americans, including buyers from some of the most well-known and prestigious US stores were over in the UK and he knew these people had heard of Lachasse through the French newspapers. This was the beginning of Hardy's popularity with what he called at the time the 'New World', and resulted in great sales figures from that customer base which persisted throughout his career.

At the time of Hardy's launching at Lachasse he was commuting into central London from Essex and appears to have enjoyed the parallels this had with his mother's previous working life. He took the same train as Mary had and even ate lunch in the same restaurant as she would have done in Oxford Street. He comically recalls in *Just So Far*, how he used to greatly enjoy the fish in parsley sauce on those days when he accompanied his mother there, but, all those years later, and after having his palate enlivened by his travels, it no longer seemed to have quite the same appeal.

Inevitably the commuting and the repetitious lifestyle finally took its toll and he decided to rent a flat in Pont Street, just off Belgrave

Square, where he was soon to immerse himself, with the help of a set of creative friends, in interior design and decoration, a passion for which he maintained throughout his life. Hardy rented property until he finally made the purchase of a country house in Oxfordshire when he was in his late 60s. He lived in numerous apartments in London, all of which were concentrated in the central south west locations of Belgravia and Kensington.

When Mrs Shingleton died in 1937, it was decided that the business which bore the name 'Miss Gray' would close down. Hardy, with no lack of confidence, suggested to Shingleton that perhaps Lachasse could move into its Brook Street premises, and seems to have even suggested that the house be renamed as *Hardy Amies*.

The motivation for this appears to have been less about his own self-promotion and more to retain the connection with his mother's career, as it was in Brook Street that she had worked for all those years, and Hardy would clearly have loved to immerse himself further in her spirit and legacy. How seriously Mr Shingleton took these suggestions is not really clear, as the Munich Crisis of 1938 appears to have been a major preoccupation among the population at the time, and undoubtedly took on a high level of significance for business owners.

Also at this turbulent time, but on a more personal level, came the news that Mary Amies was suffering from cancer. In a poignant paragraph in *Just So Far* he describes his rather buttoned-up father breaking the news to him in the upholstery department of John Lewis. Herbert Amies was obviously in tight control of his emotions as Hardy recalled that the two of them continued turning over the chintzes from which they were to choose fabric for Mary's bedroom curtains, as he learned of his mother's prognosis. He wrote: 'The scene is fixed forever in my mind, and seemed to be so typical in its deliberate avoidance of theatricality.'[4]

Mary suffered for another year, with several debilitating operations having no positive effect on the cancer. Hardy's devotion is heartbreakingly obvious in his writing. He felt it unjust that Mary, whose talent and personality had had such a positive effect on his own career, was only able to see the very beginning of his achievement, as she died aged 59 in 1938, shortly before he was to see major success.

He appears to have regretted the lack of emotion he and the family showed during her last months. He speaks of great remorse at 'all the moments I had squandered', and the times he dashed from her bedside in order to fulfil some trivial engagement. He did say that she took his hand while on her sickbed and poignantly told him how pleased she was that he was following her into dressmaking and that she had 'ardently wished it' for him. Summing up the tragic loss in the interview with Naim Attallah, he says, with great understatement and discretion: 'She had been ill with cancer for so long that there was an element of relief; it was only afterwards that I was moved.'

Part Two

Wartime Service

Chapter 5

A Singular Soldier

Hardy's progress at Lachasse could have gone in any number of ways, but for the Munich Crisis of 1938 and the looming threat of war. Relations with Mr Shingleton were by this time not particularly cordial, even though Hardy had been offered a three-year contract, the terms of which he seems to have found favourable. In the spring of 1939, when the rumblings of conflict were beginning to be heard around Europe, Hardy took his friends Nina Leclercq, a fashion editor and stylist, and Alexis ffrench (*sic*) on a trip to Cannes.

Alexis ffrench was a major figure in Hardy's life for the next twenty years. An antique dealer whom Hardy greatly respected for his knowledge of, and good taste in, furniture and interiors, he was a married man but appeared to have a very close and seemingly intimate relationship with Hardy, which came into prominence in different ways throughout his life. He was nine years Hardy's senior but was, like Hardy's mother, to die tragically young.

On their return from Cannes, Hardy felt once again that the time had come for him to be recognised in his own right as a designer, and not simply as the driving force behind Lachasse. The fact that he was known as Mr Hardy, in the manner of those working in couture houses, was at once pleasing but at the same time a source of annoyance for him. Happy to be known by the same name as his mother, he felt that he deserved the recognition as the head designer, of being known by his surname. Apparently Mr Shingleton felt that 'Amies' was a difficult name for people to get to grips with, and this small disagreement was just one of many that were apparently becoming a regular feature of the two men's relationship.

Hardy was no doubt already feeling constrained at Lachasse, sensing that around him the reputations of other young, independent London designers such as Norman Hartnell were disrupting the superiority of the Paris houses, and he would love to have been a part of that in his own right.

Hardy's dissatisfaction and restlessness was, perhaps fortunately, defused when the onset of war made it apparent that things were inevitably going to change at the business.

As he said in *Just So Far*: 'once the shock of the calamity of war had worn off, I began to accept it philosophically. To me, as I think to many others, it was to be an escape.'

Hardy decided to join up in 1939, after it became apparent that the Lachasse premises were to be requisitioned as a fire-station, and his talent for languages was to influence his forthcoming military career. Being a fluent French speaker and highly competent in the German language, Hardy was a natural fit for the Intelligence Corps. While initially working as a member of the Fire Brigade, Hardy spotted an advertisement in *The Times* for linguists with at least two European languages to join the Corps of Military Police. Hardy was 20 years old by then and could have waited for a while before being called up for active service, so his desire for adventure compelled him to take the initiative and apply.

He even called the chapter in *Just So Far* which opens in the mid-1930s 'The Great Adventure Begins', and it is not at all hyperbolic to suggest that this was indeed the actual start of a career of monumentally diverse achievements. Many wartime careers were by their very nature unusual, and in many cases unique and, even if Hardy's was not the most dangerous or life threatening, it was certainly fascinating and vast in its adventures.

His experience of Europe as a younger man meant that Hardy had a very circumspect view of the impending conflict. His desire to escape from the routine he was in and to take on a new challenge was in no way prompted by any 'burning desire to defend the Homeland'. He reveals in *Just So Far* that he could never bring himself to have 'a fighting hatred of the Germans'[1] like so many of his compatriots, as he obviously had a great respect for the country's spirit and character, leaving aside the onward march of Nazism.

His boss, Mr Shingleton released him from his employment contract 'with rather ungracious alacrity' according to Hardy, and he was soon off to Aldershot to become acquainted with his new role as a private in the British Army. He always maintained his fascination with clothing of course, showing an analytical interest in the wardrobe of the British soldier.

In *Still Here* and *Just So Far*, Hardy characteristically details the items of uniform he was issued with before beginning his training. These were 'puttees' or leg-bindings, knee-breeches, and two pairs of white woollen gloves. Hardy commented on the gloves: 'we all thought these were tremendously smart and wore them on every possible occasion',[2] The use for these never actually materialised for Hardy however, as he was diverted from military police training and sent back home to await further instructions.

Hardy was more than a little relieved by this news as he describes his time at Aldershot as being 'extremely uncomfortable', having been endured in 'bitterly cold weather'. Apparently the men had had to walk a mile 'at least it seemed as far as this – from the station with a full kit bag, a tin hat, a heavy overcoat and a rifle'.[3] Mr Shingleton was pragmatic – once he recovered from his surprise at his young staff member's return. The sudden suspension of Hardy's military duties meant that the Lachasse spring collection could be planned, ready for launch early in the new year.

Consequently, the young designer was to be found presenting his spring collection in early 1940 wearing his British Army private's uniform, complete with hob-nailed boots. He just could not resist.

Chapter 6

The Designer Diversifies

Hardy's three years living, teaching and working in Europe effectively became his 'university' education. He had become fluent in both French and German and had immersed himself in the people and the culture of both nations. This provided him with a good grounding for his eventual role in the war effort. After successfully launching the 1940 spring collection at Lachasse, in his jaunty army private's uniform, Hardy was recalled to military training.

He was directed to go back down to the dreaded Aldershot, but this time to an Infantry Officers' Cadet Training Unit, and he seems to have found it 'just like being back at school' – and in a good way. For Hardy, the appeal lay in the fact that, due to the unique circumstances of being called up for service, the unit consisted of thirty or forty 'trainees' who ranged in occupation from head waiters to university professors. He revelled in conversing and socialising with such a wide range of characters and, no doubt, having the opportunity to pass on his own wit and wisdom.

He and his peers frequently found opportunities to mock the lack of sophistication and *sang-froid* of their military superiors. In his first autobiography he recalls that it was during those months when for the 'last time in my life I had a belly-laugh that made me ache and lie completely helpless on my bed'. This was due to an incident with one of his colleagues, the famous scholar and travel writer Patrick Leigh-Fermor. On returning from a merry night out in the nearby town, 'Paddy', as Hardy refers to him, decided to lean out of their barrack-room window and quote from Shakespeare's *The Merchant of Venice*. Upon hearing this, their much-mocked sergeant yelled back 'If you aren't careful you'll be the Robert Brooke of this war!'[1] This was supposed to be a reference to the First World War poet *Rupert* Brooke, who died aged 28 during active service. The sergeant's lack of cultural education which caused him to misname the writer, obviously caused great hilarity among the sophisticated and literary Hardy and his chums. Laughing so uproariously at the seemingly less-well-educated sergeant does indicate a certain level of snobbery among the group. This reputation for haughtiness certainly followed Hardy throughout his life but, according to the art historian David Freeman, Hardy's friend and sole heir, 'He would tell you himself that he was a snob, but he wasn't. Hardy could talk as easily to a Duke as a dustman.'

On a more serious note, the men were frequently reminded that they definitely had to pass their infantry officer training before they could be put forward for the Intelligence Corps. The particular department was initially called the Field Security Police but was later renamed, and the recruits were left in no uncertainty about the fact that they were never to talk of their future work. As Hardy says, they actually knew nothing about what it could be anyway, and that he wondered with some degree of sarcasm whether some of them might 'end up checking passports on Wigan Pier'.

Passing-Out Day for the cadets coincided, worryingly, with the onset of the Dunkirk evacuations and Hardy states in *Just So Far* that he 'scrambled through somehow and got a "B"'. It was rumoured that the new graduates would immediately be sent out to Dunkirk, but this command was quickly rescinded. Hardy admitted that he was relieved not to have been involved in that particular episode. In an uncharacteristic expression of insecurity he declared: 'I trust that my only fear was that of making a fool of myself.' Instead, he was moved on for six weeks of training for the Intelligence Corps proper at Swanage in Dorset.

With his taste for the good things in life never far from the surface, he recalls that despite the bombings and deprivations of war going on all around, there was still fresh cream in the buns at the local Belgian patisserie and excellent lobster to be had in the nearby village of Corfe. Civilised life could still go on.

Those epicurean delights were interspersed with earnest lectures on the structure and operations of the Nazi Party, given, according to Hardy, by a tutoring officer who 'seemed to hiss hatred of the enemy in every word'. He goes on to explain that the reason for this could have been caused 'not so much by any deep philosophy as by an ill-fitting set of false teeth'.[2]

As well as Patrick Leigh-Fermor, Hardy's fellow recruits included the writer and naturalist Gavin Maxwell and J.C. Masterman, the noted academic, sportsman, and later vice chancellor of Oxford University.

Hardy described Masterman as a tall, ascetic-looking man who seemed rather older than the rest of the troop. Hardy became aware that despite arriving late for training, Masterman easily managed to get to grips with his studies and by seemingly 'never going to bed', had fully absorbed the subject in record time, such was his remarkable capacity for learning. This perhaps illustrates the calibre of men chosen for this particular branch of the services.

In Hardy's garden at Langford is a beautiful summer house wherein lies a plaque inscribed to Hardy in Latin by another friend he made during his army years, the scholar and later rather notorious politician, Enoch Powell. Powell later became chiefly known for his infamous 'Rivers of Blood' speech in the 1960s which was considered the embodiment of racism at the time, but many years before that he travelled the world on active service in the British Army. Although they met during their military training and there were later to be rumours about a possible relationship between them, this is highly unlikely according to David Freeman.

'Their paths wouldn't have crossed really', he said, 'Enoch Powell was not in intelligence. He was out in Africa on active service, while Hardy was in London or Brussels.' The two did, however, maintain contact after the war and remained close friends until Powell's death in 1998.

A rather scurrilous article was published in the *Mail on Sunday* on 16 March 2003,[3] shortly after Hardy's death. Under the headline, 'A Very Peculiar Couple', the paper suggested there had been a homosexual affair between the two men, who bunked in close proximity during their army training at Beaulieu. Hardy does mention his fellow officer in film footage used in a 1994 BBC documentary about the intelligence operations during the war, but there is little evidence to support the rumours.

According to David Freeman the newspaper was just 'making mischief'. He recalls how, in a documentary made for the BBC in 1994, the interviewer Michael Cockerell asked Enoch Powell what attracted him to Hardy Amies as they did not seem to have much in common. He recalled: 'Enoch replied, "Opposites attract and if I say it was his gaiety, it should not be misconstrued!"'

By autumn 1940 Hardy had been selected to work for the Canadian Corps as an intelligence officer under General McNaughton. This operated out of Leatherhead in Surrey and Hardy's direct superior as senior intelligence officer was John, 2nd Baron Tweedsmuir, a gentleman to whom he refers as 'a shining example of a really good man', and 'so extremely kind'. Tweedsmuir was the son of the writer John Buchan, the 1st Baron Tweedsmuir, who wrote the novel *The Thirty-Nine Steps*. The fact that Hardy held his boss in such high regard must have helped him to stay positive about a time that he described as 'months of boredom, which permeated the Canadian contingent'.[4]

With nothing much worth remembering from that time, apart from regular forays into London on his official motorcycle, which were more for fun and hell-raising than duty, Tweedsmuir was soon to advise Hardy of the next stage of his service to his country. Although the announcement was prefaced with the wartime slogan, 'Your country needs you – at last', this service was to be more in the nature of Hardy's regular work rather than capitalising on any newly learned military skills.

Just before Christmas 1940, the Chief Officer told Hardy he had been selected to participate in a Board of Trade initiative to send a collection of British designs to South America to promote exports and raise much-needed money for armaments and munitions. He was duly told by John Tweedsmuir that he could be spared from his military duties for two months in order to facilitate this venture.

Hardy was delighted to get back to designing and the excitement of being recognised as a bona fide designer by a government department, meant that he neglected to put in place any real financial arrangement with Mr Shingleton back at Lachasse. After an initial monthly retainer paid to Hardy when he first joined up as a private, his salary from Lachasse had been suspended when he became an officer and, once he returned to London, his army pay ceased too. This situation could not last and eventually resulted in the two of them having what Hardy described as 'a horrible wrangle'.

In *Just So Far*, Hardy admits that he was fairly cavalier about his financial situation and should, in retrospect, have made sure a sensible financial arrangement was in place before he started work again. After all, he knew 'that good business was being done on the collection I had left behind me', implying that the company was making money from his design work undertaken before he joined the war effort.

He explains his approach in *Just So Far*: 'I was terrified lest any hitch should occur. I had been recognised as a designer by a Government

Department: but I knew Mr Shingleton wasn't very pleased about this and would have liked to have conducted the business without my help.'

Eventually, after many uncomfortable and bitter exchanges, Hardy heard his boss 'telling me to get out and not come back'.[5] The two men parted ways and Hardy never worked at Lachasse again.

However, he was not in the least daunted and, buoyed up by the confidence that had been placed in him as a designer in his own right, he forged ahead with the next phase of his couture career. As luck would have it, a few more approaches were made for his work and now the only problem he faced was finding premises and the staff and equipment to set up independently.

The word had got out and he already had some independent orders coming in, for which he realised he had to quickly sort out premises in which to get them made.

Through his good friend Alexis ffrench *(sic)*, Hardy had made the acquaintance of a woman by the name of Madge Garland who was, at the time, Fashion Editor of *Vogue*. Garland had a very high regard for French design and 'She thought French *Vogue* the best of all'.[5] However, she had also been extremely complimentary about Hardy when they first met and, by chance, he bumped into her again at this crucial turning point in his career. By now she was Fashion Director at the London store, *Bourne and Hollingsworth,* and upon hearing the latest developments, offered him the use of some of their dressmaking and tailoring rooms. *Bourne and Hollingsworth* had been started as a drapery store by two brothers-in-law in 1894 in Westbourne Grove, West London. They had moved to premises on Oxford Street in 1902 and were thus in a prime position in central London and establishing themselves as one of the most prestigious department stores in the UK.

Hardy was asked to enter into a deal with the company in which they were offered rights to copy any of his designs for their store, but Hardy felt this would be fine as his work for the Board of Trade was for export only. There was a little compromise involved, but Hardy obviously felt he was not waving goodbye to couture entirely, despite some of his friends questioning his decision, as the Board was keen on retaining the skills of tailoring and an element of glamour in their collection.

A revered memory for Hardy was spending one of his military leave breaks in a suite at the Hyde Park Hotel and writing his signature on a wide piece of white satin ribbon. This was to become his clothing label as well as the tape which was used to tie up any beautifully wrapped parcels of clothing throughout the rest of his career. With such details in place, Hardy was now all set to launch himself independently on the waiting world of fashion.

As was the case for many working-age people at that time, Hardy found himself combining a military career with his 'day job' and his real passion for design. His youthful enthusiasm and the confidence he had gained both through his emergence via Lachasse and his new-found independence, meant he was able to approach both with positivity and gusto. The knowledge that he had been chosen for the Board of Trade's export initiative alongside such fashion luminaries as Edward Molyneux, Norman Hartnell, and Digby Morton was an enormous boost to his self-belief.

Hardy had been juggling his fashion work in conjunction with the Board of Trade with his continuing stint at the Canadian Seventh Corps, but by April 1941 he was called to a lunch meeting at the St James' Club in London, so he could be informed of his next military move. He joked in his autobiography that he was not sure of the motives of his hosts when they plied him with drink, but it could have been in order to test out his behaviour when under the influence. He obviously passed whatever test they may have been setting him as, shortly afterwards, he received instructions to take the train to Brockenhurst, Hampshire, where he would be met at the station.

The 'ordinary-looking army motor car' then drove Hardy to what was known as 'the house in the woods'. Apparently, according to Hardy, this turned out to be an 'elfin' property at the end of a long drive behind Beaulieu Abbey. This quaint building was the residence or Officers' Mess for those running the school for special agents and saboteurs, known by the title of Special Operations Executive (SOE).

Chapter 7

Setting Europe Ablaze

The SOE was set up for the purposes of subversion and sabotage. Despite its operations being undercover, it comprehensively enhanced the Allies' efforts in Europe, Africa, the Middle East and the Far East. The organisation employed around 13,000, over 3,000 of whom were women, on missions and in offices, and it requisitioned premises all over the UK, also becoming known as 'Churchill's Secret Army'.

Intelligence services were already in place before the war of course, but the organisation was not considered to be fully or efficiently formed, and the War Office had subsequently set up a department to research guerrilla warfare. In July 1940 Prime Minister Winston Churchill instructed the Minister of Economic Warfare, Dr Hugh Dalton, to form a new underground organisation which was to become the SOE.

The idea for the SOE had been formulated by Churchill, to take over the work being done by a group of departments drawn from the War Office, the Foreign Office and the Secret Intelligence Service (MI6). Legend has it that Hugh Dalton was commanded by the Prime Minister 'to set Europe ablaze!' Not everyone involved in the military supported the idea however, and MI6 head, Sir Stewart Menzies was a strong opponent, declaring it to be amateurish and a risk to his established intelligence-gathering services. Others saw it as a distraction from the job of defeating the enemy on the ground, though that was to some extent missing the point. Surely, by dispersing the forces at work, the Allies would gain an advantage over their opponents? Hardy's transfer in November 1941 to the London offices of T Section, which dealt with operations in Belgium, was the beginning of four momentous years. By this time, there were many officially recognised resistance organisations in Belgium after their king, Leopold III, was deposed by the occupying German forces in 1940. At this point the population believed that Germany would win the war, their country having surrendered to the invading forces at the end of May that year. Belgium's military forces had no idea at that stage of the possibilities of defending themselves against an occupying power. The high number of underground resistance movements, if anything, made it harder for the SOE to decide where to concentrate their support, and this decision-making fell to T Section's head, Claude Knight, and secondly, to the man who would go on to succeed him, Hardy Amies.

At the beginning of the Second World War, much of Europe was occupied and Russia had signed a non-aggression pact with Hitler. In June 1940 Italy had declared war on Britain and France, which was under occupation. Britain, supported by the Commonwealth, was alone against the Nazis. Winston Churchill felt that Britain's reputation had suffered after defeat in France, but was still determined to push on against Germany and give hope to the people, as well as convincing others, such as the USA, that Britain was still strong. Although, militarily, the country had lost some ground, he felt that subterfuge was one way forward and the different approach would cause the Germans to divert resources to try to deal with it, and this could weaken them. He also felt strongly about making a show of solidarity, or resistance, with our European neighbours.

In contrast to Churchill's enthusiasm, the setting up of the SOE did not go down well with many leading military figures, as the preference was to focus on the troops on the ground with a limited use of already established intelligence services. However, the SOE continued to evolve, firstly under the leadership of former First World War intelligence officer, Sir Frank Nelson, then Sir Charles Hambro, chairman of Hambro's Bank, who took over between 1942 and 1943. In September 1943 Major General Colin Gubbins, a man whom Hardy would come to regard as his nemesis, took over as chief executive. Gubbins had a distinguished military record and had already been in charge of training for the SOE. His approach was disruptive, favouring the blowing up of bridges and encouraging revolt and guerrilla warfare in enemy occupied countries.

This was the requisite attitude to the success of the SOE, as it had a mandate to 'create mayhem' and to 'set Europe ablaze', as Churchill had supposedly instructed Hugh Dalton. Conflict quickly spread around the world and the organisation was soon operational internationally, inspiring resistance movements, supporting exiled governments, and helping to facilitate the escape and survival of captured servicemen and women. Research and development stations were set up in Hertfordshire, for the creation and manufacture of specialised equipment such as disguised weapons and sabotage equipment.

Senior staff in the SOE were very often Oxbridge graduates and generally people with varying backgrounds and skill sets. The head of the French section was Maurice Buckmaster, previously a manager with the Ford motor company; chief recruiter was thriller writer Selwyn Jepson, and Gavin Maxwell, another writer was another senior officer, in addition to the talented and creative Hardy Amies. Several nationalities were represented among the agents and officers, including many women. The famous Violette Szabo (immortalised in the 1958 film *Carve Her Name with Pride*, starring Virginia McKenna) had been working on the perfume counter at a store in Brixton when she joined up, she had a French mother and was bilingual. (Virginia McKenna was, coincidentally, later to become a customer of Hardy Amies.) Another agent, Virginia Hall, who was considered to have been one of the greatest women agents operating during the Second World War, subsequently worked in the American Office of Strategic Services, which was to become the forerunner of the Central Intelligence Agency, known as the CIA. Virginia had been a correspondent with the *New York Post* and was a very striking and memorable lady. 'She was a tall woman with bright red hair, an artificial foot, which she named Cuthbert, and a remarkable ability to improvise.'[1]

Both Hall and Szabo are the subjects of significant displays at London's Imperial War Museum. The tragic tale of Violette Szabo, who, after two missions to France, was captured by the Germans and taken to Ravensbrück concentration camp, where she was executed in 1945. Poignantly, her 5-year-old daughter received the George Cross on her behalf from King George VI in 1947.

Patrick Howarth, who served in the SOE and subsequently wrote *Undercover, The Men and Women of the Special Operations Executive*, said of Hardy, 'Amies was a man of sufficient resource and versatility to be able to continue to do some dress-designing while serving as an officer in SOE.' However, some may think that his description of his colleague's civilian occupation is rather condescending and reveals a slightly dismissive attitude.

Hardy was made a Captain in order to lend gravitas to his position as Liaison Officer between the training school and the SOE HQ in Baker

Street, London. He found this new situation particularly romantic and mysterious, having come from the rather more prosaic, provincial Corps Headquarters, and mischievously rather enjoyed the organisation's secretive and distrusted reputation among the more long-established sectors of the Secret Service. As a gay man in civilian life, and perhaps even more significantly, in the military, he would probably have become quite practiced at living in a world of pretence and concealment. The cloak and dagger nature of the SOE and the resulting analytical manoeuvring involved, provided an attractive sphere of work for Hardy and many of the other charismatic characters who worked within it.

As Patrick Howarth says in *Undercover, The Men and Women of the Special Operations Executive*: 'Although the British had no experience of fighting against an occupying power in their own country, their armed services and police forces had already by 1940, a long history of dealing with resistance in various forms.' The SOE's overriding work was to organise sabotage and resistance in the occupied countries of Europe, mainly by dropping agents and explosives into targeted locations by parachute. They were, to some extent, considered amateurs by the established secret services because, as Hardy stated himself: 'They dealt in silence, we dealt in noise.' The circumstances of war being the major defining factor.

Hardy recounts in *Just So Far* how the SOE was regarded with distrust by the other secret and subversive departments within the military:

> It was natural that the organisations whose job it was to collect secret information and whose methods of work, and even network of agents, had been established for as long as there had been a Secret Service, were not exactly pleased to see an army of amateur saboteurs grow up.[2]

He was actually being unjustifiably dismissive of himself and his fellow officers, as in all cases they were at least as well, if not better trained than their more experienced counterparts.

The SOE's agents were sent for training to various large stately homes around the country, graduating to a facility in Arisaig, a small village on the north west coast of Scotland, if they passed their initial tests. The tough training there covered various themes, such as living off the land, demolition and assassination skills, and was overseen for a while by Gavin Maxwell. Maxwell, it is claimed, was the inventor of the 'double-tap', the name given to the act of firing two successive shots as a successful professional assassin.

The students who survived this education were sent to Beaulieu Abbey, Lord Montagu's estate in the New Forest, where officers such as Hardy, were also schooled. The agents trained there were involved in many role-playing exercises and practice scenarios for being potentially captured, interrogated, or abandoned in a strange country. There is now a memorial plaque and small museum in the grounds of Beaulieu, which commemorate the lives of those who trained for their hugely demanding wartime missions there.

The officers and agents of the SOE had to perform a dangerous balancing act, particularly the agents out in the field on missions in occupied countries. First, identifying nationals who were open to working as part of a resistance movement, then persuading them that the best way forward was to work as part of the Allied operation rather than alone in a more locally focused way. Staff at The HQ in London would need to be able to give direction to the citizens of the country they were attempting to launch resistance activities in, and this could be a delicate procedure.

The active agents whom Hardy was to help prepare for this work were usually on their way back from their three month initial training in Scotland. By the time they reached Beaulieu they were at the stage where they needed to put the finishing touches to their education in subversive activities, and this included formulating their 'cover story', which was to protect them when potentially under interrogation. These agents were of course recruited from the ranks of the Allied armies, which had escaped to England. The stories were to be recreations of the part of their lives which had been spent over here, to fill in the gaps and not arouse suspicion. This part of Hardy's life was running concurrently with his burgeoning fashion business operating out of the Bourne and Hollingsworth store. The work he had done for the Board of Trade's South American venture had proved successful and now Hardy was preparing designs for a similar North American project on his leave days from his military post.

Chapter 8

Serving King and Country

All the designers who had been called upon to work on the Board of Trade initiative were to band together and form The Incorporated Society of London Fashion Designers (*IncSoc*) in 1942. As a founder member of its forerunner, the London Fashion Group, Hardy was in a good position to take up his place. He makes some interesting comments about his designs for the next collection, which was targeted at North America and, in particular, New York. In a review which is self-deprecating and even self-critical, he says, 'it was all most difficult for anyone to wear, and far too different from the current fashion to be called "good design"'. In summing up the designs and how he had come to the conclusion that they did not sit well with current trends, he explained that it would not be considered good fashion creation 'to be ten years too late or ten years too early'. He seems to have been alluding to his talents as an innovator, but acknowledging that such avant-garde ideas might not be well received by the average customer.

As it happened, this was to be of little consequence, because the Board of Trade dropped the North American Scheme fairly early on due to the political and economic situation. Hardy's army career had begun to take precedence anyway, and he started to realise that in order to have the best chance of establishing his own house, he would need a good supporter in his corner and, at this stage, could not afford to be too self-reliant.

By chance, and in the serendipitous way his journey through the world of fashion seemed to progress, a familiar figure happened to be available to fill this role. This very significant character in Hardy's professional life was Mrs Flora Cohen, known throughout her fashion career as Miss Campbell or Cammie. Hardy had met Cammie when he joined Lachasse, and their friendship grew, due to a mutual love and understanding of the French language, design, style, and people. Hardy's description of the distinctive image of Miss Campbell in *Just So Far* is both complimentary and humorous, 'She looked rather like a neat and elegant gypsy, with improbably black hair and small, bright brown eyes. She spoke in a curious drawl which seemed affected, until one realised that she was endeavouring, with some success, to disguise a Liverpool accent,' he wryly says, 'at a very early age she had joined the most elegant dress shop in Liverpool which had the chic name of Maison Bacon.'[1] A most promising and auspicious start to a life-long career in the fashion world!

After moving to London and later to Paris to work at the House of Worth, Cammie married and briefly gave up her career. Hardy does not seem very clear on when and in what circumstances she came back to England, but once she did, she took up her work again and eventually found herself running the sports department of Worth in Regent Street. The term 'sport' in those days would have referred to a lady's casual or 'country' wardrobe, and not the trainers, shorts, and lycra cycling gear which would now be associated with a sports department! From there she joined Paulette, arriving on almost exactly the same day that Hardy began work at its sister company, Lachasse. Their shared love of everything French formed a firm foundation for their friendship and also what was to become a closely entwined working life for the next twenty years. Her bond with Hardy was cemented further when both Hardy's mother and Cammie's husband sadly succumbed to cancer at around the same time in 1937.

In a twist of fate, Miss Cammie was let go from her job at Lachasse due to expounding her views about their injudicious sacking of Hardy Amies, just at the time that the North American Board of Trade scheme was dropped. On hearing of her dismissal, Hardy offered her the chance of joining him at Bourne and Hollingsworth. However, she had already approached the team at the House of Worth, who, having heard of Amies' growing reputation, offered to engage Miss Cammie as long as she could persuade Hardy to design for her there. Thus, the decision was taken for Hardy to move his burgeoning business operation to the House of Worth, and he and Miss Cammie were destined to work together until her retirement in 1949.

After the abandonment of the North American trade initiative, Hardy was happy to relinquish his export scheme with Bourne and Hollingsworth and join forces with Miss Cammie at Worth in Grosvenor Street, settling in their own little corner, with Hardy designing and overseeing the production and Miss Cammie showing and selling. Hardy describes the period of working at Worth as being of immense importance to him. The arrangements for accommodation, staff, payment, and responsibility were undertaken by the parent company, as the House of Worth preferred not to over complicate things at such a turbulent time. Consequently Hardy was not required to establish his own workroom with all the extra administrative duties that would have entailed. Wartime rationing had come into play and overstretching the resources, even of such a well-respected house, was not advisable. Thus Hardy was able to step in and simply start designing, supported by Miss Cammie and the parent house, while continuing his military work at the optimum level.

Hardy was also happy about the fact that he felt his personal designs, being based around structure and tailoring, did not compete with the established designs of the House of Worth, which tended to be softer, more feminine clothes, so there would not be any potential conflict on the horizon. The House of Worth (London) Ltd had already started to distance itself from the original Worth of Paris by this time, and that separation became complete during the war, with the London operation being allowed exclusive use of the name in the UK.

One of the directors at the House of Worth was the appropriately named Colonel Pay, and having experience of financing fashion houses in Paris, he was eager to help Hardy with the setting up of his own business adjacent to, both physically and metaphorically, the House of Worth. At this time Hardy was also involved in the promotion of design at home and abroad with IncSoc, as well as producing elegant utility clothing for women struggling with the wartime rationing system. He spoke quite fondly of designing within these restrictions as, after his flamboyant early designs, he had settled into a fairly sober style. He also seems to have felt that the distance he had from the business while engaged with his military duties, gave him a fresh and unique perspective on designing.

His favoured style at the time was of pared-down shapes and economy of structure, which held its own very well in the world of austerity. After all, the feminine and frothy flamboyance of the fashions of the 1930s had, by necessity, given way to more angular and slim shapes, partly dictated by the shortages of fabrics and trimmings. Whatever was useful for more practical and utilitarian purposes naturally had to be syphoned off to help the war effort, so silks, wools, and other natural materials were in short supply to clothing designers.

However the world of fashion for ordinary women was still seen as being heavily influenced by *haute couture*, due to the employment of top designers by the Board of Trade. This period of time could be thought of as the beginning of the democratisation of fashion, a movement which resulted in ordinary working women having access to the sharpness of design which had only previously been attainable by high-end customers. Hardy Amies was entering the realm of couture at a very fortuitous moment and was determined that he would be recognised in his own right while doing so.

According to David Freeman, Hardy was particularly reticent and humble in his assessment of his achievements during the war and indeed he can only remember him speaking of it once, at the time of the broadcasting of a BBC documentary entitled *The Secret Army* in 2000.

He also rather self-deprecatingly declared of his subsequent career success: 'It was easy for me to rise up through the ranks [of fashion] after the war as so many of the talented had been killed.' However, as David said, 'He would have done it anyway.'

His involvement both in the military effort and in the world of couture meant that Hardy was able to encompass both elements in his designs, which had to fit the remit of the Board, providing functional and practical clothes which were stylish but not in any way frivolous.

Digby Morton, Amies' predecessor at Lachasse, had been asked by Lady Reading, founder of the Women's Voluntary Service (of which Hardy's sister Rosemary would eventually become a member), to design a uniform for her troops. This, along with other uniforms for women in the services, was extremely well received and the civilian population was very keen that their own clothing should not be seen as inferior or substandard while they kept things ticking over on the home front.

Fashion editors noted how quickly the pervading sense of war and its military image was permeating the world of clothing. Despite the lack of twenty-four hour news which we have now, the public craved information about the conflict in the press, on the radio, or 'wireless' as it was then known, and through newsreels at the cinema. Wasp-waisted silhouettes were replaced with more functional, easy-fitting practical outfits made of tweed or cotton, and flamboyant hats gave way to turbans or neat, head-hugging millinery. This was adaptable dressing, suitable for town or country, and apparel that made the wearer feel that she was ready for anything. From dashing to the air-raid shelter to digging for victory, a lady needed to be prepared!

In her book *Fashion on the Ration*,[2] Julie Summers quotes the fashion editor of *Vogue* in January 1940, talking of the styles in clothing and footwear of the day:

> They turn a brave face on a war of nerves. They fortify us with the feeling that we *could* walk twenty miles in these clog shoes, sleep out, if need be, in those ample, hooded coats; put our prized possessions in those kangaroo pockets. In this form of dress a woman would be ready for anything, even air-raids.

Hardy talks about this time as a transition period in his designing, which he was working on concurrently with his military service, describing some of his earlier output as 'artistically hideous', though he was always prepared to acknowledge how much he was learning through the experience. He felt he was now more in touch with the art of creating wearable clothes, as he was often out and about in London as a young army officer and rather disingenuously, stated that he would frequently judge a dress by 'whether I would like to go out with a girl who was wearing it, rather than just see it in my showroom'. Hardy would, of course, escort and be escorted by friends of both sexes, so this comment should not be taken as actually meaning '*to go out with*' in the sense that we might interpret that phrase today. He definitely enjoyed the cachet of stepping out with a stylish lady on his arm but that would be as far as his interest in female company would go.

In fact, David Freeman has a very sweet photograph of Hardy as a young boy accompanying a little girl who was wearing a short frilly dress in a rowing boat. He says, tongue in cheek, 'That's when he went off girls – he saw what was under the skirt!'

Interestingly, however, in Hardy's interview for Naim Attallah's book *of a Certain Age*, he offers up a somewhat surprising revelation about his personal life. Hardy says, 'I did once get engaged to a girl, but I cannot think why; it certainly wasn't because I wanted to go to bed with her.' He goes on to say, 'I actually love touching women for the pleasure of it, to hold their hands, to stroke their arms, and I love beautiful women. It gives me great pleasure to dress a woman to perfection.' This aspiration was still possible to achieve during the war years, despite the constraints of austerity.

There was also the opportunity to be more extravagant in design when working on garments for the international export market, so it was still possible for Hardy and his designer colleagues to allow their imaginations fuller rein in that department.

They were instructed to use this sector to promote British products such as Harris Tweed in order to bring in much-needed funds from abroad. This was an area that Hardy would have enjoyed, as it fulfilled his desire to work with quality fabrics which lent themselves superbly well to his favoured tailored styles. In *Fashion on the Ration*, Julie Summers describes how the idea of using top London designers was a clever tactic by the government and resulted in the support of the fashion press: 'It ensured that journalists and editors would take notice. They celebrated the fact that the simplicity of design, which had long been the hallmark of the great British fashion designers, especially Captain Edward Molyneux and Hardy Amies, was now available to all.'[3]

In fact, women's suiting was often simply re-fashioned from men's styles, and the resultant silhouette was distinctly masculine and free of any frivolous embellishment. Rationing and austerity extended to everything from buttons to pockets and belts, because everything was aimed at production with as little wastage as possible. These looks can be seen in classic wartime movies such as *Brief Encounter* and *Waterloo Bridge*, worn by iconic actresses Celia Johnson and Vivien Leigh.

As Julie Summers explains in *Fashion on the Ration*:[4] 'The trimmings of haute couture were now considered unfashionable. The lack of embellishment on costumes and dresses, and the narrow lines and slim proportions were made to feel patriotic and elegant, liberating women from extraneous detail.' To wear pared-down styles without excessive frills or trimmings was considered the honourable thing to do, whereas to be frivolous or extravagant was frowned upon. Hardy's naturally less flamboyant style meant that his utility designs were well-made and well thought out, as he did not have to forsake any strong yearning for embellishment, but was prepared to hone his skills within the parameters of what was required by the Board of Trade.

Hardy's great friend and mentor Alexis ffrench, who appears on the cover of his book *The Englishman's Suit*, had quite a degree of influence over Hardy's designing, especially in the metamorphosis of the man's suit into those aimed at women. Featured on the front of the book in a beautifully stylised 1930 portrait by the American artist Dur Freedly, Alexis had taken Hardy to meet his tailor, Mr Wyser, a gentleman of German descent who had been born in Glasgow. As Hardy recounts, he subsequently made his personal suits and uniforms for the next twenty years and 'an immediate rapport' developed between them.

In the book Hardy describes, in very technical detail, the way that Mr Wyser would explain what he was doing during the 'tryings on'. Apparently the word 'fitting' was, at that pre-war time, never used. Hardy goes on to say: 'What I learned from Wyser about the cut and fit of men's coats I applied to women.' In later life, Hardy's reverence for his tailor was the basis for a humorous anecdote, which the writer, biographer and his dear friend Selina Hastings quoted in the eulogy she gave at his memorial service in July 2003 at St James's Church, Piccadilly, London.

Hardy never betrayed the code of silence about his work in the SOE, but Selina Hastings managed to draw from him the revelation that one of the other men he encountered in the mess was the man later famously exposed as a spy: Kim Philby. 'I was riveted,' Selina Hastings states in the eulogy which is featured in the book *Well-Remembered Friends* by Angela Huth.[5] 'What was he like?' she asked, 'Oh, always trying to get information out of *me*, darling.' 'What do you mean, what sort of information?' 'Why, the name of my tailor, of course.'

In *The Englishman's Suit*, Hardy devotes several pages to the nineteenth-century dandy Beau Brummell, icon of fashion and friend of the Prince Regent. Later on in the book he declares: 'My Mr Wyser had only vaguely heard of Beau Brummell, but their instincts and tastes were the same.' Hardy's concentration on the attention to detail and expertise involved in being a well-presented gentleman, was invested as diligently in his work on ladies' haute couture.

He may have had to rein in some of the drapery and pleating which would have been a feature of his collections in the 1930s, but this insight into tailoring meant that Hardy's wartime designs were beautifully cut, streamlined and figure-hugging, while at the same time created with practicality and economy in mind. One thing which was not restricted was colour and many utility garments were made from bright, colourful, and patterned fabrics, which would obviously help the clothing to have even more impact.

Chapter 9

Throwing Himself into the SOE

Hardy's progress in the world of couture, with more clients moving to his eponymous label, mirrored his rise at the SOE. His superior there was Major Claude Knight, whom Hardy acknowledged had 'made himself ill' with the intense level of responsibility he felt for his troops. Knight, being described by Hardy as 'a most sensitive soul', had had to deal with many challenging events in his time as Head of the Belgian Section, not least when he was called upon to identify the body of a young agent who had died a particularly grisly death. The young man's parachute had caught on the fuselage of his plane over Belgium and he was dragged through the air and along the ground until the plane landed at a Norfolk aerodrome. The effects of this and other experiences took their toll and Knight was moved on; Hardy, having been promoted to major in August 1942, was the most senior officer left, and so was made the Acting Head of Section.

By this time Hardy was living in Chesham Place, Belgravia, having moved on from the Pont Street flat he shared with Alexis ffrench in December 1941. The two friends continued with their unofficial cohabitation arrangements at the new apartment, as well as enjoying trips to one of the ffrench family's country houses whenever weekend commitments allowed.

Having been transferred to the HQ in Baker Street, Hardy was enjoying the romance, secrecy, and intrigue which, to him, this new location represented. He had already diligently overseen the training of his Belgian agents, which took place initially at Arisaig House, in the north of Scotland. The agents undertook a physical regime which was designed to prepare the young people for their parachute training, a much more rigorous ordeal. This was the aspect of his position which seemed to make Hardy feel increasingly guilty and, in his own words, 'inferior', due to listening to the tales of what frequently happened to the active agents when they fell into enemy hands.

Sometimes mistakes were inevitably made and lives were lost among the agents on the ground, and we know that the officers, including Hardy Amies, harboured great regrets about this. Sometimes, reprisals by the Nazis were catastrophic and the loss of civilian and agents' lives had to be weighed up against the furthering of the ultimate cause, for the Allies to triumph.

The training that the student agents had to go through was likened to that undertaken by the Commandos, and the location of the Arisaig-Morar training camp fitted in with this image, as it was intensely remote, bleak, and austere. Hardy's moral turmoil spurred him into volunteering at the earliest opportunity to undergo parachute training himself. His determination was due to his desire to alleviate his feelings of guilt at having, up to then, 'a soft war' as he put it. It was highly unlikely that an officer such as Amies would be sent on a mission, because he would be of such great value to the enemy due to his knowledge of the Allies' strategies, and would therefore be put under extreme pressure to disclose it.

Nonetheless, in May 1943 Hardy, and his colleagues arrived at the Ringway Aerodrome near Manchester, which is now the site of Manchester Airport. They were about to subject themselves to a combination of fitness and gymnastics training and Commando-style military exercises which would test both their physical and mental faculties. Many agents who were undertaking training before being allocated actual missions on behalf of the resistance movement, initially failed in their first attempts at parachuting. It was not an exercise to be undertaken lightly.

After what Hardy described as having reached 'a state of physical exhaustion', the men were finally taken to complete their first actual parachute jump, only to be returned to base due to the high level of the wind at the scheduled time. Hardy describes the group as being 'luckier' the next day as they were able to complete a jump from a height of a 1,000ft, or just over 300 metres. This good fortune must have been widely met with more than a little disappointment! Hardy's descriptions of his feelings of terror as related in *Still Here* evoke quite a frightening experience, though one which he obviously volunteered for with resolute determination and forbearance.

With his signature eye for detail, Hardy gave a chillingly scathing analysis of the stark interior of the plane in which he was awaiting his drop. It was stripped out and covered on both the floor and ceiling with what looked like deeply corrugated paper that was in fact aluminium. He seems to have had a sense of trepidation, not just about the drop itself, but the potentially hazardous and unsafe structure he was encased in. He describes the edges of the aluminium coatings as 'unnecessarily sharp', and of being 'terrified of being clumsy and catching my chin on the corrugated aluminium on the rim' as he launched himself. Shaking as the plane banked and turned before the time of his jump, he observed that his neighbour's knees were rattling against his and he was terrified of slithering out of the exit aperture before his parachute was properly hooked up. In fact, his knowledge of everything that could potentially go wrong must have cranked up the fear factor by a very high percentage.

He acquitted himself well, however, and described a brief sensation of euphoria as he jumped out, hit the airstream, and had a few moments to take in the spectacular views below, before hurtling towards the ground. He describes the landing rather prosaically, as 'something like jumping off a very high wall', and this was in fact what the officers were expected to do next.

The following day they were taken to a tower in a large hangar and required to jump off the end of a plank which was jutting out from it. Parachutes were utilised once again, but apparently this can be a more challenging act than leaping from a plane and Hardy, for one, found it so. The kindness of a fellow officer, Henry Threlfall, helped him conquer his fears, and he concluded that 'no one seemed to worry about my little lapse'. Four more daytime jumps followed, as well as one in the darkness of night, over the course of a weekend and, having completed them all successfully, the officers were rewarded with a small parachute badge on their uniform sleeves. Hardy took great pride in this emblem, feeling that it projected a more robust image than that of his 'soft' green Intelligence Corps cap. He also felt it excused the effect of the Intelligence Corps badge which he observed was 'a badly drawn Tudor Rose motif' which he had heard described with some humour as 'a pansy resting on its laurels'. This florid phrase would surface again later when, on discharge from his regiment, he was conversing with his superior officer.

In her eulogy at Hardy's memorial service, Selina Hastings explained that although he almost never discussed his wartime experiences, during one martini-fuelled evening he apparently revealed what had happened when he was called to 'sign-off' from his SOE duties. After congratulating him and thanking him for his service, the colonel called him back:

> 'Just a minute, Amies,' he said, 'There's something odd about your uniform. What *exactly* are you wearing?' 'Oh, do you like it, Sir? I designed it myself. Khaki's such an unbecoming colour, so this is Loden, which I had sent over from Austria.' 'And Good God, man, the buttons! Those don't look like regimental buttons!' 'No, Sir. But pretty, don't you think?' Holding one out. 'Do you see? A pansy resting on its laurels.'

On his return to the SOE HQ in Baker Street, London, Hardy was in charge of T Section and was promoted from major to lieutenant colonel. In this role he was responsible for coordinating all the subversion and sabotage activities in Belgium, which were a major aspect of warfare in conjunction with the work of the troops on the ground. As a section head Hardy was involved in an operation known as 'Ratweek' in June 1943, a project to assassinate Gestapo officers and collaborators in occupied territories. This endeavour had minimal success and was soon abandoned, although it is covered in a BBC documentary about the SOE which was broadcast in 1994, and in which Hardy appears.

Hardy's second in command at the time was a young school teacher, Colin Tivey, and the third leading officer was *Ring of Bright Water* author Gavin Maxwell. Maxwell would have been an attractive and appealing character for Hardy to become acquainted with. According to Selina Hastings, Hardy was a 'self-confessed snob and he used to say that in his youth his social climbing had been so energetic he would take an alpenstock to parties'. This is a metal tipped walking pole which mountaineers used to help with their ascents, so Hardy was obviously aiming high.

Gavin Maxwell was the youngest son of Lieutenant Colonel Aymer Maxwell and Lady Mary Percy, daughter of the seventh Duke of Northumberland. The young and aspirational Hardy Amies would have found these aristocratic connections alluring enough, but he would also probably have sensed a kindred spirit in the writer who, despite a one year marriage in the early 1960s, was also secretly gay.

As Patrick Howarth says in his book *Undercover, The Men and Women of the Special Operations Executive*, he did not become aware of Maxwell's proclivities until he read a biography of him many years later. 'Only then did I learn that he had, or at least proclaimed he had, homosexual inclinations.' He goes on: 'For my part I found him a prickly character but I probably lacked the capacity to establish a *rapport* with a rare spirit.' Howarth's use of italics for the word 'rapport' is perhaps indicative of a view that other men of similar leanings would have got on better with Gavin Maxwell, and of course that could have been true of Hardy. As Richard Martin observed when talking about the concept of homosexuality in the services in war time, 'In those days "Don't ask, don't tell", was the approach in the military.'

As mentioned earlier, it is believed that Maxwell invented 'the double-tap', used in professional assassinations. This was a rather dubious distinction, as attention-grabbing assassination attempts were notorious for going wrong under the auspices of the SOE.

Prosper de Zitter was a Belgian double agent known to be informing the Nazis and was a particular thorn in Hardy's side. He approached the government for approval to target de Zitter during Ratweek but was refused permission due to the great fear of Nazi retaliation. One of the tragic consequences of an assassination or even a failed attempt at wiping out a particular opposition figure, was often that the reprisal from the Nazis could be of catastrophic proportions and would be likely to result in death on a massive scale, involving countless innocent civilians.

Such an incident was the killing of a high-profile Nazi figure in Czechoslovakia, Reinhard Heydrich. Two Czech SOE agents were chosen to assassinate him, but the task did not go according to plan. The head of the Czech government in exile, Dr Edward Benes, went against advice from forces on the ground stating that there was no value to the Allies in killing Heydrich, and that the consequences to the Czechs themselves could be enormous. The assassination went ahead, although the victim only died in hospital a week later. The debris subsequently discovered was identified as being of British origin.

According to Patrick Howarth: 'Hitler immediately ordered massive arrests, and it is believed that 5,000 people including the whole population of the village of Lidice, were killed as a direct reprisal for the assassination.' Lidice was believed to have been the hiding place of the assassins.

This apparent mismanagement of operations led many to question the SOE's practices and seems to have been the cause of many recriminations on the part of serving officers such as Hardy himself, although that particular operation was nothing to do with his specific section.

There were various successful SOE operations and these, together with the boosting of morale which the SOE is believed to have contributed to the resistance movement, would ultimately be considered of significant value, though its actual military achievements were not major.

However, one of the great successes of the SOE was the way it went about protecting the port of Antwerp in order for the Allied forces to move in and head off the advancing German troops. Just before D-Day in June 1944 the US army and the RAF dropped weapons into Belgium to supply the SOE and the resistance forces. Despite the German efforts, the port was held, bringing it into Allied hands, Belgium was liberated and the resistance came out of hiding. This was a triumph for Hardy's T Section and led to him being elevated to Lieutenant Colonel in order to preside over the winding down of the resistance network over the next six months.

The SOE seemed to attract an eclectic and creative cohort of senior staff members. Apart from Hardy Amies, there was the actor Anthony Quayle and the travel writer Peter Fleming, brother of the author Ian, as well as many experienced military officers and aristocrats from all over Europe. Many of these people would have been leading flamboyant, extravagant, and often eccentric lifestyles before the conflict threw them into their military roles.

Hardy's gay colleague Gavin Maxwell struggled with what is now known as bipolar disorder throughout his life and was invalided out of the army in 1944, eventually buying and living on a small island in the Inner Hebrides, working on his natural history projects and writing. He died in 1969, eleven years before homosexuality was decriminalised in Scotland in 1980. His isolated lifestyle was glamorously interrupted in the early 1960s when his famous, and partly autobiographical, novel *Ring of Bright Water* was made into a film starring Virginia McKenna and Bill Travers. Coincidentally Virginia McKenna had, of course, previously played the part of the tragic Special Operations Executive Resistance Agent Violette Szabo in the film *Carve Her Name with Pride*.

Hardy Amies does not seem to have ever recorded his thoughts on dealing with his sexual orientation while serving in the Special Operations Executive. The word 'gay' was not used in connection with homosexuality in those days, so when Hardy describes the regimental section of the

SOE as a 'gay house party', it obviously has none of the connotations we would attribute to the phrase today. However, his eloquent and creative descriptions of otherwise mundane aspects of military life, as well as his opinions of his fellow servicemen certainly hint at Hardy's latent sensitivity and flamboyance in addition to his obvious skill at writing. Apparently the fact that he decided to name some of the SOE missions he was responsible for after Shakespearean, theatrical and artistic works did not go down well with his more straightforward and prosaic superiors. There were, however, many other servicemen who would definitely have been kindred spirits and would have appreciated such touches.

Secret Agent Denis Rake had been a successful actor performing in Ivor Novello's *The Dancing Years*, before joining up in June 1939. His military service was eventful, beginning with the evacuation of the British Expeditionary Force from France one year later. He subsequently found himself on board the liner *Lancastria* which was attacked and sunk by enemy aircraft. His reputation for throwing himself into dangerous situations despite being thought of as 'a trifle effeminate'[1] led to him joining the SOE. His fluency in French meant that he was able to fill a much-needed role as a Morse Code operator in the French operation. He was captured by the Gestapo but escaped and was awarded the Military Cross in 1945. Sadly he died in 1976, not reaching such a grand age as Hardy, his contemporary in the Belgian intelligence department. Denis was another exceptional man whose story adds to the rich tapestry of the Special Operations Executive.

By 1943 The SOE was becoming a major factor in the military strategy of the British and Allied effort. This inevitably resulted in more casualties among its agents and more distressing incidents of the Germans disrupting and destroying their small, covert cells and centres of operation. Hardy took such news very badly and it is obvious his response to it lived with him for the rest of his life.

The D-Day Landings in Normandy in June 1944 preceded the beginning of the liberation of the rest of Western Europe. From the inception of the SOE it was always known that once this had happened the Belgian section, SPU47, would move its HQ to Brussels from London. As its Head in Britain, Hardy Amies moved out to its new base in September of that year.

Hardy acquitted himself extremely well during his time in both bases. Of the scant records that remain of his wartime service, the majority are positive and complimentary – his superiors praised his abilities. In 1942 reporting officer R.E. Brook stated of Lieutenant Colonel Amies: 'Although not military by disposition, I think he is improving with experience.'

In a confidential report in December 1943, he said of Lieutenant Colonel Amies: 'As a Section Officer, this officer was a specialist in training. For five months he then acted as section head pending a more permanent appointment. This position he fulfilled well and with competence, as he now does that of second-in-command.' Major General Sir Colin McVean Gubbins, the senior officer known to dislike Hardy (and vice-versa) and who was to become head of SOE, added, 'I concur. He is intelligent and quick.'

This is high praise, considering the fact that in his book *Undercover, the Men and Women of the Special Operations Executive*, SOE Officer Patrick Howarth writes: 'Before I was allowed to begin work I had to undergo one more interview. This was with a brigadier, a shortish, dark man with clipped speech, clipped moustache and brisk movements.' This almost cliched description of a high-ranking military man initially flags up with some clarity the characteristics which would have divided Gubbins and Hardy.

Howarth seems to have felt the same way as he continues: 'I already knew enough of the Army to recognise these as some of the hallmarks of the regular officer.' However, to his credit, Howarth goes on to acknowledge that first impressions are not always unambiguous. 'I did not at that stage know enough to appreciate that behind the conventional facade there were sometimes to be found men with a rich capacity for inventive and original thought and consummate powers of leadership. One such was … Colin McVean Gubbins.'[2] In Gubbins, at least for those military years, Hardy had perhaps met his match.

Chapter 10

To Brussels with Love

The SOE was officially disbanded on 15 January 1946 and it is thought that many of its records were destroyed in a fire at the Baker Street headquarters. Hardy was very skilled and diplomatic in his liaisons with his Belgian counterparts in the SOE. He interacted particularly well with the representatives of the military *Deuxieme Bureau* and the civilian *Surete Department* of the Belgian Government in Exile, who were treading a delicate line between the liberating force and the Germans who had been in authority while the occupation was in place. A balance needed to be maintained as the country had been greatly destabilised by the war. To have to endure the after-effects of all that had befallen them in those dark days, coupled with fear of retaliation and reprisal, would not have been easy for the Belgian people.

In his autobiographies, Hardy talks of the atmosphere of excitement which was understandably in evidence when the department decamped to Brussels. The sense of victory and euphoria was translated into what he describes as 'an unending round of parties and dinners to which we were invited'. Many of these were organised by people with whom the department had been liaising during the occupation, and it would have seemed churlish not to attend them. He refers to others as having more dubious credentials however, and says that they were often arranged by the wives of military or civilian men who had doubtful reputations as possible collaborationists. These people were often allied to others who had worked with Hardy in the London HQ, and Hardy refers to his 'Puritan sense of justice' leading him to berate himself for allowing them to try to ingratiate themselves into the British officers' good books. This he thinks they did because they believed that Hardy and his colleagues were part of that powerful institution – the British Secret Service.

He also encountered some disapproval from the Belgian Resistance who may have blamed the losses among their agents on bad management at the London HQ.' We were surrounded by an atmosphere of intrigue and often resentment', he wrote. Hardy seems to have found the Belgian temperament at the time to be very complex. On the one hand he tells of many hours spent listening to stories of supportive work and resistance efforts having been made by individuals on the ground, yet he also describes the Belgian population as a whole as having a marked inferiority complex.

After their government's capitulation to the Nazis, the Belgians were unsure of where their loyalties lay. Despite being a rich country they had had to appeal to the British for help in many ways and had not been, he felt, treated with the respect such a nation deserved by its counterparts in England. Hardy seems to blame himself for not achieving more recognition for the Belgian officers who worked as active agents with the SOE. He speaks of their 'indisputable' courage and even in his second autobiography *Still Here* written in 1984, he says: 'I think I made a mess of this last part of my relationship with the Belgians'.

He certainly found it difficult visiting the homes and families of those agents who had been captured or killed when on missions, in order to answer their questions and explain the circumstances they were activated under. He was also tasked with meeting residents who had given refuge to the resistance agents and had paid their own price on being discovered. Surviving agents were rewarded with military honours and Hardy was often the primary guest at such ceremonies, in addition to attending requiem masses held for agents who had died in action.

He seems to have spent a great deal of time reflecting on his work with the Belgians in a very intense and self-critical way. He admired their tenacious spirit and attributed it to the fact that the nation's long history of suffering invasions and occupations by foreign powers had had a marked effect. He also felt very responsible for the fate of the young Belgian men who had been trained in extreme levels of armed combat in the UK, in an atmosphere of high drama and danger, only to be returned to the humdrum day-to-day life of lowly ranks in their national army. What he does not seem to have considered is that this was surely the case for many young volunteer soldiers and conscripts involved in the war. They entered the conflict as barely formed youths and were catapulted into a totally different world, the after-effects of which would probably stay with them for the rest of their lives.

He still could not convince himself that he had been successful in his work for the SOE and also in trying to balance the interests of both the British and the Belgians, though they were ostensibly on the same side. Fortunately he seemed to console himself with the knowledge that he had always been 'scrupulously impartial' when dealing with the civilian and military sides in the country. Acknowledging the fact that he greatly enjoyed the culture, cuisine, and fashion he encountered in Belgium, Hardy was, nonetheless, longing to return to England and was grateful when he was recalled to London in April 1945.

Nicholas Worth recalls an incident which seems to sum up Hardy's attitude to his wartime experiences once the passing of time had begun to distance him from it. 'He never spoke about his SOE work', Nicholas begins:

As I was interested in the history of the company and the archive, whenever any enquiries came in about the past, they were put through to me.

Once a man contacted me and said that his mother had been in the SOE and had then become a model after the war. He had letters and photographs and asked if I would be able to show them to Sir Hardy. [...] When he came in I showed him the things and he looked at the letter and the photos and just said, 'Well, she never worked for me; I would never have had a model like that!' Then he went on, 'How the hell am I expected to remember someone from all those years ago?' That was it! He didn't want to talk about it – ever! That was the past.

One event during his time in Brussels which seems to have proved a little controversial for Hardy was the incident of the *Vogue* article compiled in the latter part of 1944 by American photo-journalist Lee Miller.

Lee Miller had been asked by the editor of *Vogue*, Audrey Withers, to travel to Brussels as a war correspondent in the autumn of 1944. Audrey Withers was a very influential woman during the war. She was not primarily a fashion expert, but an Oxford-educated production editor and publishing executive. Her close relationship with Miller helped the magazine to become an unexpectedly considerable force in war reporting, engaging with the women of Britain who were holding the fort at home while their menfolk were away fighting.

With utility wear taking prime position in the pantheon of fashion, Withers had taken the decision to include more wide-ranging and conflict-related articles in *Vogue* and, as she was already providing illustrated pieces for the magazine, Lee Miller was the ideal contributor to provide them.

In 1944 she was accredited to the US War Department and had gone over to Europe to witness and photograph some of the most momentous events of the end of the war, from the liberation of Paris to field hospitals and the survivors of some of the horrific concentration camps.

After meeting up with Lieutenant Colonel Hardy Amies she was taken to the Belgian home of the Count and Countess d'Ursel and greeted by a young lady named as the Countess Therese, the Countess d'Ursel's stepdaughter. In a draft of the piece included in a letter by Miller to Withers, she states that 'her baby-face must have been the perfect passport for her activities in the resistance movement'.

Miller goes on to talk in detail about the activities of the agent and poses the question of whether she should include such information in the article, and if it would be appropriate to use a photograph of the young lady. Apparently she had been given permission to do so by Lieutenant Colonel Amies.

However, in her letter Miller does express concern about using the photograph of the Countess Therese, and suggests confirming the permission given. She also writes of lunching 'in the mess with the boys and men who had organised the inside revolt from the outside, from England'. She explains that these soldiers and agents were of both British and Belgian origin. She speaks of meeting men who had been parachuted into Belgium on multiple missions over the course of the SOE's work, and expresses her surprise at being taken to a party by Hardy where the reception committee was made up of 'guys who go out to the fields, meet the parachutes and collect the arms'. Miller herself seems to have been surprised at the level of access she was given to the operatives of the SOE.

Early January saw a flurry of activity over the potential publication of the feature to be printed in March in *Vogue* magazine. Hardy himself had obviously begun to have misgivings over the level of access and openness, and the resultant copy and photographs that Lee Miller's visit had generated. In documents held at The National Archives it is stated that 'Lieutenant Colonel Amies had now become somewhat anxious about the probable publication in the *Vogue* of photographs of members of the Belgian Resistance Movement.'

Discussions with Audrey Withers made it apparent that she had not only been compelled to drastically cut the article, which covered the whole of Miller's visit to Brussels, but also that she was only intending to publish photographs which had been passed by the Field Censor as well as the censor at the Ministry of Information. A photograph of Lieutenant Colonel Amies and one of the members of the Resistance Movement had not been cleared for publication.

It seemed that the article had already been sent to the publishers of American *Vogue*, but Withers was very cooperative and 'readily volunteered to withdraw any picture or cut out any part of the edited article that might in any way compromise or cause anxiety to her old personal friend and colleague, Hardy Amies'. Indeed, it was said that Hardy was Audrey's favourite designer.

It was most likely this occurrence which was referenced in an official military report on Hardy penned on 31 March 1945. It states 'His personality is good and his administrative capabilities have shown up well. The only criticism of this officer is that he is at times apt to be impetuous and he accordingly needs a measure of supervision.'

A particularly complimentary and positive comment on Hardy Amies' approach to his SOE work comes in a passage quoted in the military report on the episode. The report contains a quote from the 'printer's proof' of the Lee Miller article which states:

Hardy Amies (Lt Col to you) took me there to call on his friends, the Count and Countess D'Ursel ... he was so modest and damned secretive that I didn't even find out for days that he was in Brussels, and was having to do with the preparation of Belgium all the time I had known him in London.

This seems to imply that Hardy's steadfast sense of responsibility, loyalty and discretion in his work was uppermost in his mind at the time and that he would not countenance compromising it with anybody. Summing up, the writer of the report says that 'The article by Miss Miller can now in no way injure SOE or its connections.' It continues: 'Col. Amies on his last visit to London checked over both the proposed article and the pictures to appear.'

However, the tone of the report then seems to sour and become somewhat critical of Hardy. After accusing him of using his position in the war effort to promote his civilian career at the possible expense of national and international security, the officer writes: 'no doubt the profile of Lt Col Amies in the next issue of the *Vogue* will cause a flutter in many feminine hearts when they realise that their handsome couturier is, after all, the "Scarlet Pimpernel" of this war.' A humorous comment, but no doubt such opinions would have wounded Hardy and contributed in no small way to his feelings of remorse over the episode.

An addendum to the report, added two days later, refers to an attempt to get Audrey Withers to withdraw a paragraph alluding to Hardy's work in London prior to going over to Brussels. At first she was resistant to this, but eventually agreed out of respect for her friend's feelings on the matter, and considering the fact that the situation in Belgium had changed somewhat since the original article was written.

By this time, Hardy's part in the war was over and he was awarded *l'Ordre de la Couronne*, one of Belgium's highest honours, for his meritorious service to the Belgian state. Nonetheless, he says of his last days in Belgium: 'I must confess I left Belgium with a tiny touch of bitterness in my heart. I did not think I had made a success of any of my work there.' However, he does allude to the fact that he had endeavoured to be scrupulous in his dealings with both his Belgian and British colleagues, saying: 'I tried to console myself with the thought that I had not used my position to encourage or even cover up any Black Market transactions, or whitewashing of collaborationists.'

In his autobiographies he does recall that he managed to engage his aesthetic eye during his time in Brussels. In his latter observations about his host country he praises the Belgians' entertaining and table decorating skills, as well as their French scents and millinery, commenting that he was 'vastly impressed by the appearance of the women'.

His own sartorial talents were still being put to good use during his later time in the military. Not only was he designing for the Board of Trade but he also took the time to subtly re-design his Lieutenant Colonel's uniform and have it made up by a civilian tailor. Actually this was not just unique to him. As Stephen Bourne writes in his book *Fighting Proud*, 'This was not all that unusual among officers, and those who could afford to do so opted for having a more comfortable uniform made.'

Officers like Hardy and other discerning aesthetes probably put as much, if not more, emphasis on the appearance of the uniform than the comfort. The famous black British jazz musician Reginald Forsythe, who joined up at a slightly more advanced age and also became an intelligence officer with the RAF, had his battle-dress uniform refitted by his personal tailor. Another 'confirmed bachelor', he and Hardy were kindred spirits with a great love of the finer things in life, although it is not known if they ever met. However, Reginald was not known to have had any heterosexual relationships and his friend, the American singer Elisabeth Welch, is quoted in Stephen Bourne's book *Fighting Proud*, saying 'His liaisons with other men were always very discreet.'

Chapter 11

Fighting with Pride and Panache

Hardy had found the early days of life as a private and an army cadet very satisfying. He talked of the warm comradeship and health-giving exercise, as well as appreciating the structure and rhythm of military life. Unsurprisingly, since homosexuality was not decriminalised until 1967, Hardy did not refer to any sort of discrimination he may have received due to his perceived proclivities while in the SOE. The Sexual Offences Act also had its limitations, with the legislation only covering men aged over 21 and excluding those within the armed forces.

The only clues to any such judgement from his superior officers seem to have been the references to him being 'more of a soldier in his performance than his looks', taken from a confidential report by Lieutenant Colonel R.E. Brooke written in June 1943. Also: 'He is far tougher both physically and mentally than his rather precious appearance would suggest.' taken from another military report in The National Archives.

It was well known among servicemen that homosexual activity on a mild and surreptitious level was going on in the military environment at any given time. Up to a certain point it was tolerated due to the extreme circumstances into which men were forced by the war, for it was not just those with suppressed homosexual tendencies who were likely to indulge in secret activity. Deprived of female company, many heterosexual and, of course, bisexual men indulged in covert liaisons, not least due to the proximity of their comrades in cramped and highly-charged environments.

Ian Gleed was a heroic, twice-decorated Spitfire pilot who published a memoir about the Battle of Britain entitled *Arise to Conquer*. He was killed in 1943 when his plane was shot down over Tunisia. Ian was homosexual and, as Stephen Bourne states in *Fighting Proud*, his book on gay men serving in both world wars: 'he could not be open about this. He had to keep his sexuality secret or risk being court-martialled and thrown out of the RAF.'

Ian was from a medical family but, rather than become a doctor, he chose to join the RAF and relished the excitement of flying. He and the writer W Somerset Maugham met and became friends and, in 1942 when Maugham penned his wartime work *Strictly Personal*, it is believed that one of the young RAF pilots who featured prominently in it was Ian Gleed. This was confirmed in 1955 by another gay author, Hector Bolitho, whose work concentrated heavily on the military. His book *A Penguin in the Eyrie*, spoke of the lives of many young wartime pilots. In it he describes how Maugham recalled knowing one of these men 'somewhat more intimately' than the others he had encountered in both Britain and France during the war.

There are many accounts of Gleed's courage and impeccable record during his wartime service, before he made the ultimate sacrifice in 1943. When his wartime memoirs were released, the publishers Victor Gollancz were concerned that his apparent bachelor status could raise eyebrows among their readership. He was asked to concoct a story about a heterosexual relationship in order to deflect these concerns. Many years later accounts emerged about Ian Gleed's relationships with other servicemen and these confirmed Hector Bolitho's earlier revelation, confirming that the overwhelmingly macho image created around the Battle of Britain and its pilots was not always entirely accurate.

Hector Bolitho himself was an exceptionally talented writer who worked as a journalist and was involved in a professional capacity with the royal family and high-profile political figures of the day. At the outbreak of war he joined the RAF Volunteer Reserve. He kept extensive diaries and some of his accounts of air-raids and their consequences on London's population and infrastructure are among the most emotional and harrowing to have been written at the time.

In his latter role in the SOE Hardy may not have experienced the highly-charged atmosphere encountered by men thrown together on the front line, but during his training and early military service, he is likely to have encountered some interest from other servicemen.

Another dressmaker and designer, Neil 'Bunny' Roger, was in the army serving in the Rifle Artillery during the Second World War. He was later to go on to become one of Hardy's *angels*, or financial benefactors, in setting up the couture house, and also having the good fortune of launching a fashion business of his own, thanks to a donation from his father. Both designers enjoyed the patronage of the beautiful actress and star of many wartime films, Vivien Leigh.

Neil Roger was a flamboyant character, known by some as a 'dandy', and euphemistically 'a life-long bachelor'. He was sent down from Oxford for allegedly participating in homosexual practices, and this event spurred him into indulging his creativity, setting up his own fashion house in Great Newport Street in London in 1937, the year of King George VI's coronation and when Hardy was designing his sensational *Panic* suit for Lachasse.

Bunny was very well liked and Roy Allen, an apprentice to the tailor Mr Ernest, who began his career at the house in 1957 at the age of 15, recounts a story about his lack of grandeur, and his consideration and care for others:

> Bunny was on his way to one of the shows at Hardy Amies wearing a dusty pink velvet suit that he had made for himself. Because I had worked on the Hardy Amies collection, my mother had been invited to the event and, as it happened, I had made her a dress and coat to wear out of a very similar dusty pink fabric. My mother was on her way in and Bunny rushed up crying, 'Look we are twins!', and promptly took my mother's arm and walked into the salon with her.'

Mrs Allen was delighted to be escorted into the event by such a charming and sartorially elegant gentleman!

Bunny's dressmaking career was, like Hardy's, to be interrupted by the war, and he served in the Rifle Brigade in Italy and North Africa.

Decorated for his heroism during the famous Battle of Monte Casino in Italy in 1944, he never seemed to lose his glamorous tendencies. When spotted later in the bombed-out monastery at Monte Cassino, legend has it that he was wearing a chiffon scarf and had a copy of *Vogue* in his pocket!

It does appear to be wrong to believe that all overtly gay men serving during wartime were victims of homophobia. Accounts written at the time suggest that many homosexuals who were prepared to own their true selves were consequently accepted 'without reservation'. In fact some of the men who seemed to take risks with their behaviour in the same way, were actually some of the toughest and most 'macho' heterosexual soldiers, thrown as they were into circumstances which were far outside the boundaries of their usual lifestyles.

As Steven Bourne says in *Fighting Proud*: 'Over five million men served in World War II. Of these, it's likely that at least 250,000 were gay or bisexual.' Many of the more camp soldiers of the time were liked and well respected by their more macho colleagues as long as they were brave, reliable, and competent soldiers. They were even more revered if they indulged their theatrical and flamboyant nature by joining ENSA, the Entertainments National Service Association, typically glamming up as female impersonators. Despite Hardy's yen for the theatre and his enthusiastic participation in school dramatic productions, there does not seem to be any evidence of him taking part in any sort of theatrical venture during his service years.

His time must of course have been completely taken up with both his SOE work and the furthering of his design career throughout the war, but soon he was to leave all of that behind, for a new era was beckoning for Hardy Amies as an independent and potentially highly successful businessman.

Hardy's designing career had continued running concurrently with his military service, both with the Board of Trade and his personal fashion work. At this point in the war, with the international situation becoming more grim, the Board had issued a notice[1] in relation to the clothing industry. 'the encouragement of good styling is one of the ways in which the government can assist that industry'.

Coupled with the rationing of clothing, the restrictions on imports were considered to be having a damaging impact on the nation's morale. Consequently it was decided that, within the boundaries of austerity, the Board of Trade would introduce a scheme to produce utility clothing. The designs were to be kept simple and minimal in order to conserve any fabrics and other materials which could be diverted to the war effort. The scheme was widened to include furnishing and housewares in addition to clothing.

Transportation and damage to factories, as well as the reduced workforce, were having a limiting effect on clothing production and this had been foreseen by the government in 1940. They had decided to launch a utility label which became known as CC41 standing for Civilian Clothing Order 1941. It was under the auspices of this initiative that the Board launched The Incorporated Society of London Fashion Designers or IncSoc with the aim of promoting British fashion abroad.

Utility clothing was already being manufactured, but had not been proving popular compared with the stocks of clothing which were at that stage still available from before the outbreak of war. Customers were put off by the rather dreary name 'Utility', even though the clothes were on the whole not drab and dull, but simply manufactured along more austere lines and with an eye on thrift and control of resources. The initial perception of the concept of utility seemed to have led to it being confused with the word 'uniform', which convinced customers that it would hamper their efforts at presenting their own individual style and image.

Eventually it was accepted that the limits and controls put in place for clothing manufacture were to the benefit of consumers, as the fabrics on offer were smaller in number but higher in quality. The introduction of higher quality fabrics and the intervention of the Board of Trade in removing purchase tax from almost all utility goods, meant that utility clothing production became more competitive and the resulting garments more desirable.

To help encourage women to take pride in dressing in the new way, the Board came up with an exciting and innovative scheme. There had already been an initiative to promote the UK's top couturiers in the export market by introducing them to American customers in particular, and Hardy Amies had experience of this as he had been at the forefront in contributing to the collection sent to South America in 1941.

This time the Board decided that Harry Yoxall, managing director of the Conde Nast publishing empire and the founder of London *Vogue*, should organise the fashion designers into the body which became known as The Incorporated Society of London Fashion Designers. Norman Hartnell was to say of the initiative: 'We might even gain worldwide recognition for clothes based on a native style and dignity.'

So in 1942, when Hardy Amies became a founder member of IncSoc, alongside Hartnell, his predecessor at Lachasse; Digby Morton, and his design idol, Captain Edward Molyneux, he was delighted. Captain Molyneux had served with distinction in the First World War and had been awarded the Military Cross. He was twenty years older than Hardy and had lived and worked in Paris since the 1920s, setting up his couture house there, and becoming known for elegant lines and simplicity of shape. He had a great influence on many young British designers, particularly

Hardy Amies, and was the first chairman of IncSoc, holding the post until the end of 1946.

In his first autobiography Hardy is rather self-critical of the designs he produced for the IncSoc collection, describing it as 'most difficult for anyone to wear, and far too different from the current fashion to be called "good designing"'. Oddly enough, he removes these comments in his subsequent autobiography *Still Here* written in 1984! What he does state is that he enjoyed the experience of designing within the boundaries of the Board of Trade's austerity – or utility – scheme as, by then, he had 'settled down to an extreme sobriety of design'.

Of Molyneux, Hardy said: 'He had a great influence on me. He showed me how the sobriety of English style could become international chic.' He also recalls a conversation between himself and the revered Captain Molyneux about the style which was most appropriate for utility clothing. In *Fashion on the Ration*, Julie Summers writes: 'When the austerity regulations for utility clothing were announced, Hardy Amies said that both he and the Captain laughed. 'We have been making utility clothes for years, we said.'[2]

In the interview with Naim Attallah at the age of 83, Hardy spoke of Molyneux as having 'extremely good taste in clothes. He believed in simplicity, as I do.' He continues, 'The first dress I ever saw of his was the simplest possible garment that just buttoned up the front, but it was absolutely impeccably made.' Apparently this sighting left a lasting impression on the young designer. 'I learned that lesson and I follow it to this day', he declared.[3]

Sustainability put down many roots in fashion at this time of austerity, with the editor of *Vogue*, Audrey Withers, stating that fashion actually benefited from the restrictions in terms of the elegance and simplicity that came from the IncSoc designers. The regulations imposed put down firm foundations for scale, material, and manufacture that led to greater efficiency and less waste, although mass production is now looked upon as having gone too far.

With repercussions still abounding due to his association with the Lee Miller article in *Vogue* of March 1945, Hardy was keen to 'get out of the army as quickly as possible'. He had been praised in an official report in the same month, but reference was also made to him 'being impetuous' and needing 'a measure of supervision'. He felt this was due to disapproval from his superiors about his involvement with the *Vogue* episode, and how it was perceived as self-promotion on Hardy's part. He was very eager to resume his career as an independent designer and anxious should anyone decide that, due to his German language skills, he would be an asset during the army's occupation there. He felt 'mentally exhausted' by the struggles at the SOE and was convinced that what he saw as 'chaotic' organisation during the latter part of his military service would be continued post-war.

Having convinced himself that he had at least done his bit, and having been in no small way influenced by what seemed to be a churlish attitude over his pay during the last part of his tenure at the SOE, he took the view that it would be in the best interests of all sides to try to facilitate a smooth transition back into civilian life.

The government was keen to promote and boost exports and that, coupled with the fact that the SOE was starting to be disbanded, led Hardy to believe that the powers that be 'were not unrelieved to find someone who was not anxious to cling to his rank and pay'.

The issue of Hardy's pay being suddenly stopped was finally rectified by his superior officer Brigadier Mockler-Ferryman, who commented: 'I feel this officer has been hardly (*sic*) treated.' Thus vindicated, Hardy prepared for demobilisation. He travelled back to England, arriving at the end of March,1945. Hardy quickly reconnected with his previous personal and professional life by travelling up to Cumberland to visit old friends in the tweed mills. On his way back he received his official demob papers at the Intelligence Corps headquarters at Wentworth Woodhouse, Yorkshire.

His assessment of his demob wardrobe, which all departing servicemen were awarded at the time, was typically waspish. He found it to be 'of surprisingly good quality' but mostly 'rather unbecoming', with the exception of 'a cavalry mackintosh of excellent cut'. This latter garment was still being cherished at the time of writing his first autobiography in 1954 but, perhaps unsurprisingly, this fact was cut from 1984's *Still Here*. The mac had by then probably lost its place in his perfectly curated wardrobe, and was therefore not deemed worth a mention in the sequel.

Part Three
Business Begins

Chapter 12

Settling into Savile Row

O nce the war was over it was time for Hardy to start formulating a future for his business and an important part of that would obviously be finding the right premises. Shortly after VE Day he happened to be dining in Soho with an old friend, Geoffrey Houghton-Brown. Houghton-Brown was an antique dealer and an active figure in the sale of historic houses, and he suggested that Hardy view a very badly bombed-out premises, No. 14 Savile Row, in the heart of London's Mayfair. He said of the house: 'it has been terribly bombed, but I could see some wonderful panelling'.

Hardy quickly realised that he recognised the house as having been home to a dress shop before the war, as well as bearing a plaque on the front elevation which stated that the dramatist Richard Brinsley Sheridan had died there in 1816. On entering, Hardy and his friend Alexis ffrench were shocked to see the terrible state of the place, the result of a land mine exploding some four doors down the street. It was totally uninhabitable, but the proportions and light in evidence made it a very attractive proposition for the use that Hardy proposed for it. Some of the work done by the previous dress shop owner was still visible and would form a valuable basis for him to work from.

'I knew it was what I wanted,' says Hardy in his autobiography, 'although in all that excitement I didn't realise exactly how handsome the house was … until later.' The location in the heart of London's tailoring hub coupled with the regency proportions and imposing pillared entrance made the property extremely appealing to Hardy's aesthetic tastes.

The house was built in 1735 as part of the famed Burlington estate, which covers a vast area of Mayfair in central London. Despite there being many grander properties built by Lord Burlington and his architect William Kent, Hardy was proud to note that of the properties in Savile Row, No. 14 stood out as having a more impressive facade, with four instead of three windows. Even at the time of Hardy's first autobiography all the other houses in Savile Row had been converted into shops with vast plate glass windows stretching across their fronts, thus destroying the original facades, whereas No. 14 retained its original elegant appearance as a residential home.

As soon as his departure from the army was finalised in September 1945, Hardy officially took over the lease. The owners of the building were, fortunately, prepared to take a lower rent for his first two years of tenure in order to allow him to get the house into a habitable state, no easy task at that particular time as, after the war, building materials were in short supply.

With his reputation for tailoring, albeit in the sphere of womenswear, Hardy was delighted to be taking over premises in the prestigious Savile Row, but it was his love of architecture and all things cultural and aesthetic, which led Hardy to spend time researching the history of No. 14. He discovered that its first occupants were the Honourable George Berkeley and his wife, Henrietta, Countess of Suffolk. He assumed that that particular area of town began to become less fashionable by the time the couple moved out in 1813, as when Sheridan moved in he was struggling with debt and was, in fact, quoted in a rent book as being constantly in arrears. This situation worsened until in 1816 Sheridan was on his deathbed, unable to resist an invasion by bailiffs, and had all his possessions confiscated. The rather morbid last entry in the rent book reads; 'Dead. Insolvent.'

One of the most beautiful features of the house is a small room with a decorative window which was suspended above the staircase, and is said to have been the place from which the financially impecunious Sheridan would take refuge to observe the bailiffs periodically coming in to remove his possessions.

In mid-Victorian times Savile Row developed a reputation for being the home of several highly respected doctors, and was perhaps the Harley Street of its time. Queen Victoria's private physician was the last residing owner of No. 14 and, by the time of Hardy's visit, it would appear to have been one of the only properties in the street which had not been converted from a private residence. It was only in the latter part of the nineteenth century that Saville Row had begun to transform into a famed centre for tailoring.

Now was the time that Hardy had to finally announce his intention to run a fashion house under his own name and no longer under the auspices of the House of Worth. The Board of Trade had been invaluable to him in providing the financial cushion which meant his designing could be kept afloat, and his business, under the umbrella of the House of Worth, had been flourishing throughout the war years. The manager, Colonel Pay, was once again to become a significant figure in the life of the Amies couture house. He was by now involved in financing not only Worth but the French house Paquin, and had shown a good deal of interest in backing Hardy Amies within his growing empire. Hardy quickly deduced that joining the board of Paquin and Worth would essentially lead to him giving up his autonomy, and was not what he foresaw as his future. Through the feedback Hardy had been receiving from his loyal vendeuses Cammie and Violet, he knew that there was a demand for his work and that many clients had asked to be informed immediately if a Hardy Amies stand-alone house was ever to be established. This of course had greatly encouraged Hardy to do his utmost to try to launch on his own, but the problem now was how to finance the whole venture.

From his customer base he decided to call upon three trusted and steadfast clients to be shareholders in Hardy Amies Ltd. Top of his list, as she seems to have been one of his favourite people, was Virginia, Lady Jersey. As Virginia Cherrill, Lady Jersey was not only a successful American actress but also, for a while, the wife of Hollywood idol Cary Grant. Lady Jersey had been a customer of both Worth and Lachasse and was a devoted follower of Hardy Amies.

Unfortunately the timing was not the best, as a divorce from Lord Jersey was imminent and Lady Jersey was not in the most stable of financial positions. However, such was her enthusiasm for the up-and-coming couturier that she put forward a friend by the name of Mrs Dickie Gillson who, fortunately, was sufficiently wealthy to offer up some funding in her place. Virginia Cherrill meanwhile, still maintained a deep interest in the business and her beauty, charm, and fame were to continue to be a great asset to Hardy as he established the firm.

Hardy's father had now remarried and his stepmother, Mary Amies, also kindly sunk capital into the project. This seemingly pleasant and generous lady does not come out well in later reflections by Hardy. Asked about her by Naim Attallah, he rather disparagingly states: 'Although she was a goodhearted woman she was socially very inferior to our standards, which is an awfully snobbish thing to say, but it's true.'[1]

Talking about Rosemary's dislike of the new partner in her father's life he goes on: 'She was at first jealous of this really hideous woman. She was so ugly apart from anything else.' He then goes on with what could be described as a total lack of discretion: 'I now realise that my father was a very sexy man, and obviously she had certain tricks which satisfied him.' Thankfully both the protagonists had died by the time this interview was published! The second Mrs Amies' donation of £1,000 to Hardy's embryonic business did, however, motivate him to refer to her rather hypocritically, as his 'darling stepmother' later in the interview, so presumably he may have managed to muster some more benevolent feelings towards the hapless lady at some point.

Herbert Amies became one of the first directors of the fledgling company. Hardy's friend Alexis ffrench showed loyal support by buying shares in Hardy Amies Ltd despite needing funds for his own antiques business, as did Neil Roger, who was also running his own small dressmaking firm at the time. 'Bunny' had had a memorable time in the military during the war and subsequently set up his company, Neil Roger, in London. Buying shares in Hardy's business and later agreeing to sell them on when Hardy was trying to facilitate a buyout, was considered by Hardy as 'showing true strength of friendship'.

Among the other initial investors was Miss Agnes Linton of the Cumberland based Linton Tweed Mills, with whom Hardy had a long-standing relationship, and had visited on his return from Belgium. Hardy was a great admirer of both Miss Linton and her father, who had established the business, and praised their 'wonderful coloured tweeds' which he said had 'delighted and startled the world of fashion in the late twenties and early thirties.

While talking to Naim Attallah, Hardy eschews the idea of any great feeling of thrift or reservation where money was concerned immediately post-war. 'There was actually no feeling of austerity; everybody wanted new clothes,' he declared. 'The Americans were the ones who really encouraged us, they were on my doorstep before we even had the clothes – in fact they bought them from paper patterns.'

Hardy was initially disappointed by the general lack of support he received from other manufacturers and suppliers with whom he had worked at Lachasse and Worth. He felt let down by the fact that they did not rush to invest in his new venture, despite having seen its potential and indeed success, during his earlier career. However, in retrospect he came to value their show of commitment whereby they were always ready to supply him with cloth promptly and without demanding swift payment. This was obviously their preferred way of showing support rather than diverting their own capital away from their businesses at a time when post-war trading was not without its difficulties, despite the optimism of a newly launched businessman such as Hardy.

Hardy did approach several 'financiers' during the war, but the terms which they later wanted to lay down for the protection of their funds soon began to sound prohibitive to him. He seems to have felt hopeful during their wartime 'dinner meetings', but described the subsequent disappointing business appointments rather scathingly as taking place 'round their imitation Chippendale desks'. He was not impressed by their lack of sophistication and foresight, which must have led him to believe that, although he obviously could have done with their money, they would not have been a good fit for his business.

He did, however, have the good fortune of getting a man on board whom he described as 'a wonderfully imaginative accountant', Dick Hinds-Howell. In *Still Here*, Hardy recounts how Hinds-Howell 'guided me through my first paces and watched the business grow with almost paternal interest'.

Despite being a mere financial expert, Dick Hinds-Howell brought out feelings of enormous admiration from Hardy. In his earliest autobiography *Just So Far*, he recounts how the accountant explained and put into effect the perfect structure for a business over which Hardy ultimately wanted total control.

The way that Hinds-Howell constructed the plan for the business seems to have impressed Hardy to the point where he eulogised about it in *Just So Far*, saying: 'To this day I am amazed at the neatness of this beautiful arrangement. There is poetry in business as there is poetry in a fine rally in lawn tennis.' High praise indeed, and a very positive note on which to launch Hardy Amies Ltd.

The original staff of the business included his ever-loyal lieutenant, Mrs Flora Cohen. There was also Miss Violet, another vendeuse, who had been trained at Miss Gray, later moving to Lachasse to work for Hardy's predecessor Digby Moton. She had subsequently joined Hardy's team, which he noted was a move which was selflessly borne out of loyalty to him, as Violet did not get along well with Cammie. Miss Violet was to stay with Hardy until she felt he was well-enough established as a designer to allow her to leave without any feelings of guilt and devote herself to being a wife to the man she had married just before the outbreak of war.

Hardy also needed a tailor, and into this role stepped Mr Victor, who had replaced Mr Ernest at Lachasse in 1937. Mr Victor, had by then also left Lachasse and was working at a rather traditional company known as Russell and Allen, which was also part of Mr Shingleton's empire. He was finding the atmosphere at this company rather stuffy, and relished the thought of joining a newly established firm with the opportunity for more up-to-date, modern designs. Two other House of Worth employees, Mr Leonard and Mademoiselle Odette, who was Swiss and one of the top fitters and dressmakers at Worth, were soon to follow.

Miss Cammie had made it known to Hardy that both these extremely talented people would be very keen to join him once he launched his own line, but Hardy felt rather reluctant to poach staff from the House of Worth. This was mainly due to his feelings of gratitude and indebtedness to the director, Colonel Pay, as well as to Mrs Charlotte Mortimer, the Head of the House, who had both given him unfailing support in his early years. However, despite making advances to another admired fitter, Hardy eventually felt he had to approach Odette, who told him in no uncertain terms that she would have been offended if he had *not* asked her to come on board!

Just to compound Hardy's feelings of guilt at depleting the ranks of Worth staff, most of the technicians who worked under Mlle Odette decided to move with her, but this was quite normal practice at the time in the couture world. The acquisition of Mlle Odette and Mr Leonard was immensely important to Hardy. Their skills were invaluable, but also the sense of loyalty, enthusiasm and continuity from his pre-war operations at Worth would have made for a very promising starting point for Hardy Amies Ltd.

The business was to be overseen by a house manager, Ted Fothergill, whom Hardy already knew as he had been in charge of the mess and the office of the SOE in Brussels. In addition to the central team a number of young trainees would be taken on board as soon as possible to complete the founding workforce.

Filling the junior positions was not as easy as one might think and this was due in part to the timing of the launch of the business. So many young men were still tied up in the services, having not yet been released from their military duties and this, together with the fact that in those days young women were highly likely to leave their roles as seamstresses as soon as they married, meant that staff were thin on the ground.

Hardy describes this section of his workforce in *Still Here* as 'a lot of youngsters whom we had to train … all sorts of strange bodies, refugees and complete beginners'.

The Board of Trade were as supportive as they could be of the new venture as they could see the value that the Hardy Amies name and ethos could have in the promotion of British exports. It was important to capitalise on this with haste, as the already well-established world of French couture was consolidating its grip on the commercial market as things began to build up again after the war.

While tradesmen colonised the building, Hardy's workforce was valiantly toiling to get the designs – or models, ready for viewing. His reputation in the United States after his work on the Board of Trade's wartime export initiative stood him in good stead, and buyers from across the Atlantic were already showing keen interest in the pieces coming out of the new house.

In January 1946 orders were already in place from such large stores as Marshall Field of Chicago and Magnin of California, and the scene was set for Hardy Amies Ltd's first *in-house* fashion show.

By this time, Britain was ready for a new perspective on fashion. The editor of *Vogue*, Audrey Withers, having visited Paris in September 1945, was surprised to see that there was a sense of impracticality, even winsomeness, about the new styles being gradually made available to French women.

While it seemed to her that the British were still holding onto their utilitarian flat shoes and bulky-yet-practical warm overcoats, the French were about to cast off their wartime uniform and embrace more feminine and frivolous styles. From high-heeled shoes to flamboyant millinery, they were throwing caution to the wind in an effort to bid farewell to the drudgery and hardship of the past several years. The *Vogue* editor decided she needed to canvas opinion among British fashion experts about where they saw the direction of post-war fashion going.

The fashion critic and historian James Laver referenced historical periods following previous conflicts and decided that the women of Britain would not follow French thinking, but would instead restrict themselves to a more conservative vision, eschewing the playfulness and extravagance of their Gallic cousins. Another fashion critic, C Willett Cunnington, was similarly austere in his predictions, warning that cheap fabrics and an almost uniform approach would predominate, because women had become a larger part of the UK home front workforce, and would therefore have a more practical and parsimonious attitude to their wardrobes.

It was only Hardy Amies who seems to have trodden the delicate line between an ongoing feeling of austerity and a national desire to throw off the strictures of war and re-embrace creativity and feminine beauty. While acknowledging that many women would continue their new-found position in the world of work, Hardy also felt that they would want to embrace the freedom that should gradually emerge in the post-war years, perhaps by developing two separate wardrobes that would interact together. He envisioned a masculine style based around tweeds and tailoring for formal daywear, but in addition to that, a celebration of the female form in dresses and evening wear with full skirts, nipped-in waists, and accentuated shoulder lines.

As he said: 'her clothes will be rich and rather grand, but she won't be afraid to wear them'. Austerity was not going to take centre stage at Hardy Amies Ltd!

As fabric production and imports and exports began to take off again, the company went full steam ahead in designing and producing their first proper collection in readiness for the opening of the showroom. The cheap felt which Hardy had had to lay down to cover the floors was barely in place by the time of the first fashion show at 14 Savile Row in January 1946. Carpet was in short supply but, as Hardy said himself, this was a good thing as he could not have afforded it at that stage anyway.

In addition to all the other costs involved in setting up, Hardy was facing the potential expense of trying to furnish the property in a style to suit its George II architecture. He acknowledged that he made many mistakes along the way, but enjoyed gradually rectifying them as time went by and funds began to pour in.

His artistic and sophisticated friends John Fowler and Alexis ffrench contributed various ideas and theories on how the interiors should look. Fowler told him: 'You must give up all attempts to make these beautifully proportioned rooms look like a dress shop.'

Apparently Hardy's mother, on her deathbed, had asked Alexis ffrench to curb what she considered to be Hardy's expensive tastes. He felt obliged to pass on her thoughts to her son at regular intervals, despite probably disagreeing with her in many ways. According to Roy Allen the premises were, 'Stunning, like a country house.' Hardy's office was in one of the grand reception rooms and looked more like the morning room of an elegant regency residence. His secretary, however, was stationed in 'a little room under the stairs', which was not much bigger than a cupboard, but had the advantage of being attached to her boss's office.

Coping with the disadvantages of the tall and draughty old house must initially have tempered the excitement of setting up and launching the business. This may have added to the frayed temper of Miss Cammie who, 'never stopped complaining of House Manager Ted Fothergill's shortcomings'. The stress of all this appears to have led to a sustained spell of ill health for Fothergill, who was constantly having to deal with a workroom of 'temperamental and excited women', who were being stirred up by their imperious head vendeuse.

In her book *It Isn't All Mink*, Ginette Spanier, Directrice of the Paris fashion house Balmain, backs up this view, describing the world of the vendeuses in haute couture at the time as extremely frenetic and highly-charged.

Interestingly, Mme Spanier highlights the fact that she placed great emphasis on her Paris vendeuses displaying an English emphasis on good manners. 'I insist that the vendeuses should stand as the customers come in,' she says in *It Isn't All Mink*, 'the vendeuse is an important part of the nervous system of the Couture.' However, she recalled that her boss, Pierre Balmain, referred to these powerful ladies as 'enemy number one'.

Mme Spanier describes the vendeuses as going 'into a collective state of paralysis', whenever they see a new collection for the first time.'[2] Apparently, once they have built up a relationship with their clients and sold them the outfits which they believe show them off to their best advantage, the vendeuses find it difficult to move on to persuade them of the virtues of the next collection.

> They cannot see the collection as Balmain and his assistants see it, in terms of a work of art and beauty and excitement, instead they see it in terms of money, of business. This is all very well, but as they stand there brooding, they forget how important enthusiasm and encouragement are.[3]

This clash between art and business is obviously a source of stress in any couture house. Presentation of luxury and fantasy is an expensive process and the result is that many couturiers like Hardy and Norman Hartnell did not amass vast riches from their high-end clients, even when a collection sold reasonably well.

Mr Fothergill must have found the idea of balancing the creativity of Hardy Amies with the financial side of the business rather challenging, and ultimately he missed most of the first few months of operation at the business after being struck down with double pneumonia, eventually returning but being replaced at the end of 1946. Despite all this Hardy's vision for his new collection was a huge success and his tailored yet feminine clothes were extremely well received. This was a great achievement, especially when we consider that Hardy was an innovator in Savile Row at the time, as all the other tailoring that was being produced there was very definitely aimed at the gentlemen's market.

In suiting, the silhouette was still firmly rooted in the wartime austerity image with nipped-in waists, jackets curving out over the hips and neat, fairly short skirts. The skill of the tailoring was exemplary with perfect form-fitting and attention to detail obviously paramount. In overcoats, shoulders were large in order to accommodate suit jackets beneath, and the bottom of the coat would naturally be fuller too.

More extravagant shapes were just around the corner, however, as in Paris Christian Dior was soon to launch his New Look, with its tightly fitted neat jackets over voluptuously full skirts, a look that was to influence the world of fashion and herald the final abandonment of austerity.

Hardy's love of tweed and earthy natural colours was a signature aspect of the collection and expressed his 'country into town' philosophy. Brown, a colour not particularly loved by urban ladies, was a favourite of Hardy's, and its use would have been quite innovative in upscale, urban city settings. As Nicholas Worth says, 'Hardy was a stickler and loved the rules of fashion, but he also bent the rules. He wore brown and tweed in town.'

Hardy's very presence in Savile Row was like a vibrant canary arriving in an aviary of blackbirds and ravens. As Richard Martin of the Cotswold Woollen Weavers explains: 'He was the first womenswear designer on Savile Row and that was a very difficult thing to do. They were all very wary of interlopers.'

Nicholas Worth agrees:

> All the couture houses were in Mayfair – Digby Morton, Lachasse, Hartnell – and then for Hardy to start up in Savile Row was quite something. ... Hardy didn't really like the comparisons with 'Dear Norman', as he called Norman Hartnell, but the two of them were both very much the first to do something which was, at the time, very different.

Richard Martin again:

> Hardy and Norman Hartnell were the first people to produce tailored garments in a particular niche, unencumbered by Paris. Before that it had always been things coming over from Paris to London. Hardy saw that he could create something to rival that by taking on the premises in Savile Row.

After the first show orders flooded in, despite a feature which would probably have alienated many modern buyers. Perhaps with an eye to distinguishing the structure of men's tailoring from women's, part of Hardy's single-minded approach to his first autonomous collection was to draw attention to the hip-line, even going so far as to insert canvas-covered pads to the area.

Of this he rather indiscreetly says, in *Just So Far*: 'Of course it took a long time for our fatter customers to get used to the idea.' This would almost certainly have been considered a very un-politically correct comment for a designer to make nowadays – even if they were likely to be thinking it. However, in post-war austerity Britain there were not likely to be too many overweight ladies and, in the high echelons of society from which couture customers were inevitably drawn, slimness was considered an enviable asset.

The famous quote from the Duchess of Windsor, 'One can never be too rich or too thin', would only have worked on one count with Hardy. He enjoyed producing clothes for the female form and despite having no sexual urges towards women, appreciated their shape and how good they could look in the right clothes. 'All good designers must be body lovers,' he says in *Still Here*,[4] 'I love seeing beautiful bodies and I love touching them and being touched.'

That first collection in 1946 was not only well received by the home audience but the delegations from abroad were also impressed, and this was to set the foundation for a business model that would continue for the next four decades. As Roy Allen recalls: 'The first shows were always on his birthday, July 17th, and then we'd break for the summer.' A lovely annual celebration for the boss.

Having received many orders from the United States Hardy was personally invited by the Marshall Field buyer, Anne Sheehan, to be present at the store's first show of imported British and French clothing since before the war. Hardy jumped at the chance and in *Just So Far* he recounts that his journey to the States was rather uncomfortable, as in those days air travel was 'almost military in its austerity'.

Presumably it cannot have been as gruelling as his tense flight in the tin-can that took him for his parachute jump in Manchester however! He was met in New York by a group of stern looking businessmen who turned out to be the executives of Marshall Field, all of whom were as apprehensive of him, the first European fashion designer they had ever met, as he was of them. However, they got to know each other over 'enormous steaks and several scotches', and after that, all got on like a house on fire. In *Still Here*, Hardy skips over some of the details of this first business trip to America forging contacts for his label, but the information he gives in the original *Just So Far* is fascinating to the modern reader and social historian.

Hardy spent a frenetic few days visiting all the stores he had previously had dealings with in New York, and then took a train out to Pittsburgh where an English female friend was living with her steel-magnate husband. He also wanted to visit a store in the town as he wanted to see places other than just the large cities while in the United States. He had been warned that New York did not represent the whole of America, as indeed it still does not today. He received something of a shock when he arrived at Marshall Field in Chicago, as Anne Sheehan broke the news to him that she was leaving the company. In his own rather catastrophising way, Hardy recalls that he momentarily 'wondered if she had been sacked because she brought me out there', and that he had to be 'calmed down'. After this temporary drama he was reassured that Ms Sheehan was only leaving as she wished to retire and write a book!

The highlight of this trip appears to have taken place the next day, 9 May 1946, the day of the Marshall Field fashion show, which he describes in

Just So Far as 'one of the most exciting experiences in my dressmaking career'.

Hardy was extremely gratified to see that the obviously affluent audience was taking an enormous amount of interest in his collection. Among the other collections on show, the Hardy Amies clothes appeared simple, but with clean lines and an 'easy to wear' appeal. Beautifully fitted sheath dresses, ingeniously constructed skirt suits displaying exquisite tailoring, and capacious overcoats with statement collars were the signature styles of the new couture house. Hardy's only reservation about what was on display at Marshall Field seems to have been that the clothes did not fit the models perfectly, or 'mannequins' as they would have been called were the show being mounted in London.

However, this description applied to all the houses which were showing, and as he said himself: 'I must say our own efforts looked pretty good'. So good in fact, that 'they were practically the first to be sold, because they were easy to wear'.

After this glorious experience Hardy's American adventure continued via a trip on what he describes effusively as 'the fabulous train, The Twentieth Century Ltd'. Everything from his sleeping berth to the food on offer in the dining car seems to have exceeded Hardy's expectations as he travelled back to New York in great comfort from Chicago.

From New York he sped on to Boston where he was called upon to give a lengthy speech to a Ladies' Luncheon club. He recalled speaking for an hour and a quarter and being rather surprised by how transfixed the audience were, hanging on his every word. Despite the fact that he was speaking off the cuff, he felt that he was fairly well prepared as he had had to answer many press questions and enquiries from those he had already met in the previous few days.

However, this did not prevent him from expressing his surprise at how enthralled the audience seemed to be; on asking one of the ladies present afterwards if he had actually been as impressive as was indicated by the 'tumultuous applause', she replied: 'My dear sir, we would have been as interested if you had read from the telephone book, for we are all fascinated by your voice: it is the first British voice we have heard since before the war.' High praise indeed![5]

Such was the endorsement of Hardy's designing skills that he came away from his trip with 'open orders' to the value of about £8,000 – about

£350,000 today. This meant he was able to select models from his next collection to send out to the United States, without awaiting the buyers' visits. This was partly because there was such a shortage of stock in the stores after the war. Nonetheless, it was a fine tribute to a newly established design house, and a brilliant launching point for Hardy's international breakthrough as a 'living label'.

Chapter 13

Establishing the House of Hardy

After this initial and most gratifying trip to America, Hardy had to start the process of firmly establishing the staff, processes, and routines for the fledgling business. There were now so many orders that they needed to be divided fairly between all the vendeuses or saleswomen, within the separate workroom structure, and furthermore it became apparent that many more staff were going to be required. Hardy paid multiple visits to colleges and art schools in an effort to recruit young workers, but still more reliable and experienced staff members were obviously necessary.

A great step forward came when Hardy realised that the faithful Cammie was still regularly in touch with a well-established and experienced saleswoman whom they had all got to know when Hardy took up his position at Worth.

Madame Marthe was a French lady married to an Englishman and steeped in the world of fashion, as her mother was the owner of the French fashion newspaper *L'Officiel*. She had always used Mlle Odette as her fitter at Worth, and was thus rather upset when Odette had moved to Hardy's new establishment. Coincidentally, one of the tailors, Mr Leonard, was also getting restless at Worth and somehow, through the collusion of Cammie and Marthe, it became apparent that were Marthe to move to Hardy Amies, Mr Leonard would probably also make the change, bringing his workforce with him. Enough time had passed since Hardy himself had left Worth for him to feel that he was not instrumental in causing a mass exodus from the company and, in the autumn of 1946, the arrival of these additional personnel helped establish a strong staff base for the house. Naturally, the clientele that Mr Leonard and Mdme Marthe brought with them was also a great asset to Hardy.

As is the case in many businesses, people often move on and seldom stay with one company for any length of time. Hardy claims never to have incentivised any of the Worth staff members to jump ship and come to him, but simply made it clear that they would be very welcome if they did make the decision to do so. That did not stop him still feeling in some ways apologetic to the company, and especially to Colonel Pay, the director at Worth with whom he had a history that spanned his career in the military as well as in couture.

As a comfort to himself, he notes in both *Just So Far* and *Still Here* that both Worth and Lachasse continued to prosper even after the departure of some of their core workforce.

Established haute couture staff were obviously extremely skilled in their work and expected great commitment and application from any young employees who wished to take steps towards joining their ranks. Unusually for the professional world at the time, couture was considerably dominated by female talent, and those who had risen to positions of superiority often struck fear into new entrants, particularly young men! Roy Allen observed of Mme Marthe: 'She was a tyrant – we were all scared of her. The vendeuses were all scary.'

Before Hardy settled down to work on his Autumn Collection he took the opportunity to take a holiday with some friends at a villa near Cannes. Tellingly, the only one of these friends that he names in *Just So Far* and *Still Here* is Alexis ffrench the antique dealer who had already played such a significant part in the progressions of his life and his career. In the autobiographies he refers to the trip in nostalgic terms. They had all 'known and loved France before the war and this was a most exciting return to well-loved sights, smells and flavours'. Such an idyllic description perhaps gives the reader a hint about the hedonistic nature of the vacation.

Of course, in the days when *Just So Far* was written and at the outset of his career, Hardy would never have alluded to his sexuality in any overt way. He continued to gloss over it in *Still Here*, even though that book was penned in 1984. Whether that was because the AIDS pandemic was emerging at the time, bringing with it an unjustifiable level of fear and prejudice against the homosexual community, we cannot know. Perhaps Hardy believed his business could be affected, or he simply still preferred to keep his private life out of the public eye.

Hardy had become acquainted with Alexis in the 1930s and he became one of a small but very influential coterie of friends, which included the interior decorator John Fowler of Colefax and Fowler, and Nina Leclercq, who eventually became Fashion Editor of French *Vogue*.

Alexis was married to Anne, and between them they had four children: Alexis was father to one daughter from his previous marriage, and Anne had three daughters, also from an earlier marriage, whom Alexis helped bring up. Although Anne had come from a family of landowners in New Zealand, she was largely brought up among the country set in England. The family was very wealthy and she and Alexis had at least two residences in the United Kingdom, which facilitated separate lives whenever it seemed to suit their circumstances.

In *Just So Far* Hardy recounts how the couple offered him a room in their Kensington flat when he first began work at Lachasse in 1934, and subsequently 'gave me a family life for the next twenty-two years'. Anne was a customer of the Lachasse couture house when Digby Morton was in charge and moved on to Hardy with enthusiasm. Once absorbed into the ffrench's large family, Hardy found a communal support group similar to that which he had had when he first moved out to Europe as a youth. As he said in *Still Here*, when discussing his confirmed 'bachelorhood': 'This does not mean I am not a family man. I am.'

In an interview with Sally Brampton published in the *Independent* newspaper in 1999, ffrench is described as Hardy's mentor and he admits to 'a liaison' which spanned twenty years. However, 'That doesn't mean it was based on sex,' he says. 'We got on well together, respected and loved each other.' Hardy refers to Alexis teaching him a great deal about 'food; more of course about antiques and decoration', but it is to his wife, Anne, that he seems to defer, stating that she 'never failed to command respect'. As previously stated, the couple were a major factor in, and influence on, Hardy's life until Alexis's early death from bone-marrow cancer in 1956.

Back in the workplace, Miss Violet Allen, who had been one of Hardy's great assets at Lachasse, retired to devote herself to housewifely pursuits and this was the point at which the highly qualified Betty Reeves, who had joined Paulette as a junior at the same time as Hardy began work at Lachasse. Betty's cordial working relationship with Violet made customers feel very comfortable and led to a greatly loyal following among Hardy's clientele, many from the aristocracy. This was later to lead the new house to its most high-profile client, Her Majesty the Queen, or Princess Elizabeth as she was when Hardy Amies Ltd began its relationship with her.

Speaking to Naim Attallah, Hardy could not express his devotion to the monarch in any more fulsome fashion. Asked about his great admiration for her, he said, 'for many reasons – her politeness, the order of her mind, the way the palace is run, the way she has never failed to keep an appointment'. He states that he would die for the monarchy, saying: 'It's one of our most precious assets"

As business picked up Hardy realised that he would need another dressmaker in addition to Madame Odette, and at this point Maud Beard joined the ranks, specialising in what Hardy called the 'softer models to make' since she had great skill at draping jersey and chiffon.

Hardy was soon off on his transatlantic travels again, setting sail for New York in September 1946 as the guest of the department store, B Altman and Co, who were to present a show of his models at the Plaza Hotel. As fulfilling as that must have been, Hardy's social engagements appear to have been the highlight of the trip, especially in the company of a designer whose name, Omar Khayam – referencing the Persian classical poet – seems to have tickled Hardy.

This ebullient fellow creative – 'a poppet' according to Hardy – was his partner on one particularly entertaining evening. The two had dinner after which they 'took a taxi and cruised slowly down Fifth Avenue'. As it was the time when the new collections were on display in the windows of the large department stores, the two would leap out to scrutinise the displays and Omar 'would proceed to tear most of the dresses to pieces, adding colourful details about the various designers' private lives'.[1] In a true sense of fairness, he apparently did not spare his own either!

One can only imagine the thoughts of the taxi driver as the flamboyant pair jumped in and out of his vehicle as they toured the shopping streets of New York after dark. The fact that he would have been keeping his meter running must have made the experience worthwhile, even if it was a little bemusing for him.

This evening of jocularity may well have been equalled for Hardy by the breakfast party he attended at the home of the actor Edward G. Robinson once he had left New York and flown to Los Angeles. There followed a night at the opera in San Francisco before he flew back to New York to catch the first night of Lady Windermere's Fan, in which Cecil Beaton himself supposedly acted in addition to designing the costumes.

On Hardy's return the business was running well, apart from the fact there was still a need for a good manager with a sound knowledge of the couture business. Madame Marthe recommended a young man named

Stanley Cox whose parents had both worked with Marthe at the House of Worth. Stanley himself had held a position in the stockroom for Edward Molyneux before he joined up for war service and was, by this time, back there but apparently not enjoying the work.

Stanley impressed Hardy from the moment they met, as he felt he had an instinctive love of figure-work, accounts, charts, and percentages. Despite the fact that the executives at the House of Molyneux were somewhat apprehensive about the young Stanley's readiness for such a responsible position, they released him to Hardy Amies Ltd and Hardy subsequently described him as 'a remarkable person', and 'tremendously respected throughout our House'.

Hardy described himself as the kind of person who 'adores figures, if I don't have to work them out', and presumably if they are distinctly in the black column. This affection and enthusiasm obviously engendered the great respect that Stanley Cox enjoyed from his employer in his role as house manager and company secretary. Stanley remained with the house until he retired in 1976, and was described by Hardy in *Still Here* as 'a man of integrity coupled with a respect for business procedures in general and a knowledge of the slightly dotty trading habits of the *haute couture*'.[2]

In an obviously heartfelt endorsement, Hardy speaks of his indebtedness to Stanley, not only for his loyalty and service from the earliest days of the business, but for his even-tempered and fair behaviour in all his interactions and relationships within the house. He valued his meticulousness and attention to detail hugely.

The business was soon doing so well that Hardy was compelled to create more space and, serendipitously, it so happened that some floors in the house next door became available in the summer of 1947. There was already another tailoring business on the ground floor of number 15 Savile Row, but the upper floors were quickly acquired by Hardy Amies Ltd as leasehold from the ground floor occupant. The house was by no means as grand, large, or architecturally admirable as no 14, but it was certainly functional for the initial use as fitting rooms, and gradually for more operations as and when the tenants moved out. Hardy found the slow progress of these transitions very wearing and was relieved to be able to take a holiday in the health resort of Grindelwald in Austria, before the launch of that year's Autumn Collection.

Although Hardy had made many visits to the United States at the invitation of some of the top department stores out there, his work was also being very well received in the Canadian market. There was a sense that the clients in cities like Montreal were rather offended by the fact that they seemed to be below the United States in Amies' list of priorities. Therefore, by 1947 a visit seemed long-overdue. Two stores, Eaton's and Henry Morgan's, were supporters of the label and had been since before the House in Savile Row was opened. Both companies were based in Montreal and Hardy later recalled that although he made the visit independently, representatives from both stores appeared to be awaiting him, vying to be the ones he chose to chauffeur him from the railway station. He made a good attempt at ameliorating things between the competitive stores and divided his time accordingly, overlooking each one's attempts to promote his visit as being primarily for their benefit.

A representative of the Henry Morgan company had the pleasure of driving Hardy into the Adirondack mountains at the weekend but – unlike most tourists who pay peak-season rates to travel to see the autumn colours of North America – the discerning designer was unimpressed. He later wrote:

The countryside was ablaze with the reds of the Autumn maple. At the risk of losing a lot of friends, not to mention a lot of customers, I have to record that I thought the colour horrible, but then I have always disliked all those shrubs which we cultivate for their autumn leaves rather than their summer flowers.

He was nothing if not firm in his views. Hardy seemed rather truculent in his opinions and seemingly did not adapt or modify them even when being hosted on the other side of the world.

Something which found more favour with him was his journey from Detroit, which he visited after Montreal, back to New York on the *Twentieth Century* locomotive. On his previous rail trips he had merely had a sleeping berth but, this time he upgraded to a 'drawing room'. As much as he evidently enjoyed the space and luxury, he bemoaned the fact that it meant he 'sat solemnly by myself when I would much rather have gone along to the dining car' at mealtimes. However, as he said: 'I suppose it is one of those things one ought to do once in one's life.' His sense of superiority won the day.

Around this time a very valued and loyal staff member joined Hardy Amies and he was a man with an impressive pedigree in the mind of his new employer. Peter Hope Lumley was the son of Kathleen Molyneux, who managed the Edward Molyneux Couture House on behalf of her brother. Therefore, Peter was the nephew of Captain Edward Molyneux, whom Hardy considered the ultimate role model in the world of fashion. Having worked with his uncle for a while and not having got on particularly well with him, Peter was happy to move to Hardy Amies, which was by then becoming a well-established and respected house. He still worked on a contractual basis for other companies, but Hardy Amies was to be his only couture client.

Peter was to take on the role of Press and Public Relations Officer. This job had, rather surprisingly, been under the remit of Miss Cammie up until then, and Hardy refers to Peter's arrival at the end of 1947 as 'the beginning of a most happy relationship'. He was later the recipient of the sum of £10,000 in Hardy's will.

One of Hardy's other loyal and trusted lieutenants, Mr Ernest, who had been one of the tailors at Lachasse, also joined the house later in 1948, establishing a workroom in the upper floors of No 15 Savile Row. His skills were greatly admired and some of his designs were easily identifiable by the way he worked with asymmetric cuts and architectural shapes.

That October Hardy was awarded the Order of the Crown of Belgium and this seems to have finally laid to rest the ghosts of his latter wartime experience in Brussels. As he says in *Just So Far*, he was 'immensely pleased' by the bestowing of the honour, showing how much the self-critical opinion he had of his work there still played upon his mind. Interestingly, by the time he penned *Still Here* in 1984 he appeared to have let go of his negative feelings, or perhaps they just diminished with the passage of time, for the award was not mentioned.

Hardy's thoughts soon returned to the important things in life – decor, taste, and etiquette. He travelled to the US again in the spring of 1949, travelling both there and back on the *Queen Elizabeth*. Despite the luxury of the liner, Hardy could not help but note that the interiors were 'banal' and the food 'pretentious'. However, he was impressed by the exemplary service and organisation on the ship. He referred to the voyage as the time when he cemented his love of the card game Canasta, which he was apparently addicted to for the rest of his life, barely leaving the card tables while on board.

He was also very impressed by the style of the other passengers. He made many trips to the United States from the late 1940s up to the end of his career, such was the popularity of his work over there. On his return in the middle of 1949 however, things were not so positive in the workrooms of Hardy Amies Ltd. There was an obvious clash of personalities and working styles between Mr Victor and Miss Cammie and this was exacerbated by Victor's desire to start a business of his own.

The inevitable soon happened and he gave his notice, which Hardy reluctantly accepted. Hardy said that they parted as the best of friends, and he was comforted by the fact that in Mr Ernest, he was already fortunate to have the perfect replacement. Ironically, Miss Cammie 'did nothing but bemoan the loss of Victor' for the following season.

Hardy was at pains to assert to Miss Cammie that Mr Ernest's character was totally different to that of Victor. What is more, Ernest was now trying to re-establish himself after quite a long time out of the world of haute couture, having had a long break for wartime service. However, Cammie's lack of patience and volatility made for a fraught atmosphere in a small workspace. Indeed, work was coming in at such a rate that more staff were obviously going to be needed, and now there was the extra space in No 15 Savile Row, Hardy set about establishing more workrooms and showrooms and filling them with staff.

Among all these plans, however, was the persistent problem of Miss Cammie. After just a year in his new position, Mr Ernest had made it known to Hardy that he would have to leave the business unless arrangements were made that meant he no longer had to work with the irascible *grande dame* of the house. Hardy pondered on the problem and worked out that although Miss Cammie presented herself extremely well and was never anything less than elegant in her dress and deportment, she must in fact have been over 70 years of age by this time. By all accounts she was as tidy in her home environment as she was in her personal presentation, residing in a bijou apartment in Chelsea which she kept as neat as a new pin.

Despite Miss Cammie's temperamental and often confrontational nature, Hardy admired his long-standing colleague enormously. He thought of her as one of the most capable saleswomen in London and was full of praise for her knowledge of dressmaking and her sewing skills. For many years, she was the embodiment of the world of couture at that time and appeared to live and breathe the business. This almost physiological connection to the work of the couturier is summed up by Ginette Spanier in *It Isn't All Mink*: 'My enthusiasm is a genuine thing. If I don't feel it for something, then I cannot sell that thing. I don't think. I look. I enjoy.'[3] Hardy and Cammie were in many ways kindred spirits, and both had a love of the good things in life and a very discerning view of the world. In his autobiographies Hardy refers to the times when she would telephone him at home in the evenings so they could converse at length, for which there was not always time during the working day.

Hardy appears to have felt that Cammie could have been his equal were it not for her intransigence, along with her haste and lack of attention to detail where orders and record-keeping were concerned. All of this was manageable when the two were working together at the outset of the establishment of the house, but as the business grew and more staff were coming on board, Miss Cammie became a destabilising influence, and one which did not help to create a calm atmosphere.

She was unerringly rude to any new, young members of staff, with the result that some of the junior assistants who were assigned to work with her would hastily leave the business as they found it such a trial. All of these rather negative factors were now expanding and this, coupled with the fact that Hardy and his other colleagues were noticing a decline in Miss Cammie's health, meant he felt he would have to take action.

The prospect of Mr Ernest being forced out by Miss Cammie's intolerance and pugnacity meant that Hardy had no choice but to confront his responsibility to restore harmony in his burgeoning business. It is obvious from the amount of deliberation he recalls in his books that he did not take the prospect of dealing with Miss Cammie's failings lightly. He describes a scene in which he could tell she was irritably assessing one of the garments being discussed at a costing session, as making him aware that she had become 'a very sick, obstinate old woman, and that the time had come for me to do something about it'.

He recognised that her knowledge, skill and experience were now being outweighed by the growing flaws in her character, and that many of his customers did not like her and some even feared her. Her overwhelming loyalty and the relationships she had built up with Hardy himself as well as some of his original staff members was still strong however, so it was with a heavy heart that he drew up a plan of action to facilitate Miss Cammie's 'retirement' from the house.

This decision necessitated consultation with Hardy's solicitor and business advisers and it was decided that making a fair but final severance was the best course of action for both parties. It says a lot that Hardy's secretary brought him a fortifying glass of brandy before the momentous meeting with Miss Cammie took place.

He recalls it being tantamount to having to ask his own mother to leave the family business, and all the platitudes and mollifying phrases he began the interview with fell on stony ground as Cammie immediately took up a defensive position, especially where references to her health were concerned. This inevitably led to Hardy having to be cruel to be kind, and thereafter the end was in sight and 'it was all over in fifteen minutes'.

It was to be a sad end to a very significant relationship in Hardy Amies' life. Miss Cammie had been a mother figure to him and it was a source of heartbreak that she would only communicate with him through solicitors after she left the company. He managed to get her to accept a reasonable deal, though her pride precluded her from taking a pension. This situation was alleviated by her sale of the small group of shares she had, which Hardy worked out should have kept her comfortably until she had calmed down and was prepared to talk with him again. She maintained contact with her close colleagues Marthe and Odette, but Hardy deduced that her opinion of him as her employer was rather critical during any conversations she had with them. He made further attempts at contact over the ensuing year, but Miss Cammie was still very resistant to his overtures.

Having given up trying to heal the rift, Hardy was badly affected by the tragic way Miss Cammie's life seemed to end. He received a phone call from the wife of a doctor who attended her in the latter stages and discovered that the varicose veins she had suffered from for many years had accelerated into several cancerous wounds, which by the time she was taken to hospital were too far advanced to be treated.

Miss Cammie's funeral was rather a pitiful affair with Hardy, Mme Odette, and Mlle Marthe, the doctor and his wife the only mourners. Although Hardy knew in his heart that he had done the right thing by forcing her to leave her post, he still felt he had gone about it in the wrong way. Up until the end he had wondered if there was a chance of a reconciliation between himself and such a long-serving and fondly loved employee and friend, but it was a forlorn hope and was always to be a source of self-reproach for Hardy.

Her death cast a long shadow over the man and the Hardy Amies' business, as she had been such a ubiquitous part of it from the beginning. It also caused a great feeling of loneliness in Hardy; he reveals in *Just So Far* that he was henceforth reluctant to share things too closely or take anyone into his confidence where the house was concerned, as he always feared that things could turn out badly, as they had with Miss Cammie.

During the late 1940s Hardy put a great deal of effort into establishing the business at home as well as thoroughly pursuing the export market. After a chance meeting he took on a young executive called Bill Ackroyd, whom he had met some years before when Ackroyd was working at his father's woollen mill in Yorkshire. An aesthete, Hardy realised Ackroyd had a considerable grasp of the finer things of life and a deep understanding of etiquette, behaviour and appropriate dress among what he referred to as 'the county set'. Along with a distinguished military record resulting in the award of the Military Cross, he was also from a wealthy background and invested money in the business as well as becoming, as Hardy described him, his 'personal assistant'. With Ackroyd's arrival and a more harmonious atmosphere in the workrooms, Hardy felt that at last the business was settling into a comfortable order and routine.

Around this time, Neil Roger actually moved his dressmaking operations into the Savile Row premises and Hardy credits both Ackroyd and Roger with boosting his profile and enhancing the enthusiasm at the house. 'They were of immense help in building up our reputation,' he says in *Still Here*. Hardy gained business knowledge from Bill Ackroyd, and Ackroyd's father also gave him invaluable advice which led to a financial restructuring of the company. Hardy was content with the way the business was going, at this point he was happy with the scale of everything and felt reluctant to speculate with larger ventures, concerned that such ambition may lead to losses. He seems to have been keenly aware that it would have been a mistake to gamble on more staff and higher outgoings while there was the ever-present possibility of going through seasons where business could slacken off. Financial advice and actual monetary input from the Ackroyds appears to have had a reassuring effect and calmed the ship as Hardy Amies Ltd entered the 1950s.

Ackroyd, and indeed some of Hardy's other friends, were also a link to the higher echelons of society. Hardy had already begun to attract very famous celebrity clients such as Lady Olivier – otherwise known as the beautiful Oscar winning actress Vivienne Leigh – as well as his loyal customer and investor from the early days, Lady Jersey. In addition, he was well known for having a young set of clients, which together with his appeal across the Atlantic, lent Hardy a reputation for being a forward-thinking, diverse, and modern designer. This, coupled with his growing appeal to the aristocracy, made for a comprehensive and enviable customer base, which was to exemplify the business throughout his career.

He talks in *Just So Far* about taking on a 'second generation' of skilled staff. Young women he had first encountered at Lachasse who may have taken time away from couture to raise families, were returning to work and keen to join his burgeoning business, as well as daughters of some of the more established staff members who were now entering the workforce and were equally enthusiastic. Having experience at, or hearing about, the world of fashion from their mothers or aunts encouraged them, but being able to join a new, young house obviously held great appeal to these younger seamstresses and saleswomen. Another younger lady, Sheila Ogden – originally a customer at Lachasse – had also come on board, so Hardy had assembled what he saw as a very harmonious quartet of vendeuses. Marthe and Betty had been joined by Sheila and another enthusiastic new recruit, Monica, in all of whom Hardy felt confident of the discretion and personal attention that his sophisticated clientele expected.

Chapter 14

Management and Expansion

By mid-1950 Hardy was satisfied with the composition of the house, but was aware that he could easily expand and move forward with various new ventures. One of these was his appreciation of how little competition there would be if he advanced his foray into the American market. Already popular there, he was conscious of how little there was in the way of US businesses that dealt in handmade clothing, and that those that did were heavily influenced by French design. His instincts told him that the way to have any significant impact on the market over there was to not only introduce his couture range, but also to offer a ready-to-wear collection alongside it. An alliance was made with the emerging New York designer Charles James, and this association was to stand Hardy Amies in good stead with the market available across the Atlantic.

This connection which had been established in the late 1940s had already helped to raise the Hardy Amies profile in the United States and led to the launch of his ready-to-wear boutique. Nina Leclercq spearheaded this with regular forays overseas, to which she would take a large ready-to-wear collection, intending to show at a top hotel.

The attraction of their customers being offered the chance of the glamour and cachet of the Hardy Amies name without such a significant financial cost, led to the large-store buyers flocking to these shows, which subsequently became a biannual event. Hardy himself accompanied Nina Leclercq on some of these expeditions and his reputation and status grew exponentially as a result.

To actually establish a physical boutique operation back home, necessitated another aspect of business planning for Hardy. He had already deduced that he could utilise some of the workspace in Savile Row for the designing and fitting of a boutique ready-to-wear range, but the subsequent manufacturing of larger quantities of garments was something he had never investigated before.

Brothers Alex and Simon Brenner were businessmen with a strong background in clothing manufacture, and their mother had previously been a much-loved client of Hardy and Miss Cammie. Hardy approached them and they quickly came on board; Hardy Amies Boutique Ltd was launched in 1950 to run alongside the couture house.

Hardy's original doubts about the boutique side of the business were swiftly dispelled once Nina Leclercq actually took on the job of running the operation for him. From his first conversations with Nina, Hardy had recognised that she would be a perfect fit for the role, as she had gathered a great deal of experience of buying and selling ready-to-wear clothing while working for Fortnum and Mason in London, before repatriating to France to edit French *Vogue*.

As with many of his staffing issues Hardy does seem to have had great empathy with his fellow businessmen and would never have considered ruthlessly plundering their workforce. Even if he felt strongly that a person may be a good fit for his business, as well as potentially fulfilling their potential and enhancing their career by joining him, he would never actively encourage someone to leave their present employer. However, there were obvious signs that Nina was more than a little enthusiastic about the boutique initiative and regaled Hardy with tales of how popular such ventures were among the French customers, and she was filled with enthusiasm when Hardy put forward the idea of starting his own.

Hardy was therefore delighted when, while he was visiting her in Paris, Nina dropped a very unsubtle hint that she would love the job of running Hardy Amies Boutique. He must have been extremely flattered that this distinguished doyenne of fashion was prepared to give up her prestigious position at the Paris-based edition of *Vogue* to work for what was, in effect, a fledgling business. By the summer of 1950 the boutique was well and truly up and running and Hardy was having to expand the workspace at Savile Row to accommodate the staffing and logistical elements of the venture. Starting out with a small range of ready-to-wear suits and coats, Nina soon added dresses, sweaters, blouses, scarves and gloves, and sales quickly advanced along with the growth in the couture line. These garments were eventually made in workshops in the East End in what is still the heart of clothing production for London's 'Rag Trade', as well as at a factory in Weymouth, Dorset.

The Savile Row premises were by now home to showrooms, workrooms, and an actual retail outlet selling the boutique items which were made in-house. Certain items like Scottish knitwear were bought in so there was also a wholesale element to the business, as well as the export side. All this made for a fascinating mixture of fashion and industry, with intricate finance, tax, and business practices, which Hardy described as being 'a complicated piece of machinery' with himself at the head.[1]

Nina Leclercq had visited the United States with an extensive ready-to-wear collection in May 1951 and this further enhanced the popularity of the boutique with buyers from many top stores keen to place orders. The attraction of buying into the Hardy Amies name without committing to couture prices was to prove hard to resist for discerning customers. Launching the boutique proved a master stroke of business planning by the designer. Some at the company were not so keen on the idea however. Obviously Hardy himself was desperate to ensure that the business at the boutique was not having an adverse effect on the couture arm of the company. Any fears proved unfounded as the couture side of the house continued to prosper. However, couture was a well-established feature of the world of fashion, especially in Britain and France, and those who had worked in it for a considerable amount of time were wary of the encroachment of ready-to-wear under the same umbrella as an established design house.

Mme Marthe was a particular opponent of the boutique in the early stages. Being of French origin and with a mother, who owned a highly regarded fashion newspaper there, she actually regarded the arrival of the boutique as a grave threat to the couture line. Marthe went as far as to muster support in her opposition to the venture among the other staff, which resulted in Hardy having to set up different shows of the designs for couture and those for the boutique. It was apparently some years before both sets of designs were shown together, but once established, that became the norm for most fashion houses of the day.

It says a lot for Hardy that such episodes of insurrection did not always end with a parting of the ways between himself and the staff members involved. The house seems to have remained a congenial place throughout the heyday of the 1950s and early 1960s. Hardy was happy with his business and content with his clientele and, in that way, seems to have been admirably satisfied with how everything was falling into place. In *Just So Far*, he talks of how a group of small houses had evolved into 'London haute couture'. Despite the fact that the businesses fell into the formula of aiming for the overseas export market, they were not overly dependent on fulfilling that expectation.

Having been asked if he would actually like to launch a business in Paris, at the time of writing *Just So Far* Hardy said, 'No, I prefer to work in London. I understand the Englishwoman's attitude to dress, maddening through it may be at times. They have style, which transcends fashion, and even chic, on occasion.'[2] He did, however, maintain a routine of making regular visits to Paris, where he was on familiar terms with many of the top designers, throughout his career.

To sum up his attitude to the way an Englishwoman of the time dressed, he said: 'English ladies often try to look like French ladies. The secret of their charm is that they never succeed.' This may sound like damning with faint praise, but it is obviously tempered with a good deal of affection which would have undoubtedly endeared him to his clientele. His affectionate side came out in his treatment of his staff, and he often expressed paternal tendencies too.

Looking at the young apprentices entering his workrooms, he considered the fact that they may continue working for him five days a week for twenty years of their lives, and he felt the responsibility of this, saying: 'My House must be a harmonious and decent habitation as well as an efficient shop.' The well-being of his staff does appear to have mattered a great deal to him.

At the end of *Just So Far*, he states that 'we are sunk without workers', and obviously realised that the quality of his staff was of paramount importance to his reputation. 'Everything should be done to encourage craftsmanship; it is now as important as design,' he declared.

In *Still Here* he acknowledged that the hub of his operations was Savile Row and that there he had 'a band of people not only of great loyalty to their craft, as well as to me, but also a group of highly skilled and experienced artisans'.

He felt that his reputation as a designer was obviously a large part of his success, but his skill as a couturier meant he had 'been able to bring out the best in all the people who work for me'.

Mr Roy Allen, who is mentioned as a long-serving staff member in *Still Here*, acknowledges this, but also recalls that Hardy had an acerbic side to his personality which sometimes came out in his dealings with staff members.

He recalls speaking to his boss one day and observing that the business was running so well 'partly because of the loyalty we all feel', to which Mr Amies replied, 'What's loyalty?' in a rather dismissive way. The young Mr Roy was slightly crestfallen at this response, and obviously felt less than valued at that particular moment as a result of the casual put-down.

The pay structure in the house was not over-generous, but back in post-war Britain, as Roy Allen says:

> You were definitely expected to feel grateful that you had a job. We were given two weeks holiday a year plus Bank Holidays. I started on two pounds and ten shillings a week in 1957. You stayed on that for three years as an apprentice and then you had a year to prove that you had learned enough to be promoted, otherwise you were put back down as an apprentice. You had to be quick too, because at that point the work was piling up, we were so busy. Later on I was running my couture workroom and doing boutique work to make my workroom pay.

As the boss, as well as in his personal life, Hardy definitely had an air of superiority which would inevitably rise to the surface on occasion. Another of Mr Roy's anecdotes tells of one such incident which took place when he departed after attending a dress fitting with the queen. A palace staff member revealed to him later that Her Majesty had commented 'He is rather grand, isn't he?' as Hardy left the palace.

To his credit, pomposity and grandeur do not seem to be traits which Hardy either denies or felt ashamed of. One recollection in the earlier autobiography tells of a rather touching episode when he invented a personal motto. It was a description of how he felt about the couture business, and he had it translated into Latin: 'Less than art, more than trade'. The closest translation into Latin would appear to be: '*Impar arte, negotio superior' artis*'. Despite the self-confessed pomposity of inventing a personal motto in the first place, it does seem a good way of summing up the fashion world.

What Hardy seems to have meant was that the creative and artistic aspects of the business are highly admirable, but without good business sense to promote and progress the company, those aspects will never reach their full potential. He revered the balance of creativity with the financial and technical aspects, and appears to have been good at maintaining it, albeit through surrounding himself with those who could cover all sides of the business.

Hardy also claimed that his fashion vision was evolutionary rather than revolutionary and, as such, chimes well with the sustainability drive that dominates morally conscious fashion today. He had no desire for the new clothes he produced for his clients to make their existing wardrobe appear out of date or lacking cohesion.

Speaking of his undoubtedly well-off clientele, he accepted that they were very reluctant to spend money recklessly but acknowledged that 'this is contrary to what most people think'. At the same time, Hardy would not compromise on the quality of fabric or amount of labour he put into a garment so, in today's world, his theory and ethos could be considered a forerunner of the concept of sustainable fashion. The mantra 'Buy Better, Buy Less' is much repeated in today's fashion circles, and is thought to have first been coined by the designer Vivienne Westwood.

One concept that Hardy Amies voices in the chapter entitled 'The Designer' in *Just So Far*, would probably not resonate so easily with today's young woman. He references the fashion critic C. Willett Cunnington, saying that when a woman dresses, she 'assumes the shape which she knows instinctively will be most attractive to men'. Hardy goes on to say: 'When it is argued that women dress for women, I know that it is nonsense', though he does acknowledge that 'women are madly interested in what other women wear ... and love to outdo them.'

This latter theory is a perennial concept which is represented not only among the woman on the street and her circle of friends, but by the level of interest we now have in the wardrobes of celebrities and members of the royal family. I personally recall the excitement which was generated during the 1980s and 1990s over the clothes worn by the late Princess Diana. Thinking back to when I would pore over the pages of *Hello* magazine to rate the outfits the princess had worn over the course of a year, I was probably judging some Hardy Amies designs, as the company was still producing clothes for her during that period.

Obviously the royal ladies had, and still do have, fully comprehensive wardrobes for all different times of the day and night. Hardy's interpretation of the lives of many of his clientele back in the 1950s was almost as vast in its catering for all events and occasions. In portraying his average customer's day-to-day life and the resultant needs of her wardrobe, he said: 'At night she may go to a ball looking like a streamlined edition of an eighteenth-century Marquise', and then 'the next morning she has to be the efficient little housewife. For this she must wear a suit.' Obviously the duties of this particular little housewife were more likely to have been instructing her cook and housekeeper, planning her family's social engagements and maybe a little light shopping, rather than the full roster of chores that many women balance alongside a workplace career today.

Even the daywear these ladies would have worn regularly was often not made with the comfort and practicality that today's buyers would look for. The wide, structured skirts that were introduced in the wake of Dior's New Look were often stiffened with horsehair, making them almost as impractical – and even as uncomfortable – for woman to wear as a crinoline would have been.

Hardy reflected that both himself and Dior had a nostalgic eye for the clothing of bygone eras. At the same time he acknowledged that the designer had to have two things in mind: the shape that both he and the woman he was dressing desired her to be, and the sort of life that she led. 'They do have to shop, they do have to fly to Paris', was how he summed it up.

As someone who adored designing whole ranges of ladies' fashions and colouring them meticulously in my small exercise books as a child, and the mother of a daughter who has trained and now works as a womenswear designer, I am not entirely in agreement with Hardy Amies' view of female designers. In the same chapter, 'The Designer', in *Just So Far* – a chapter which interestingly has been left out of the follow up *Still Here* – he claims that he did not 'think any girl should ever be encouraged to think of herself as a potential dress designer'. He felt that women would only be able to design for other women if they were of the same shape as themselves – in other words, they would not be capable of designing objectively. To give some context here, however, the following words are obviously very much of their time, and the belief behind them would not stand up to scrutiny these days: 'she should become a dressmaker and only move on from there to designing if she feels she must. Many sensible young men realise that a girl who is a good needlewoman usually makes a good wife.'

Nowadays of course, there are eminent fashion designers and couturiers of both sexes working in the worlds of men's and women's design, and they have largely all been trained in needlework and technical skills, in addition to having their creative talents nurtured.

Despite the dressmaking skills of Hardy's mother being obvious to him throughout his childhood, he does not appear to acknowledge any sewing talents of his own within the confines of creating clothes or tailoring. His major loves in the world of needlecraft were embroidery and tapestry, which he perfected throughout his life, and he was well known for whiling away whole transatlantic flights by working on a needlework project. His later companion David Freeman talks about his hobby: 'The Royal College of Embroidery at Hampton Court Palace used to plan out the designs for him.' David explains, 'It's all been exhibited. People still remember him stitching away on Concorde or in airport lounges.'

Speaking in the early 1950s about the young male apprentices in his workrooms, Hardy says: 'If he can learn to make a tailored jacket correctly he will always be able to earn not less than £8 a week. I wish I could do this.' It is surprising he could not, having been introduced to the skills of the dressmaking world by his mother at such a young age. However, the fact that he investigated other career paths before settling down into couture obviously stood Hardy in good stead for running a successful business in the world of fashion. He sums up the requirements for this in three words: 'invention, intelligence and taste', and acknowledges that this is not a combination of attributes that can be taught, or indeed learned. He was quite sanguine and pragmatic on the matter of taste, saying, 'Taste cannot be taught, but can be acquired. You must be born with the good taste of wishing to acquire good taste.' That, Hardy Amies certainly was.

This approach obviously helped Hardy overcome what were self-confessed failings such as his inability to draw a competent fashion sketch. In the very detailed outline of the composition of the house once it was established, he mentions that he always had at least one and often two artists either fully trained or learning on the job. 'I have no natural aptitude for drawing', he readily admitted.

However, he was blessed with the ability to visualise a dress from its basic concept to 'walking across the floor', and even 'Hatted, booted, befurred and bejewelled'. He also found it effective to picture the garment in its proper milieu, be that Claridge's Hotel, the promenades of Paris, or at Royal Ascot.

What would normally happen at the beginning of the design process is that one of the graphic artists at the house would draw a fairly anatomically correct human female figure. Hardy did not favour exaggerated abstract figures as some designers did. Hardy would then add his 'tracing' of his design over the top. Once this stage had been reached his confidence was such that he would go so far as to add colour with ink or paints until 'quite a handsome result' had been achieved. He did not, however, consider any of his own sketches suitable for submission to fashion publications or to store buyers and customers overseas.

That said, over the years Hardy seems to have grown in confidence at drawing and sketching. By the time he penned *Just So Far* in 1954 he alluded to the fact that he could produce 'fairly presentable sketches' which, coupled with his ability to verbalise and present ideas through choosing suitable cloth and describing shapes, would eventually make it easy to put across the concept for a collection.

He had great respect for his fitters and did not blindly press forward with any ideas that they thought would not work in practice. Not only that, but within his chosen translation of 'haute couture' as high sewing, Hardy always acknowledged the input of the customer herself in the design. In the boutique, he accepted that they sold clothes, but in the couture business, Hardy was at pains to point out that 'we execute orders'. By this he meant that a lady would come in to order a suit for example, have two or three fittings, and express her own opinion as to the detailing and trimming of the finished garment. It was considered to be a 'cooperation between designer, tailor and customer, with the saleswoman as a sort of vigilant referee'.

Hardy himself would also visualise his concept for a completely new collection and produce some rudimentary illustrations of what he had in mind. The young assistants would then take these ideas and develop them, simultaneously adding their own creative flourishes and producing copious drawings of whole garments as well as detailed illustrations of features such as pockets and fastenings. Interestingly, Freddie, Lord Teignmouth, was at this time, one of Hardy's most trusted sketchers.

The artists worked in what was known as the studio alongside Hardy's right-hand man, Bill Ackroyd, and it was also here that the garments would begin to be created and fitted onto models. By his own account this room was, back in the early 1950s, rather compact, which led to him having to turn down young people who would have relished the opportunity to spend some time working at the house, in the role of what today would be known as an 'intern'. Much as he would love to have had them, 'I haven't room physically to fit them into the house.'

The junior staff members who were installed in the workrooms needed to be adaptable, highly competent, and very fit! Once assisting at a fitting, if the required trimmings, fastenings, or other details were not at hand, the junior would be dispatched down four flights of stairs – and back up – to get them. Mr Roy Allen recalls how he would run up the stairs 'two at a time and I still do that to this day'. Determined to keep up his fitness levels both mentally and physically, he retains the work ethic learned in Savile Row in older age. Indeed he can still be spotted around London, as smartly dressed as you would expect of a man who had worked in the hallowed temples of tailoring, dashing about, not least when in danger of over-running his car parking time! He affectionately says of his years at Hardy Amies: 'I do miss that life. It was mad – always on the go, working really late.'

One memorable event Roy recalls from 1969 when he was 27 was the famous rooftop concert performed by the Beatles at the headquarters of their Apple Corps, which was just up the road at number 3 Savile Row. Once the music started resonating around the neighbourhood most of the staff of the nearby businesses came out to listen and to try to catch a glimpse of the 'fab four' until, after complaints from the more staid members of the community, the Metropolitan Police arrived to break up the proceedings. 'We went outside to watch and we loved it,' says Roy. It was quite an event, as it was to be the last public performance by the Beatles.

From the catering staff and cleaners, through the apprentices and saleswomen, or vendeuses, right up to the tailors, company secretary, and Hardy himself, by 1954 there were over 200 people working in Nos 14 and 15 Savile Row. Hardy Amies Ltd had become firmly established as one of London's top couture houses and the business was going from strength to strength.

Chapter 15

The Queen is Here!

In 1950, Hardy Amies Ltd received their first visit from the King's eldest daughter, Princess Elizabeth. The future queen was accompanied on a trip to 14 Savile Row by her sister, the glamorous Princess Margaret. Alongside the young future queen, Princess Margaret was at that time one of the most famous beauties in the world. Comparisons with the likes of Elizabeth Taylor and Ava Gardner were not unusual in the fashion and showbusiness press at the time.

There is some discrepancy in the accounts of how the young princesses' interest in Hardy Amies was first sparked. It may have been that his designs were seen being worn by one of Elizabeth's ladies in waiting, Lady Alice Egerton, whose mother, the Countess of Ellesmere, was a long-standing client of Hardy's and coincidentally, the grandmother of Lady Sarah Faringdon, a future friend of Hardy's. However, many women in the upper echelons of society were also his clients by that point. The fashion press was obviously another source of information and, by then, Hardy's profile was sufficiently high that any fashion-conscious young woman would have been aware of his presence in the world of couture.

The young Princess Elizabeth was at the height of her elegance and beauty at that time and would have been a dream to dress. Norman Hartnell was the sole designer to Her Royal Highness, Elizabeth the Queen Mother, but her daughters were also employing the talents of Hardy's idol, Edward Molyneux. Hardy's pride at being asked to produce a selection of designs for the princess must have been enhanced by the fact that he was now going to follow in the footsteps of the man he saw as a huge inspiration.

That first visit to the premises in Savile Row took place in Hardy's office and sounds remarkably informal. Hardy describes it in *Still Here*, saying, 'everything was relaxed but also totally businesslike'. The princess was soon to embark on her first overseas tour since her marriage, and had decided that she would like to take some clothing by Hardy Amies with her to Canada.

Rumours had been circulating for some time that Princess Elizabeth had been admiring the clothes of her lady in waiting, Lady Alice, but once the first visit to the showroom was announced, the level of excitement among the staff was, understandably, off the scale.

Hardy recalls the response of Betty Reeves, one of the premier salesladies, 'She came up to me, and in a state of great excitement said, "It's happened".'[1] All the staff had been aware of the murmurings of the royal interest in the house, and were on tenterhooks waiting for signs of an imminent summons.

Betty's excitement must have been at fever-pitch once she realised she was going to be the sole assistant to Hardy to be present at the princesses' inaugural visit. Her reward was a smile and a handshake from each of the young royal women who, as Hardy said, behaved as 'any of the high-born English ladies on whom I had previously waited'.

The spontaneous timing of the royal 'command' does not seem to have fazed Hardy, but it did come at a time when he was trying to navigate something of a crossroads in the fashion and design world, with Dior's New Look having created a sensation with its rebellion against the constraints of wartime restrictions and its flamboyant use of fabric and shape.

Hardy felt that he and various other British designers had already recognised the need for romantic escapism and he almost implies that the ideas behind the New Look were an organic progression from the fashions of the early forties. 'There was to me a feeling in the fashion world of a romantic revival around the corner,' he said.

However, he acknowledged rather grudgingly that the frivolousness and extravagance encapsulated by Paris's top designer of the time could probably not have emanated from Britain in quite the same way, such was the pervading air of austerity and restriction in the UK. Understandably perhaps, for a person of such creative instincts, he was finding the drudgery of the post-war years in England very tedious. The utility laws, rationing, and regulations were, he felt, a large ugly boot still stamping on top of the exuberance he felt the nation needed.

After a fully committed period of wartime service in the military, which sliced through the centre of his burgeoning career, perhaps he deserved to harbour such feelings of repression and stultification and to seek ways of escaping from them. As Julie Summers says in her book *Fashion on the Ration*: 'While people in post-war Britain were constrained by continued rationing and austerity, Parisians were relishing their freedom.'

In fact, the New Look received a mixed reaction among the British press and public, with some being of the opinion that it was like dangling jewels in front of those who could not afford such fripperies, when the quality and quantity of fabrics available at the time were not economically – or practically – possible to attain.

However, it was to be a royal gesture that helped the New Look begin to sweep over the United Kingdom in a flood of enthusiasm and approval. In 1948 Princess Margaret had asked Norman Hartnell to adapt an existing coat for her to wear at her parents' Silver Wedding celebrations. Having become aware of the New Look and being possessed of the hourglass figure that could wear it to its utmost effect, she charged him with modifying the garment with all the features encompassed by the latest French trend. By having him do this and not produce an entirely new piece of clothing she simultaneously demonstrated that the royal family recognised everyone was still living in austerity Britain, but that there was a light up ahead to lift the nation's collective mood. 'It seemed that at last fashion had turned its back on the war for good.'[2]

By 1950 Hardy Amies had perfected his idea of how he wanted to incorporate these forward-thinking features into his creations, and this was what he planned to do in the designs he intended to present to Princess Elizabeth. The company did not have much time to prepare the sketches to show the princess, as Hardy retells that after the initial visit, 'a few days later we were summoned to Clarence House'.

However, he must have long been pondering on the prospect of having the opportunity to dress the future queen, as he also said confidently in *Still Here*: 'I had already a good idea of what kind of clothes I thought would be appropriate for a royal princess.'

The flamboyance and extreme features of the New Look had been slightly modified three years on from its launch, and this seems to have been reflected in Hardy's designs too. Post-war he had largely stuck to a template not far removed from the styles that were popular in the late 1930s and he acknowledges that it needed someone with the illustrious reputation and gravitas of Dior to really launch the post-war fashion era by throwing an incendiary device into the world of couture.

By 1950 things were looking up considerably, the atmosphere was enlivening and designers felt that they had almost been given permission to allow their imaginations to run riot and fulfil their remit of lifting the mood of the population – or at least the female element of it.

No longer were designers still constrained by the austere wartime styling, which was exemplified by wide shouldered, long-line jackets and short, narrow A-line skirts. Instead hems were elegantly lengthening – though not to the degree first shown by Dior in 1957 – shoulders were narrowing, waists were cinched in, and generous amounts of fabric were utilised to maximise the impact of the full skirts.

This was the template Hardy had in mind when he began to formulate his image of the clothes he would create for Princess Elizabeth. The commission of the first royal order was two overcoats, two day dresses, and two evening dresses, a small consignment by couture standards but obviously to be subsumed into the full collection with which the princess would be travelling to Canada in 1951. The Hardy Amies contribution was described by the designer himself as 'modest', but 'at the time we were all immensely proud to have been asked at all'. It was, of course, their first experience of designing for a princess and, as such, needed a great deal of consideration of the various factors which always have to be considered when producing clothing for the public-facing role of a member of the royal family.

Appropriately at the time, the style of shaping in a dress or coat was known as the 'Princess Line'. This is created by a number of seams down the torso which are slightly nipped in at the waist and expanded gradually over the hips to give a flowing elegance to the skirt.

Hardy created a coat and dress in this way and, despite knowing that the obvious way to complement the abundance of the skirt was to pair it with a wide brimmed hat, he had to acquiesce that, for this particular client, this was highly unlikely to be permitted. Royal hands and arms were for waving or holding bouquets of flowers and not for steadying large-brimmed hats in an unexpected gust of wind. Furthermore, it was of paramount importance that the public see the face of the very important visitor, so an equally fashionable close-fitting hat would almost always be worn instead.

In the event, the Hardy Amies' clothes the princess wore on the tour of Canada in the autumn of 1951 were declared a success and considered perfect for the requirements of his royal client. Norman Hartnell, already established as the primary designer to the princess, praised Hardy's efforts and was even said to have declared that he was glad of the chance to share the responsibility with someone else and to have someone else to occasionally 'take the blame'!

Hartnell had been designing for Queen Elizabeth the Queen Mother for many years and had been awarded the Royal Warrant for dressing her in 1940, and the same accolade as Dressmaker to the Queen herself in 1957. He and Hardy shared similar backgrounds, having grown up in London soon after the turn of the century. However, whereas Hardy had such pride in his mother and respect for his father's achievements, not to mention a life-long bond with his sister, Hartnell seemed ashamed of his family.

His parents had owned a pub in Streatham, South London, and this seems to have been the root cause of his feelings of alienation. Once he was accepted in the higher echelons of society, he always bore in mind that none of the ladies he dressed would have ever set foot in a pub, as that was not the done thing right up to the mid-twentieth century. Society was still governed by what would now seem antiquated rules and divisions, and Hartnell was not keen for anything in his background to be in any way at odds with that. He managed to navigate his way through these concerns and was, of course, eventually fully accepted by high society from the royal family downwards.

Hardy appears to have been very satisfied with the results of his first commission for the princess. He felt that the cold climates of Canada suited his design talents, as it required the use of heavy, structured fabrics and therefore the necessary tailoring for which he was famous. This was definitely his forte, as was proved when he subsequently looked back on the next collection he designed for Princess Elizabeth, for a tour of Kenya and South Africa. The collection he was to produce for that visit was not one that he could claim to be completely happy with.

The reason for this appears to have rested with the fact that the temperature in those countries was so much warmer and therefore necessitated the use of finer, more lightweight fabrics, which do not lend themselves to the structure and formality of design that was his strength. Heat and humidity can also have a detrimental effect on the performance of fabrics, as well as the way they react to movement and travel, and the impact that has on creasing and other wear and tear.

However, it was a learning experience for the house as he sums up the outcome by saying resolutely in *Still Here*: 'If a lack of experience was responsible .... I am glad to say now that it was a fault we managed to correct on subsequent lightweight designs for the queen.' That tour of Kenya and South Africa was to be memorable in a rather tragic and momentous way.

After the success of the clothes for the Canadian tour, Her Majesty wrote a poignant letter to Hardy from Clarence House in September 1951 informing him, in confidence, that the poor state of her father's, health suggested that she and Prince Philip may have to tour Kenya and South Africa in his place early in 1952. The queen's father, George VI, had been unwell for some time and, during the period that the princess was in Kenya with the prince, he rather unexpectedly died. The tour was cut short and the couple returned to London with the knowledge that she was now the queen, with all the responsibility that entailed. It was at this point, of course, that Hardy Amies officially became a dressmaker to Queen Elizabeth II, a title of which he was rightly proud.

In *Just So Far*, Hardy was at pains to avoid referring to any of his customers by name, but finally relented during the last chapter. Written in 1954 when he had approximately two years of dressing the queen behind him, he writes of his pride in the honour that had been bestowed upon him. His obvious admiration for Her Majesty shines through the page as he writes: 'To me Queen Elizabeth II typifies all that I admire most in English women's attitude to dress.' He had previously described the rather more frivolous and acquisitive attitude of American ladies' to clothing, by stating that they are 'not the best dressed women in the world. They are the *most* dressed women in the world.' Unlike the British woman of the day, who valued the quality and heritage of an outfit, he seemed to have the impression that novelty and innovation mattered more to her US counterpart than investing in fewer garments that would serve her well for years.

At the end of *Just So Far*, in his vision for the future, Hardy correctly identifies what probably is to this day the greater part of the United States' contribution to global fashion. Summing up, it is what is now considered classic, but what was at that time just emerging, and is a combination of denim jeans, t-shirt, and sneakers.

However, he did not foresee, or at least did not look forward to, the total domination that this kind of outfit was to have, saying: 'Blue jeans are a sartorial triumph for men – I refuse to discuss them for women.' Little did he know that within a decade jeans would start to feature in most young women's wardrobes and that by the latter part of the twentieth century, they would be ubiquitous.

At the time Hardy was fairly generous in his assessment of American clothes design. He acknowledged that it was a good thing that, due to their love of sports, travel, and a wide range of leisure activities, their designers were pioneers in placing comfort high on their list of attributes for good design. However, that did not mean he would countenance the lowering of standards that nowadays means a pair of jeans is just as likely to be spotted at an evening performance at the theatre as at a ball game in the park. 'I see the influence of American clothes everywhere,' he says in *Just So Far*, but goes on to speak of how they are fine for 'the young at play', but 'they look as silly in London as does an Englishman in New York with bowler hat and furled umbrella.'[3]

By contrast, the queen was known to always dress appropriately whatever the occasion. She would appear so effortlessly chic that the clothing receded to a supporting role, while the focus moved on to the event or meeting she was attending without unnecessary distraction. This he felt was the epitome of respectful, understated style which he saw as being at the centre of the majority of British design.

Whether this ethos still holds true in today's mercurial, fast-fashion climate is debatable. In many of Hardy's thoughts it is possible to spot the seeds of today's concepts of sustainability and ethical clothing aspirations. Obviously, coming through the war era he was bound to understand the importance of economics, thrift and longevity in clothing but he definitely relished the opportunity to utilise top quality fabrics and produce a high-end product. However, this was always with the hope that his clients would buy better but therefore buy less, if that was proscribed by their personal budgets.

In the case of the queen, who was of course in rather a unique position, her working wardrobe needed the 'wow factor', but she has always been known for a certain level of frugality in her private downtime at home. Her daughter, the Princess Royal, is of course well known for not only having a particularly rotating wardrobe, but also for having garments adapted over the years to suit new trends, rather than investing in whole new collections. It harks back to that dress coat of her Aunt Margaret, which Hartnell adapted back in the early 1950s at the onset of the New Look.

Hardy as a baby with his mother, Mary. *Personal Collection*

Hardy as a child in a rowing boat, when he was said to have been '… put off girls'! *Personal Collection*

Hardy at Ski School in Feldberg in Germany's Black Forest in 1930. Hardy seated far right. *Personal Collection*

Hardy larking with his army mates during training. Hardy saluting, far right. *Personal Collection*

Swanage Army Intelligence training camp in 1940 with Hardy 4th left, second row down. *Langford Archive*

Hardy's identity papers as an officer in August 1940. *Langford Archive*

RECORD OF SERVICE (including Extra-Regimental Employment).

UNIT. (N.B.—The unit in which the officer is at present serving must not be shown.)	HOME.		ABROAD.			
			With Expeditionary Force.		Elsewhere.	
	From	To	From	To	From	To
* In the ranks.						
JUNIOR Intelligence Pool	18·5·40					
8· war Intelligence Course Swanage	8·0·40	0·7·40				
2nd Intelligence Course Swanage	13·7·40	10·8·40				
I.O. i.a VII Corps	12·8·40					
Posted to M.I. i.x Pembroke College Oxford	15·4·41					
Posted to M.O.i.	15·4·44·					

* Enter first any service in the ranks.

10   11

This book is not to be taken as a proof of the identity of the holder.

INSTRUCTIONS.

1. The unit in which the officer is at present serving must not appear anywhere in this book.

2. This book will be issued to every serving officer.

3. It will be carefully kept by the officer and be produced whenever required by a superior officer under whom he may be serving. It will not be shown to unauthorised persons.

4. Except where specially stated, officers will make entries in the book themselves. The accuracy of entries must be vouched for by an officer's C.O. or his other superior officers. Past entries must be vouched for by the C.O. on the authority of the duplicate copy of Army Form B. 199A.

5. The authority for all promotions must always be stated.

6. The officer will enter his usual signature at the foot of this page.

7. Pages 8, 9, 10 and 11 need not be completed by officers above the permanent rank of lieutenant-colonel.

........................Signature.

........................Rank and Regt. or Corps.

Date....................

2

OFFICER'S RECORD OF SERVICE.

Surname of Officer AMIES (Block capitals.)

Christian Names EDWIN HARDY

Personal Number P/130398

Regiment or Corps INTELLIGENCE CORPS

Nature of Commission EMERGENCY (e.g., Reg., Reg. Retd., R.A.R.O., S.R., T.A., T.A.R.O., Emergency, Short Service, Temp. and Temp. Short Service, etc.)

Date of Birth 17·7·09

Industry Group

Occupational Classification

Full Name and Address of Next-of-kin, showing relationship— (In pencil)

Year of Birth		17·7·09
NOTE.—The above particulars will not be filled in until instructions are issued by the War Office.		20·11·37
Age & Service Group together with Suffix 'C'		17/C

Part of the record of Hardy's service in the Intelligence Corps. *Langford Archive*

Photograph used on a card sent to his father at Christmas 1941 showing Hardy in uniform when working in T-Section at SOE HQ in Baker Street, London. *Langford Archive*

The exterior of 14 Savile Row after restoration in the late 1940s following extensive bomb damage during World War II. The two doormen were a feature of the time. *Roy Allen*

Suspended above the staircase at Savile Row was a windowed area which was connected to a small room which ran to the back of the house. Here a previous occupier, the playwright Richard Brinsley Sheridan sat to watch his creditors and bailiffs taking away his property during the later months of his life when he had become bankrupt. *John Rowland*

Hardy's Office at 14 Savile Row during the heyday of the House in the 1950s. *Roy Allen*

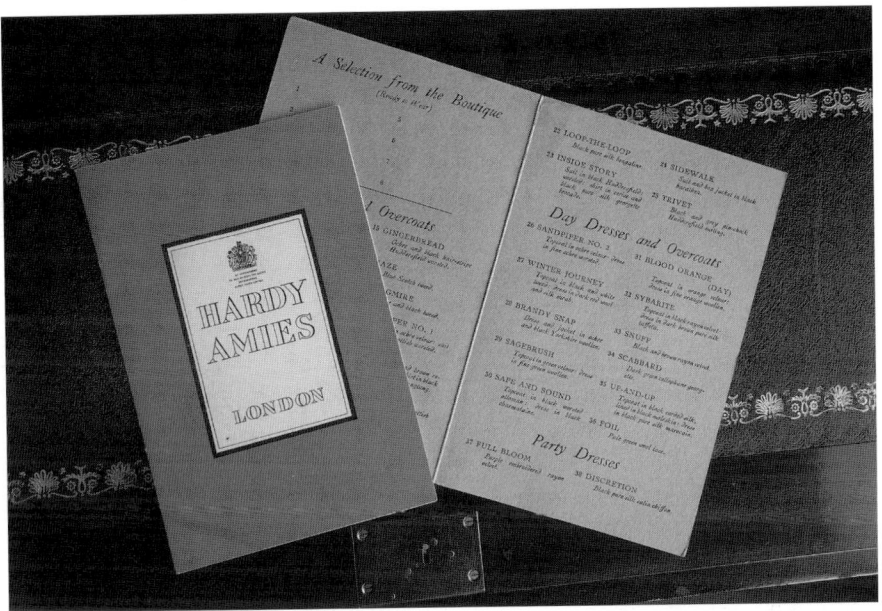

Fashion show brochures, 1960 and 1952.

Model wearing an elaborate evening dress and coat, with left to right: Hardy, Mme Marthe, Miss Betty, tailor Mr Ernest, an assistant and Mr Leonard. *Roy Allen*

Hardy with model girl at a rehearsal for a catwalk show in the 1950s. Left to right: Lord Teignmouth who worked as a sketcher for Hardy, vendeuse Mme Marthe, the Queen's dresser Miss Betty Reeves, an assistant and the tailor Mr Leonard. *Roy Allen*

Hardy and Alexis ffrench in Pisa in the 1950s. *Personal Collection*

Hardy at Savile Row in the 1950s with Lady Pamela Berry, who had been president of the Incorporated London Designers during World War II.

Hardy in the drawing room of his home at 17b Eldon Road, Kensington, London with Henry Moore's work 'Two Standing Figures'.

Mr Roy Allen, long-serving tailor at Hardy Amies, from 1957 to 1995. *Author's Photograph*

1930 portrait of Alexis ffrench by the American artist Dur Freedly, which is on the cover of Hardy's 1994 book 'The Englishman's Suit'. *John Rowland*

WINCHESTER   Salmon

Rosemary in her Women's Voluntary Service uniform during World War II. *Langford Archive*

'The Queen wearing the dress which was designed by Hardy Amies for the State Banquet at Schloss Augustusburg, Germany in 1965. Photograph by Cecil Beaton.' Copyright: *Royal Collection Trust*.

The Royal Warrant Crest and Citation Plate awarded to Hardy as head of Hardy Amies Ltd in July 1955. *John Rowland*

The Queen in the dress embroidered with Californian poppies which was first worn in Hollywood in 1983. She later wore it again on her Canadian tour in 1984. *Getty Images*

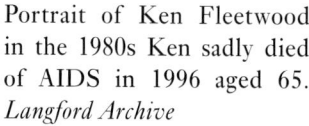

Portrait of Ken Fleetwood in the 1980s Ken sadly died of AIDS in 1996 aged 65. *Langford Archive*

Needlepoint chair cover created by Hardy. He was very talented at needlepoint and was often to be found working on a piece in an airport lounge or on a long-haul flight. *John Rowland*

China and table linen designed for sale under the Hardy Amies name in the 1970s.
John Rowland

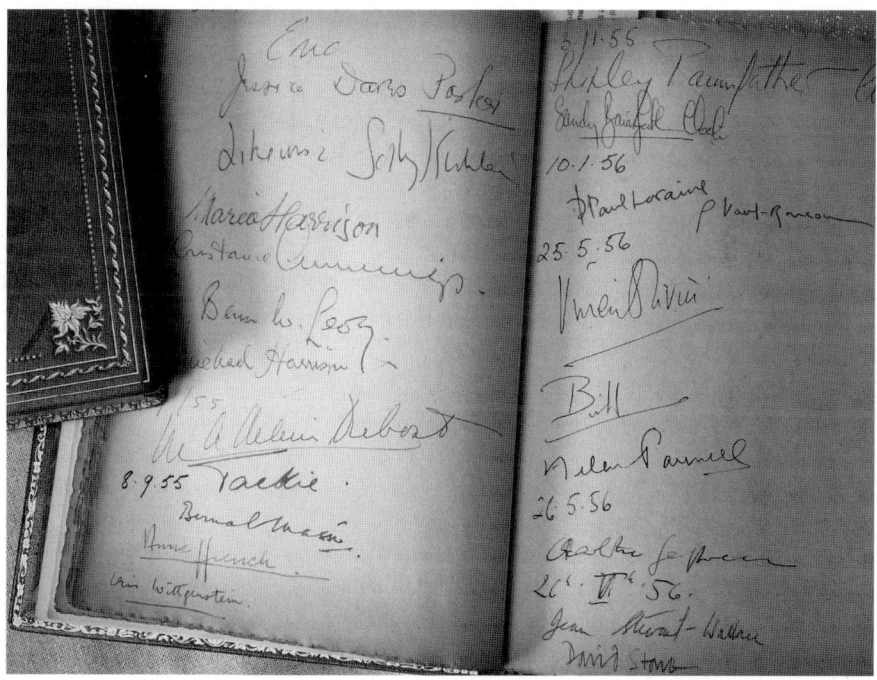

Page of the visitors book from Hardy's London home in 1956, showing the signature of
the film star Vivien Leigh, then Lady Olivier, the wife of Laurence Olivier. *John Rowland*

The Old School, Langford. *John Rowland*

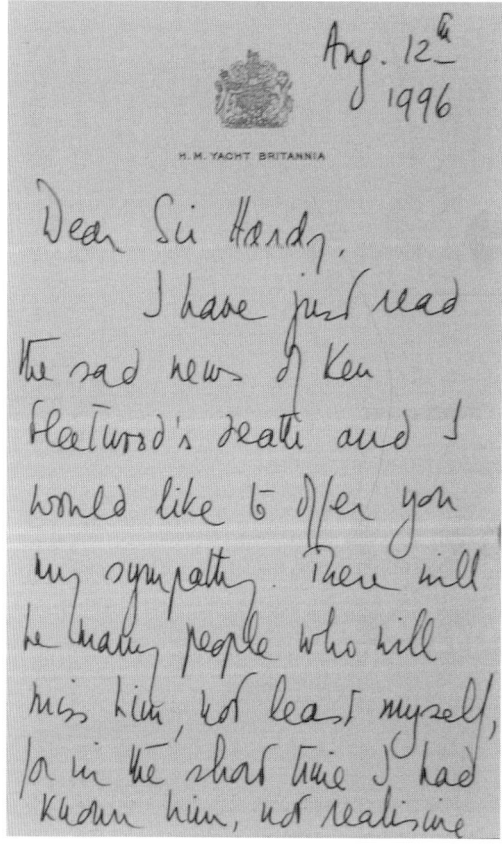

Aug. 12ᵗʰ 1996

H.M. YACHT BRITANNIA

Dear Sir Hardy,

I have just read the sad news of Ken Fleetwood's death and I would like to offer you my sympathy. There will be many people who will miss him, not least myself, for in the short time I had known him, not realising

Personal letter from the Queen to Hardy after the death of Ken Fleetwood in 1996.

Hardy's office in the present day. 14 Savile Row is now the premises of J.P. Hackett, menswear designers and retailers. *John Rowland*

The needlepoint rug sewn by Hardy and featuring his favourite flowers, which was draped over his coffin at his funeral in 2003. *John Rowland*

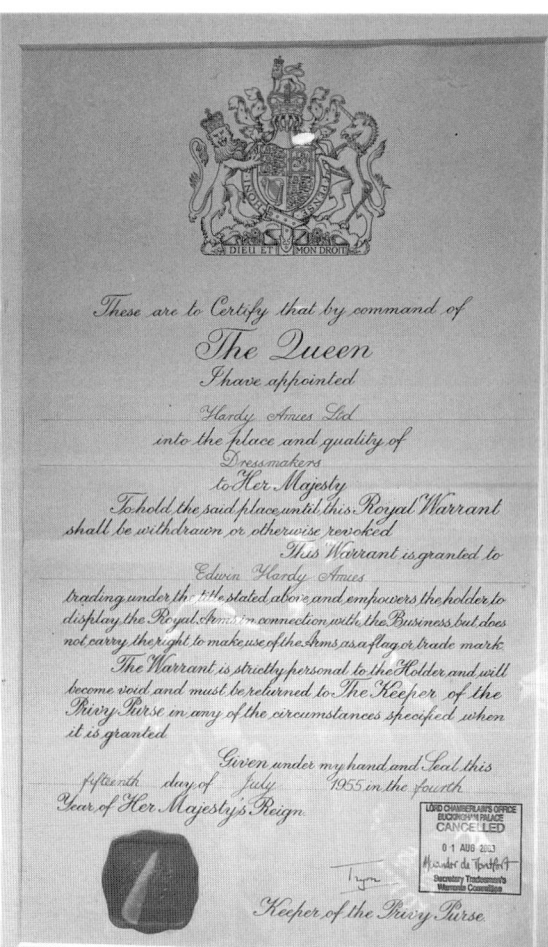

Royal Warrant certificate returned from Buckingham Palace, having been cancelled at the request of his heir and executors after Hardy's death in 2003. *John Rowland*

David Freeman in the sitting room of The Old School, Langford. *John Rowland*

One influence on the queen's prioritising of frugality was her redoubtable dresser, Miss Margaret MacDonald, known affectionately by the queen as Bobo. Miss MacDonald had started work in the royal household as a 22-year-old Scottish nursery maid when the princess was a mere infant and remained in her service for the next sixty years becoming one of the closest people to Her Majesty. She was even known to refer to her as her 'Little Lady'.

With the arrival of Elizabeth's sister Margaret in 1930, the chief nanny at the time was required to devote more attention to the new baby, thus leaving Elizabeth primarily in the care of Bobo. Their bond was cemented and according to the queen's biographer Sarah Bradford, Bobo 'was the one person whom Elizabeth trusted absolutely outside her immediate family and had considerable influence over her, encouraging her to follow her own thrifty principles'. Margaret MacDonald had a sister, Ruby, who was later to take over from her as nursemaid, growing close to Princess Margaret, while Bobo graduated to the role of the queen's dresser. The queen valued her as a close confidante and also as a valuable link to the goings-on and the politics among the staff, something upon which she placed a great deal of importance. Bobo herself was known to be tough and considered herself answerable only to the queen. She did not acquiesce to various senior courtiers and it was said that her power lay in the fact that she gave unswerving loyalty and devotion to Her Majesty.

According to Sarah Bradford, Bobo's closeness to the queen from the early days is illustrated by the fact that she referred to Elizabeth in private, and when conversing with her, by her childhood nickname: Lilibet. This epithet has now, of course, been given wider prominence by being chosen by the Duke and Duchess of Sussex as the name for their daughter. It is also stated in Bradford's biography *Elizabeth*, that Margaret MacDonald claimed that on the occasion of waving his daughter off for her tour of Africa in early 1952, the ailing King George VI entreated her to 'Look after the Princess for me, Bobo.'[4]

Bobo's influence, and even her status in the royal household, was revered by all the other courtiers and staff members. She was a formidable force in the palace, or wherever the queen was residing, and was well known for being more angered or offended by any mistakes or failings on the part of the other staff, than the monarch herself would ever be. This was partly down to the history between the two. Having been nominally brought up by Miss MacDonald from when she was a very young child, it was in some ways natural that the queen would defer to her carer and teacher. This probably later translated into an understanding that Bobo was Elizabeth's 'eyes and ears', as Sarah Bradford puts it, within the royal household, and therefore held great sway over the rest of the staff.

Hardy acknowledges her position when, in *Still Here*, he talks about his pride at being invited to watch the queen's coronation in 1953 from a viewing platform facing the Victoria Memorial opposite Buckingham Palace. 'It was a moment of great pride for both of us,' he says about himself and his assistant Betty Reeves, as they watched the queen leaving for Westminster Abbey. Apparently the seats were organised for them by Margaret MacDonald, despite the fact that in Sarah Bradford's biography she refers to Hardy as being something of a 'bête noire' to Bobo.

Perhaps by the time of the coronation relations were cordial. In *Still Here*, Hardy recounts his first visit to Buckingham Palace, when MacDonald instructed him that if just carrying sketches, he was permitted to use the Privy Purse entrance, but that his staff should always use the side entrance. Hardy was humble enough, if he was accompanying his staff or was carrying bolts of fabric, to be perfectly content to use the side entrance too.

Sir Roy Strong, art historian, writer, broadcaster, and landscape designer, recalls a drinks reception he attended in the late 1960s at the palace. He spotted Hardy, who told him gleefully: '"Do you know Roy, this is the first time I've been permitted to enter by the front door", because, of course, he would always have to use the tradesmen's entrance on the right-hand side.'

An incident which happened much later almost caused Hardy to have a rather unexpected close encounter with Her Majesty. Chris Stratmann, Hardy's relief chauffeur recalls:

> We had been invited to eat at the Kensington home of Hardy's friends Derek Granger, the literary critic and writer and his interior designer partner, Ken Partridge. It was the day of the unveiling of the newly regilded Albert Memorial in Kensington Gardens and we must have taken the wrong route back through the park. To my horror I was driving along and suddenly came face to face with the queen's car. Needless to say I had to reverse very quickly.

Bobo, as Her Majesty's dresser, is said to have greatly enjoyed her role liaising with the queen's dressmakers and was never backward at keeping them in their place, assuming a senior role throughout all their visits. According to Sarah Bradford, Hardy was once thought to have made an ill-considered remark which, when Bobo heard of it, was interpreted as a criticism. This unfortunate incident was not forgotten by the redoubtable Bobo and their relationship was prickly thereafter. 'He was never forgiven. Elizabeth loyally stuck by him but there were battles which Bobo inevitably won.'[5]

Hardy does not allude to this in his own autobiographies and, of course, his relationship with the monarch remained steadfast. Bobo's power was not in doubt however, as she consistently restricted the couturiers, reminding them that their role was limited to the clothes they were designing and did not involve having any input regarding shoes, bags, or accessories. As Gyles Brandreth recounts in his book about the queen's long-standing marriage, *Philip and Elizabeth*: 'She kept them in their place, both by the manner with which she handled them, and by not allowing any one of them complete control over Elizabeth's appearance.'[6] She even kept an eye on the cost of accessories, which perhaps explains the queen's later habit of sticking to one particular design of black *Launer* handbag and corresponding shoes, frequently designed by the leather goods company *Rayne*. The queen herself was known to be relatively frugal in relation to her clothing, and this is revealed in another letter to Hardy which, before it goes on to discuss other matters, refers to a rather large bill she recently received from him.

However, the canny Hardy appears to have employed some subterfuge in getting around Bobo's determination to allow him no input into the queen's accessories. Among the collection of extremely detailed, personal, and friendly handwritten letters which were sent to her designer, Her Majesty thanks Hardy for his many Christmas and birthday presents.

The Christmas presents seem to have been chosen carefully in order to be memorable and popular with the younger members of the royal household at the time. Every year a seemingly lifelike and durable soft toy animal, ranging from a lion to a dachshund, was sent and, according to Her Majesty's thank you notes, these were displayed, year on year, on top of the grand piano at Sandringham House. The children loved the growing menagerie but apparently it caused consternation among the royal pets, particularly the dachshunds!

The birthday presents Hardy sent to the queen were, however, more calculatingly chosen. Many letters refer to the beautiful handbags and gloves Her Majesty received, which would perfectly match dresses and coats he had designed for her. Although the queen enthusiastically informed Hardy of how much she was looking forward to using them, no doubt the controlling Bobo would not have appreciated the '*dressmaker*'s' impertinence and attempts to get around her enforced constraints.

To accompany him to the coronation Hardy chose his trusted assistant, the saleswoman Betty Reeves, who held a very dear place in his heart. As mentioned earlier, Betty had been a junior in the millinery showroom at the House of Paulette when Hardy started work at Lachasse, then, before joining the forces during the war, she moved to Lachasse. At that point she met Hardy's mother, Mary, on one of her visits to the company, and realised what a huge influence Mary, and her career, had had on the young, aspiring Hardy.

Betty empathised and totally understood how poignant the occasion of the coronation was and how proud Mary would have been to know her son had not only by then launched his own house, but was also Dressmaker to Queen Elizabeth II. Betty was considered by Hardy to be the perfect vendeuse, in the style of his dear mother, and according to her employer had the perfect combination of reverence and confidence when dealing with her clients, whether royal or otherwise.

The terrible downpours of rain on Coronation Day in June 1953 did nothing to dampen people's spirits, nor to detract from the vision of the young and beautiful new monarch officially taking on her formidable life-long duties. With no hint of envy, Hardy lavished praise on the dress designed by his peer, the more established royal designer, Norman Hartnell, for the occasion. Hartnell had operated from his own impressive premises in Bruton Street, Mayfair, since 1934, when the young Hardy Amies was just emerging at Lachasse.

'Norman Hartnell had done an absolutely superb job and I can think of no one who could have done it better.' he graciously recounted in *Still Here*. 'Throughout the Coronation I remember thinking "This is Norman Hartnell's day."' Hartnell had also designed the six dresses for the queen's Maids of Honour and, in the spirit of competition, Hardy would perhaps have been wryly amused by the account given by one of them, Lady Anne Glenconner, of the gowns. 'The dresses weren't lined, which meant the underside of the embroidery was uncomfortably scratchy,' she writes in her autobiography *Lady in Waiting*, 'They had also been made extremely tight.'[7]

Lady Glenconner goes on to describe the queen's appearance on that momentous day. 'The queen looked absolutely ravishing,' she writes, 'The dress was exquisite ... covered with embroidery of the rose, the thistle, and all the different emblems of the British Isles and the Commonwealth.'[8]

Hardy appears to have had a more cheerful outlook on life than his co-designer, but that is not to say that there was any resentment on Hartnell's part for the young upstart coming along the track behind him. In *Still Here*, Hardy talks about how much time is taken up in fittings for clothes for a royal tour, and says: 'there is no reason, therefore, for any jealousy to exist between the designers, and when I first started my work with the queen Norman Hartnell wrote me a very kind letter which, in a nutshell, said just this.' It dawned on Hardy as the momentous day of the coronation progressed, that he was indeed now Dressmaker Number Two to the queen as they were already working on the collection for the queen's next tour to Australia, later that same year.

In *Still Here*, Hardy goes on to recount a memorable evening of a Gala Performance of Benjamin Britten's opera *Gloriana*, which took place six days after the coronation as part of the ongoing celebrations. Hardy was fortunate enough to have been given tickets by a friend, David Webster, General Administrator of the Royal Opera House. Being loosely based on the life of Queen Elizabeth I, the opera was thought to have been a carefully considered choice, but turned into a 'disaster' according to Hardy.

'It had seemed such a good idea,' he writes, 'but the tale of the jealous love of an ageing virgin queen for a young courtier proved to be terribly inappropriate for the occasion.' It seemed to him to be 'even discourteous to the new queen'. Moving swiftly on from that supposed error, Hardy recalls the sartorial aspect of the evening to have been a huge success.

Hartnell had once again designed the dress the queen wore, which Hardy described as 'splendid'. He also noted that the queen was unsurpassed in the way she carried off jewellery having, of course, probably the most glittering collection in the world at her disposal. Her magnificent wardrobe of tiaras provided the finishing touch to any evening outfit and Bobo MacDonald proudly told Hardy that the queen was 'the only person who could put on a tiara while going downstairs'.

Hardy recalls being asked whether the royal jewels were of such status that designers were asked to design dresses with specific pieces of jewellery in mind. He replied that that was not the case, and that they would produce as beautiful a dress as they could, 'knowing full well that the queen will have some suitable piece of jewellery to go with it'.

He modestly reflected on how the queen's jewellery collection was so exquisite that the clothes, especially the eveningwear, often took second place. He acknowledged that Hartnell was the 'king' of the embroidered evening dress, but also that, on many grand occasions, the Paris-made clothes of visiting dignitaries were often considered to be superior to those of the English ladies. When the queen was present however, British jewels were always the primary focus of attention.

Hardy Amies' own role was of course to focus on the dresses and suits that the queen would possibly choose to wear. Once Princess Elizabeth had been elevated to the role of monarch and moved into Buckingham Palace, all fittings and viewings took place there in order to fit in with Her Majesty's hectic schedule.

His next commission was for the queen's Australian tour to take place later in 1953. His position was now considered stable enough for him to design a collection with the expectation that it would sit alongside that of Norman Hartnell. Hardy understood that the clothes should be fashionable yet not too forward-looking, and that the overriding need was for them to be functional, practical, decorous, and comfortable for the queen to go about her essential business in. He does claim to have suggested brighter colours and bolder patterns for her, in order to make her more easily visible on royal tours and visits. As we know, Elizabeth often said, 'I have to be seen to be believed'.

In *Still Here*, Hardy describes the process of preparing a collection for a royal tour. It begins with:

> the queen's devoted dresser requesting us initially to go to the palace with sketches of clothes we intend to propose. A series of fittings at the palace follows and eventually the wardrobe is delivered to the care of the queen's dresser, who is then responsible for its packaging and transport on tour.

Hardy is at pains to point out that, although he leads the team which creates the collection for the queen, he is not 'the all-important person'.

The team was made up of the tailor, the fitter, the vendeuse and the designer, and although the personnel stayed largely the same, there were inevitably changes over the course of the time that the house was creating clothes for Her Majesty.

It is, however, the man at the top who must inevitably come up with the theme or vision for a collection and Hardy undoubtedly felt the weight of what was both a great honour and an important responsibility. As he says in *Still Here*: 'I can allow myself a grain of pride in having been permitted over these past thirty years to contribute one tiny spot to the superb panorama of her successful reign.' At the same time he acknowledges that he 'must share this pleasure with the team of craftsmen and women who actually made the clothes'.

It is significant that he closes his first autobiography, with this humble and gracious statement written in October 1953: 'A girl in the workroom who is making a good buttonhole is surely as near God as a designer. I sometimes think nearer.'[9]

Hardy always seemed to credit his staff with providing a very firm foundation for his work with his demanding and confident clientele. He obviously greatly valued the knowledge, intuition and skills of his female workforce, in particular Betty Reeves and her successor, Sheila Ogden. Betty was the original vendeuse responsible for the queen's wardrobe and, being the same height and as he said, 'equally neat of figure', she was perfect for the job.

In her dealings with his clients Hardy said she 'had the perfect style of a professional vendeuse: a mixture of bossiness and servility', although it is probably the case that the latter characteristic triumphed in her work with the queen. She was not averse to telling a duchess or a lady that a desired model would not suit them if she believed that to be true. However, Hardy does not record whether she expressed her thoughts similarly forcefully with Her Majesty the Queen.

Hardy was, of course, forced to leave Betty and the female fitter to their own devices for a good deal of the time that they were dressing the queen. He would dutifully sit on a chair outside the door of the royal fitting room as the ladies assisted Her Majesty with putting on the dress and assessing any areas of positive or negative feedback. He describes, 'listening to the light murmur from within, interrupted quite often by the queen's silvery laugh. Sometimes there is an ominous silence but this does not always mean there is any trouble afoot. It is merely an indication of concentration.'

After this short wait while Hardy was able to sit and take in the grandeur of his surroundings, he would be duly summoned to observe how the dress looked, as the queen obligingly assumed different postures and performed small acts such as sitting, waving or lifting a cup of tea, in order to display how the garment would react to each of those situations.

The dependable and hugely capable Betty would be doing her job very well and Hardy knew he could rely on her skills and personability. The queen rewarded Betty one Christmas with a brooch in the shape of the royal cypher and she assiduously wore it on what the House of Amies called 'Palace days'. Imagine Hardy's surprise when Betty announced one day 'that she was leaving the firm to go and get married to Teddy Knox, a member of the popular stage comedy act, The Crazy Gang'. Apparently, after this, the House of Hardy Amies 'never saw her again'. During the 1940s and '50s it was normal for a woman to leave a job upon marriage and not return, whereas nowadays this is unlikely to happen, and a woman is now also free to continue in her job or career after having a baby.

Hardy's mother Mary was probably one of the few exceptions to this, having returned to her beloved job as a vendeuse after having her family – even taking them with her in the case of the young Hardy and his fortuitous visits to Lachasse during his early childhood years. Hardy himself comments, in *Just So Far* (although his view may well have changed with the advance of women's liberation), that often the glass ceilings on women's rise in couture, would indicate that once they reached a certain career milestone, their best option was to leave and get married.

Betty Reeves was succeeded by a lady who took a similar path to his mother, Mrs Sheila Ogden. Sheila, however, had rather a different background. She had been a debutante, subsequently married, had a child, and was divorced. Seeking her independence and being in the fortunate position of having a ready-made clientele drawn from among her society friends, she took up the role of a vendeuse, bringing her knowledge of the preferences of her social circle to the House of Amies. Like the departed Betty, she became a great asset to the company, not least in her work with the queen. By this time, the very fact that Hardy Amies was associated with the queen as well as other members of the royal family, was to see the company enjoy huge success both in the United Kingdom and overseas.

Chapter 16

More Than Friends

Despite all his loyal and trusted employees, up until the early 1950s Hardy did not have a protégé – a person that could be seen as another leading light to carry on the company's vision with equal commitment as its originator. However, in 1950 Hardy met Ken Fleetwood who was a student with a burgeoning talent for sketching and a growing knowledge of art and music and, most importantly, a love of couture, all of which obviously drew the older man to him. This was to be the beginning of one of the most important relationships in Hardy's life, both professionally and personally.

Ken had come from a poor background in Wigan in the north of England but, coincidentally, his mother, like Hardy's, had excellent sewing skills, particularly in the exacting field of tailoring. Unlike many small boys, the young Ken seems to have been greatly influenced by this aspect of his mother's life as he was growing up, another significant feature of his personality which closely mirrored Hardy's. Hardy described Ken in *Still Here* as 'in essence an artist ... by nature a dreamer though with his feet kept on the ground by a strong streak of northern common sense'. His talent for sketching was one of the primary reasons that Hardy knew Ken would be indispensable to him. He recognised his creativity and his romantic imagination, which was to work perfectly in tandem with Hardy's design skills and business prowess. He describes Ken as a close friend, but this extended further over the years right up to his relatively early death in 1996, not least because he was quickly accepted as part of the family by Hardy's beloved sister, Rosemary.

Hardy acknowledged that Rosemary was the most important person in his life and, in the absence of a wife, she was certainly his most significant female attachment figure. When interviewed by Naim Attallah, Hardy says: 'It never occurred to me that I would marry. I did once get engaged to a girl, but I cannot think why; it certainly wasn't because I wanted to go to bed with her.' He rounds off this surprising story with: 'I thought perhaps she would make a good wife to me, but she was sensible enough to say no.' This tale does seem to be rather ambiguous and perhaps even Hardy's sharp mind had lost its grip on the reality of it in retrospect.

His sister Rosemary, despite – as he put it – never really understanding his lifestyle, which 'perplexed her', appears to have bonded with the significant male figures in her brother's life, Ken Fleetwood being a prime example and later David Freeman, who was to inherit Hardy's estate.

After that initial meeting with Hardy, Ken finished his studies at St Martin's School of Art in London and went on to work very briefly in theatre design, an area of expertise and experience he shared with Hardy's fellow couturier Norman Hartnell, who also started out in the theatrical world. He was to work briefly for the renowned ballet and stage designer Loudon Sainthill. However, once he moved on to his new path and joined Hardy Amies Ltd, Ken was to remain there for the rest of his career, apart from his National Service in 1953. He was initially taken on by Hardy for his illustrating and sketching skills, an area that Hardy himself was happy to acknowledge he had no particular talent in, but he quickly graduated into the realm of design.

When the two men met, Ken seems to have been well known for stumbling through life in a rather shambolic way. His living arrangements left a lot to be desired; seeing him go from run-down, shabby student accommodation to dingy flats, Hardy stepped in and offered him a room in his own house and later a basement flat at Eldon Road, Kensington. It appears that Hardy may have felt guilty about the poor young man's chaotic lifestyle once he began working for him, as it drew people to question how little he must be paying him. As Jon Moore, the designer who later worked with Ken at the house, remembered: 'Ken was hopeless at organisation and never had any aptitude for domesticity.' It seems he had another strange quirk too, which hints at something of the personality traits of a hoarder. Sir Roy Strong recalls finding out a rather odd fact about him after he had died: 'He couldn't stand getting presents. When he died they found cupboards full of them – all unopened.'

This chaos extended into his professional life, as represented by Jon Moore's recollection of the way he worked as a designer. 'Ken drew endlessly and his desk was piled high with sketches, one on top of the other until he was completely overwhelmed', Jon remembers. 'When he was off work I just used to spend a whole day tidying his desk – and then he'd just start all over again when he came back!'

Ken was also not in the best of health after eighteen months of National Service, having suffered damage to his liver while in the forces, and Hardy's housekeeper was tasked with taking over organising his diet and rebuilding his strength. Thus, a life-long bond began to be established between the two men. Hardy's later companion David Freeman believes there was probably a brief physical relationship between the two in the early days, but that it probably petered out fairly quickly.

Once Ken became established at Savile Row he focused fully on the womenswear aspect of the business, which allowed Hardy to concentrate his energies more on the men's tailoring which was being introduced as part of the licence trading of the company abroad. Something which is surprising, considering Hardy's own disappointment and frustration at not being given credit as a designer at Lachasse, is the fact that it took nearly twenty years before Ken was outwardly acknowledged as a premier designer at the house.

It is obvious from reading *Just So Far* that he had a pragmatic approach to his business and would have embraced any diversification with great alacrity. His reputation for wonderful tailoring inevitably led on to the incursion into menswear and this was what took up most of his own time once the womenswear side of the company was fully established and flourishing.

He would have felt extremely confident in allowing a visionary such as Ken Fleetwood to take the helm of his already well-established women's couture line, if it gave him the freedom to plough more energy into menswear, which obviously flowed naturally from the company's proven strengths in female tailoring. Indeed, in *Still Here* Hardy says of Ken: 'He knows my mind better than any other.'

Designer Jon Moore, who joined the company as Ken's assistant in 1979, refers to Hardy and Ken as being like the 'oldest married couple you could ever meet – they fed off each other',' he goes on: 'if one was away they would ring each other up religiously every morning'. By the time Jon joined the company Hardy was significantly involved in the global licensing business and frequently off on his travels. 'Ken was in charge at 14 Savile Row', says Jon.

Hardy and Ken's relationship is obviously significant and can be compared to those he had in his earlier years with his great friend Alexis ffrench, and before that, fleetingly with his former German boss Jonny Witte. Obviously in the case of those two situations Hardy was cast in the role of the younger, almost student-like partner, and now he was the mentor and more experienced figure to his protégé. Both men enhanced each other's lives culturally, and music and art were prime areas of mutual interest. Ken had very good musical skills and a 'pitch-perfect' singing voice, whereas Hardy of course was constantly tuning his ear to musical appreciation even though he admitted he himself could not sing. Jon Moore continues: 'Ken was the enabler for Hardy to hold court. Hardy would always be the one to dominate a situation and Ken would take a back seat.'

In many ways Ken drew together all the aspects of Hardy's life up until then and created a world where business and pleasure coexisted. He was a cultured, intelligent and creative young man, and yet he also showed pragmatism and skill at knowing what would keep the company current and innovative. He also possessed a shrewd business brain and despite his flair, imagination, and vision, he was down to earth and focused – and singularly unimpressed by many of the skittish fantasies of the fashion world.

Remembering Ken Fleetwood, Roy Allen describes him as rather a daydreamer: 'He got bored quickly and would often walk off in mid-conversation with someone,' he recalls. It seems that Ken needed a lot of reassurance and approbation when it came to his work and the younger staff members were on hand to provide this, whereas perhaps the 'boss' was not. Roy Allen recalls:

He would be all right leading up to the shows, but then a couple of days before he would sort of lose it. Then we would all have to reassure him and after that he would be fine and it would all work out wonderfully.

I remember once we were working on a collection which was going to be presented at The Mansion House in London. A couple of days beforehand Ken turned around and said 'Oh, I can't be bothered with this. You and Jackie will have to do it.'

So a young lady called Jackie Marx, who worked as a sketcher for Ken and the equally young and fairly inexperienced Roy were left in charge! 'Jackie and I were thrown in at the deep end,' Roy continues, 'and I was still quite shy in those days.'

The event was being hosted by a glamorous TV presenter of the day, Katie Boyle (well known for her hosting of the Eurovision Song Contest) and Roy remembers being completely over-awed when this broadcasting luminary approached him for guidance about the running of the fashion show. 'I couldn't believe Katie Boyle was asking me what she should do,' he remembers. 'But she was absolutely lovely.' Just to add to the young staff members' anxiety, they had been made responsible for the valuable furs and jewellery that had been used to accessorise the outfits in the show. 'It came to the end and we didn't actually know what was supposed to happen to the valuables,' Roy explains. 'Anyway, the people in charge at the Mansion House said they could be put up at the Tower of London overnight for safe-keeping. That was quite a story!'

Jon Moore goes further in his assessment of the senior designer's character. 'Ken was a Scorpio,' he reveals. 'He was really funny but could also be extraordinarily nasty. I knew that if we had a really good day with him, in a few days we would get a really terrible day, which we all dreaded.'

At the peak of the house's success, Hardy was away a great deal. When he returned and decided to begin to assimilate himself back into the day-to-day workings at Savile Row, which for so long had been Ken's domain, it often caused fireworks which did not go unnoticed among the staff. 'We had these awful directors' lunches with sandwiches in Hardy's office,' remembers Jon Moore. 'Ken and Hardy would start to have their differences of opinion and it would all kick off! All the rest of us would just be sitting there staring at the ceiling while they argued with each other!'

Ken Fleetwood apparently disliked the unstructured styling of the late 1960s and early 1970s clothes, and Hardy agreed, as tailoring was so important to him. The 1980s brought the opportunity to revive some of the structure and powerful features of the 1950s' heyday of womenswear.

Of course menswear, at least in urban settings, would always be encapsulated by tailoring and both Hardy and Ken were perfect ambassadors for the personae of the dandy-like man-about-town as depicted in the portrait of the late Alexis ffrench on the front cover of Hardy's book, *The Englishman's Suit*.

As mentioned earlier, the relationship between Alexis and Hardy, which was the precursor to that of Hardy and Ken, had been equally close. The portrait of Alexis on the cover of *The Englishman's Suit* is a beautiful memento of their relationship. In the delightfully whimsical portrait of Alexis, two perfect little dashes of pink represent a pair of coral cufflinks, almost like tiny hearts on the cuffs of Alexis's shirt. 'Hardy wore them to the memorial services of all his friends and I wore them to his,' David Freeman reveals. Richard Martin spoke of Hardy's choice of the portrait of Alexis for the cover of the book as a bold gesture:

> I don't think he could have got away with a book with a cover like that a couple of decades earlier. It was almost a celebration of him throwing off the hidden life of a gay man up to the decriminalisation of homosexuality in Britain, which he and so many others had had to conceal. It was like a fanfare. If you read *The Englishman's Suit* with the thought in mind that here was a man who had lived a hidden life and now he can write this book about men's dress in such a flamboyant way, I think that must have been important to him.

> It is not so true now, but, like a lot of gay men of his age, he lived half his life when it was illegal, and consequently their attitude to their lives was always split. Hardy could compartmentalise his life in other ways too. He could be quite workmanlike and then at the drop of a hat could become a kind of prima-donna or eighteenth-century fop. Hardy did a lot of things differently.

Richard talks of the veil that must have been lifted from the lives of men such as Hardy who had grown up concealing a fundamental part of their personality, and in some ways the essence of their being, who, when homosexuality became legal, were able to grow into their own persona. 'He could be as camp as he liked,' he laughs. Richard also tells a humorous story about a surprisingly negative view that Hardy held about the merits of Italian tailoring in the 1980s and 1990s:

> He intensely disliked the way that Italian suit jackets at that time were designed to button very low down. He used to say, 'They button so low that when a man is adjusting his jacket he actually looks as if he is adjusting his genitalia.' To be honest I couldn't understand why that would put Hardy off!

As much as he enjoyed the convivial company of the whole ffrench family, who were a stylish, creative, and well-educated clan, it is hard to dismiss the view that Hardy and Alexis had formed a deeper and probably more intense bond during the twenty-two years before the latter's death from cancer. Ken Fleetwood was considered the person who most significantly filled the gap left by the loss of Alexis. Once Ken was established as a rather elevated form of lodger in Hardy's London home, the two would stroll across Kensington Gardens towards Savile Row together on workday mornings before being collected by car and driven the remaining short distance to Hardy Amies' HQ.

They used this time to discuss business, but surely some personal and creative topics and mutual interests must also have been the subject of the conversations. Both Hardy's self-penned accounts of his story are scant on very intimate and personal detail. As he says: 'I have told the story of my life only to illustrate how I became a dress designer and how I came to found a dress business.'

However, it is easy to weave other characters into the story, and it would be folly to think that all of his friends and business associates did not play their own part in formulating many aspects of Hardy's legend. From his mother's early influence, not to mention his father's involvement in the origins of his love for travel, right through to friends he made once his career was established, they all seem to weave intrinsically into the fabric of his life story.

The fact that he was fortunate enough to have a career in such a creative industry meant that there never seemed to be a cut-off point where his professional world ended and his private life began. Hardy was able to continue with his burgeoning design business all through his wartime service, and this also facilitated his smooth pathway through adult life. Everything about Hardy Amies had its roots in style, taste, and etiquette.

Perhaps it is not so surprising that a man of such talents would be drawn to similar characters to himself, and also that sometimes he would chance upon those who were not only like-minded but also happened to possess those filaments of creativity that Hardy himself actually lacked. The German, Jonny Witte, may have been a kind of mentor and guiding force to Hardy in the world of business and he also undoubtedly awakened the younger man's understanding of intimate relationships, but it was the arrival of Alexis ffrench who truly spanned the compass of Hardy's personal, artistic, and professional life.

Hardy did not, of course, allude to the precise nature of his relationship with Alexis, or any of the other men in his life, even in the later *Still Here*. When describing Alexis, however, he is effusive both in his praise for his friend's good taste and urbanity, and also for the influence he and his family had on large parts of Hardy's life over many years.

Alexis was of course also inherently connected to the business, perhaps not surprisingly as it was an intrinsic part of Hardy's persona. From buying shares at the outset, at a time when Alexis himself was establishing his own antiques company and needed to target all his resources there, to being with Hardy on the night he first saw the future premises at Savile Row, the pair's lives were tightly entwined.

Alexis was constantly tempting Hardy with items of exquisite antique furniture, either for the house or his own private residences, and in *Still Here*, he declares that, 'had I not been a dress designer I might well have been an interior decorator'. This he attributed to his close associations with both Alexis ffrench and John Fowler, who of course founded his eponymous design business with his fellow interiors expert Sybil Colefax in Bruton Street, Mayfair, coincidentally the location for the Norman Hartnell Design House.

Of the two interior designers, however, Alexis was by far the most important in Hardy's life. Alexis was from a distinguished Irish family but does not appear to have been on the same footing financially as his second wife, Anne. Hardy speaks of him being 'anxious to be financially independent from Anne', which sounds strange to a modern ear, but in those days was probably a reflection of the theory of male dominance which would have prevailed in society. This also facilitated an element of independence for each of the marriage partners, which was perhaps fairly common among the higher, more monied echelons of society, because the ability to create distance between them enabled them to carry on separate lives, only having to come together when it was mutually desirable to do so.

Anne was older than Alexis and seems to have absorbed Hardy almost as a surrogate 'son' into the country-based family side of the arrangement, as simultaneously Alexis was perhaps orchestrating an external, exclusively male life for the two friends in London.

Alexis's transfer of his antiques business from premises in Kensington to a new base in Pont Street, Chelsea in 1935 became the vortex for Hardy and himself to become more closely entwined. At the same time as Hardy was enjoying being invited by Anne to play the role of older brother to her daughters as they enjoyed debutante balls and other events which Hardy revelled in being involved in, Alexis was securing and renovating a 'very smartly decorated flat', which just happened to be above his antiques shop. There were rooms there for both Hardy and himself.

It all sounds like a very civilised and mutually agreeable arrangement as, in return for Hardy and his male housekeeper looking after, or 'keeping Alexis during the week', a room was made available for Hardy in a cottage in Kent, situated very close to Anne's own country house. Hardy describes this cosy idyll in *Still Here* with the words, 'Happy Days!

The ffrench clan were an extremely cosmopolitan family and this held great appeal for Hardy. His fluency in the German language brought him close to Alexis's sister Yvonne, a writer who shared a flat with Countess May Voss, a chic Italian lady who, by the 1940s, had had two German husbands and spent time all over Europe. According to Hardy, these two older women, along with Anne ffrench, all 'took me under their wing' and seemed to open up enormous opportunities for him to develop a style of living that was truly European. One of Anne's daughters became a German princess by marriage and as we know, Hardy found it difficult dealing with the extreme and polarised hatred of the whole German race that he sometimes encountered after the war.

Hardy stated in *Still Here*: 'I got much more than I deserved from the ffrench family.' Apart from Alexis and Anne, their extended family of relatives and well-connected friends seems to have provided him with a very valuable education in art, culture, food, and language that enhanced his status as an English gentleman and an accomplished European. Tellingly, the chapter of *Still Here* in which he goes into intimate detail of his life with the ffrench family, is entitled, not 'Me' but 'Moi'.

Hardy had, of course, always been drawn to large family groups since leaving home for Europe as a youth, and did not seem to really return to that kind of environment with his own family until much later when he and Rosemary both resided in the idyllic Cotswold village of Langford, where they both lived out their days. Descriptions of Alexis's great taste, style, and accomplishments punctuate Hardy's writing in both autobiographies.

Although Hardy loved opera and classical music, Alexis apparently preferred popular music with the exception of the opera, *Pelléas and Mélisande*. He was also in possession of a talent for music and writing, composing several popular songs. This both enchanted and intimidated Hardy, as it was reminiscent of his own father's 'above average beautiful baritone voice', which Hardy did not inherit. 'I was a terrible disappointment to him,' he says in *Still Here*. Despite admitting to an inferiority complex about this, Hardy soon moved on, once he discovered the gramophone and was able to foster a ravenous interest in listening to music, which was sparked in the 1920s in the opera houses of Germany.

When Hardy first took on his own house in Eldon Road, in Kensington, West London, Alexis's influence was all around. Not only did he install the gramophone on which to listen to his preferred French music as well as opera, but Alexis's style and taste in interiors was given free rein. Their bond fully encompassed their lives, both professionally and personally.

Hardy managed to take both Alexis and Anne on one final continental holiday before Alexis died in 1956. Alexis had long experienced poor health and had had a heightened perception of it for many years. He departed from orthodox medicine, much to his wife's dismay, and was a devotee of an Indian doctor, Chandra Sharma, who would later come to be known as a homeopath and herbalist. When in 1954, during the early stages of his final illness, Alexis visited Dr Sharma, he was prescribed what were obviously homeopathic remedies intended to 'remove toxins' from his body.

The way in which this manifested itself was to produce a painful rash on his upper body which, under the guidance of his wife, led to Alexis having to call upon conventional medicine to 'cure' it. Dr Sharma was obviously crestfallen at this and – in an act which appears to reflect the closeness of the two friends – asked Hardy to come into his office to talk to him about it. The account of this meeting in *Just So Far,* seems to fly in the face of today's sacrosanct code of doctor-patient confidentiality, regardless of how intimate the friendship of the two men was.

Sharma explained to Hardy how the conventional medicine Alexis was receiving to combat the effects of his attempt to purge Alexis's body of toxins was, in his opinion, simply repressing his underlying health crisis. According to Hardy, Dr Sharma told him: 'I find Alexis a patient who might be cancer-prone.'

This turned out to be true of course, as Alexis was stricken with bone-marrow cancer and died two years later – although obviously that is likely to have been apparent to any medical practitioner and does not necessarily reveal any particular insight on the part of Dr Sharma.

Hardy was obviously impressed, however, and goes on to talk at length about how he, while acknowledging how fortunate he is to be 'blessed with a healthy body', pursues a homeopathic approach to any medical issues he encounters thereafter. Sensibly, he qualifies his total faith in the doctor's herbal remedies by stressing that different plant-based medications will probably not always have the same effects on different people, telling his readers with dramatic emphasis that Chelidonium, a plant which he describes as one of his 'constitutional remedies', may be 'poison to you'.[1] A rather alarming thought!

Hardy became a fully signed-up client of Dr Sharma, revealing that his potential patients 'were interviewed totally naked'. Although he seems to have visited the doctor for his herbal remedies, Hardy also seems to have found comfort in personally growing the plants which formed part of his medical repertoire, later in his garden at Langford, Oxfordshire, where he lived in close proximity to his beloved sister, Rosemary. He did not intend to use them to self-medicate, but the implication is that he found a holistic comfort in surrounding himself with the mental and emotional feeling of well-being he gained from the herbs, which appeared to him to be instrumental in keeping him in good physical health.

He talks of their beauty in the garden, but also of how the herbs he grows for cooking give him immense satisfaction too. The garden was a great source of pleasure for Hardy, in terms of its sense of space and comfort but also as another vector of his taste for design and a visual expression of his character and experiences. He was also prone to sentimental quests for plants that had a particular family connection for him, noting that he scoured horticultural catalogues to find a climbing rose called Richmond which had been grown by his parents in their garden, eventually having to make do with a close substitute.

Hardy's long-serving chauffeur, Bill Howat, remembers how Hardy would plan his weekend visits to Langford around the flowering of his garden, particularly the roses: 'In the summer he would sometimes say, "I must go down on Thursday because the roses will just be coming out." He always had old English roses at the house and at the Barn.' The Barn was another village property, which Hardy later acquired as a guest house.

Nostalgia for past eras of design in clothing and interiors was something that bound Hardy and his friends together throughout his life. Alexis had been an inspiration in terms of taste and style and now Ken Fleetwood, who had stepped into his shoes as a hugely significant figure, brought the same emphasis to his lifestyle. In the same way that Ken had no admiration for the floaty clothes of the 1970s, Hardy abhorred the look spearheaded by Mary Quant in the 1960s, of which he said unequivocally: 'As a man of taste, I disliked the vulgarity of the mini-skirt.'

Sir Roy Strong describes Hardy as 'the master of the put-down', and when referring to Mary Quant's skills as a dress designer, recalls him saying: 'Mary Quant – what a shame no one told her how to put a sleeve in.' Sir Roy continues: 'The thing is Hardy didn't recognise how things were changing and people like Mary Quant and Jean Muir were working with that. Society had changed and women were becoming emancipated and they were working.'

Hardy had obviously taken a dislike to Mary Quant after a comment she made, and which he reports in *Still Here*,[2] referring to the 1960s as a 'watershed', Hardy reveals that he 'was more than peeved when I read that Mary Quant had said that *haute couture* was dead. The implication was that she had killed it.' He goes on to explain that after his initial fury at the comment had subsided, he realised that the young designer had actually meant that 'the influence on dress design of the *haute couture* was beginning markedly to decline'.

In fact, in his diaries Sir Roy recalls a conversation he had with Hardy shortly after the death of the acclaimed designer Jean Muir who, like Mary Quant, was a pioneer of the more practical and pared-down style of dressing which emerged for women in the 1960s.

Jean Muir had been suffering from cancer but had told practically no one, dying very suddenly at the age of 66 in May 1995. Sir Roy was a great admirer and friend of the designer and speaks in the diaries of his shock and grief at her passing. A month later, meeting Hardy at the *Country Life* Awards, Sir Roy was stunned at Hardy's response to the sudden death. He writes: 'He shocked me when I said to him, "Wasn't it a shame about Jean Muir?" "No," he replied, which was not nice.'

It is no surprise that he goes on to say, in a later chapter of the diaries 1988–2003: 'Hardy Amies only gets more crabby as he gets even older.' However, he rather generously states: 'I suppose at almost 90 you can get away with anything.' Sir Roy felt that a designer such as Hardy should have been ready to move with the times. 'But Hardy never listened to advice.'

This is in stark contrast to Hardy's recollection of the British unveiling of Dior's New Look. The first showing of the styles in the UK took place at Blenheim Palace and Hardy wrote in *Still Here*, 'I have seldom been so moved by the sight of clothes as I was when I watched the stream of thirty superbly coiffed and shod mannequins gliding through Vanbrugh's hall and library.'

Ken Fleetwood was able to carry Hardy's vision forward and this was evident in the fact that he nimbly stepped into the role of the queen's dressmaker on occasion.

However, his higher profile took a while to develop as Hardy does seem to have looked upon Ken as a sort of project in the early days. He realised Ken's potential and valued the enhancements he made to his life both in business and personally, but it took some time for Ken to be seen at Hardy's formal social events and to be allowed the full run of the premises at Hardy Amies Ltd. He certainly had to adhere to the rules in the same way as the other younger staff members did at the house, in terms of upholding the discretion of the clients at all times. This is not surprising, as Hardy himself had learned during his early days in the rarefied world of couture, the preservation of the client's dignity and mystique was always paramount.

Chapter 17

A Very Special Relationship

After joining the company in 1950 Ken quickly became established as a major figure in the House in Savile Row. He eventually ran a studio next to Hardy's office, with its own staff directing the tailors and cutters in the workrooms beyond. As Hardy says in *Still Here*: 'he was given complete control and a free hand to plan collections and to buy cloth in my absence. I never found fault with his choice.'

By 1952 Hardy Amies Ltd was flourishing, although as Hardy said, the business of haute couture was almost always underfunded as 'its stock in trade is extravagance'.

Fortunately, Hardy himself had a good business brain and surrounded himself largely with people who were astute, honest and reliable, unlike some of his fellow London couturiers who fell by the wayside due to either a lack of financial acumen or exploitation by those around them. This was the case for Norman Hartnell, who died with very little wealth, having lost his country home, Lovel Dene, due to the mismanagement and opportunism which was prevalent among his trusted business staff.

Many of Hardy's own friends and contacts also find it hard to understand how an accomplished and highly successful person such as Hardy did not accrue a great deal more obvious wealth over his time in business. The whole premise of couture is to present a rarefied world based in luxury and, to some extent, fantasy. To look at the photographs of Hardy's office and showroom in the heyday of the 1950s is to see a luxurious and opulent backdrop for the glittering, beautiful and almost unobtainable creations that emerged from the mysterious backrooms of the 'salon'.

Beavering away in the upper reaches were the men and women, not greatly well-remunerated as we know, who produced the sparkling gems that were to be modelled by the glamorous mannequins in the beautiful setting of the showroom. This dichotomy was a recipe for a 'perfect storm' which could be summed up by the phrase 'to live beyond one's means'. As

Mr Roy Allen said: 'At some points Mr Amies made money but at other times he didn't – but he would *always* spend a lot.'

Richard Martin expanded on this but, not having known Hardy during the heyday of the house, his comments do not reflect the success of the business: 'He certainly had style and position, but it seemed as if he had no money. He was constantly running to catch up. I don't think the business was ever particularly successful financially. He was always punching above his weight.'

Viewing Hardy from a point at which his star was on the wane, Richard observed that Hardy seemed intrinsically bound up with the identity he felt he had through the couture house. 'The shop on Savile Row was a fundamental part of Hardy's life, and of himself,' he says, 'And without it he absolutely wouldn't have felt himself to have been *Hardy Amies*.' As Sir Roy Strong says: 'Hardy was a self-creation.' Perhaps there is nothing wrong with that.

Later on, when Hardy Amies was known more for the menswear side of the business, Richard believes that he became disillusioned with how he had to balance his true creativity with acceptance that the emphasis was on other facets of his reputation:

> I think it rankled with him a bit that the only thing that was making money for him at that stage was the production and selling of umbrellas with his name on in Korea. [...] I think he thought, 'Why should a top British designer have to make umbrellas in Korea, when a French designer like Dior didn't ever have to do that?'
>
> ...
>
> That kind of highly tailored structured kind of Savile Row thing was quite esoteric, particularly for women. The French designers like Dior didn't make any money from the couture.

A quizzical observation about Hardy's finances is made by Sir Roy in his diaries (1988–2003) Speaking on the day of Hardy's funeral, at which he gave the address, he comments:

> It did strike me how little, apart from the residence, Hardy had of any value. It was strange that he purchased reproductions of prints

of the Stuarts when he could so easily have acquired originals. There was not a single decent picture in the house, not one. Nothing in the least personal suggesting an accumulation through the decades. That I thought was odd.[1]

There was, however, one portrait in which Hardy did invest. In 1989, he purchased an original oil painting of *The Winter Queen* by Gerrit van Honthorst. Hardy had a fascination for Elizabeth Stuart who was the daughter of James I of England. In 1613 she married Frederick, who became King of Bohemia in November 1619. Their rule was extremely short, and the following winter Elizabeth fled to the safety of Frankfurt through terribly cold and harsh conditions at the onset of a Jesuit uprising. She escaped through this severe weather and the affectionate title of The Winter Queen, already bestowed due to the couple's reign of just one winter, stuck. After the king's death Elizabeth was supported by Lord Craven, who supposedly built Ashdown House in Berkshire as a retreat for her. Hardy's fascination with the story could have developed because Elizabeth's daughter Sophia had a son George, who became George I of England and the first of the Hanoverian dynasty, which eventually led to Queen Elizabeth II. The fact that Hardy was enthralled by the Stuart period and had subsequently dressed the present monarch, appears to have compelled him to purchase the portrait. As David Freeman puts it, 'She was his pin-up'. Hardy later sold the portrait and it is now the property of the National Trust at Ashdown House.

Apart from the money that was contributed when Hardy launched the business in 1946, significant financial injections came from Neil Roger and the man who was to become Hardy's de facto personal assistant, Bill Ackroyd. It is rather curious, however, that although Ackroyd is referred to in the first of Hardy's autobiographies, he seems to have been expunged from the second.

Could this be because, despite his financial acumen, he also had rather a frivolous side and was known to have treated No. 14 Savile Row as more of a louche gentlemen's club than a serious workplace? Neil Roger, while also inclined towards carefree and indulgent hedonism, had an overtly justifiable presence at the house as he established his own studio there alongside Hardy's. Both men, of course, had distinguished wartime service records and cannot be dismissed as totally capricious. Bill later became Sir William Ackroyd.

Reading Hardy's second autobiography *Still Here*, does give one the impression of a growing business with the emphasis shifting more to the commercial rather than the creative design side, at least for the founder. Perhaps this is inevitable with the level of success Hardy Amies Ltd was having and the resulting demand for diversification. With the growth of the licensing deals they were making abroad, Hardy was travelling more and therefore had less of a hands-on approach to the domestic business.

To be profitable internationally and to be able to rest assured that his original business was in good hands, was key to the success of the burgeoning company and it is probably in no small way a credit to the comprehensive nature of Hardy's skills that he seems to have been able to balance these two factors. The accolade of royal patronage had helped to promote Hardy Amies Ltd around the world and ironically, this in itself led to the designer being pulled in many directions, one of which was inevitably away from having a hand in many of the company's designs. The Korean umbrellas were not a source of fulfilment or satisfaction for him!

Before that, however, a great deal of royal magic was bestowed upon Hardy and his company. As he grew to be more and more valued and trusted by Her Majesty, Hardy naturally found his influence on the royal wardrobe, in small ways initially, was also growing. Despite the doughty Bobo leaving the collective couturiers in no doubt that she did not believe they should have any input over and above submitting their designs and producing the dresses thereafter, Hardy for one found himself able to infiltrate one area that had previously been out of bounds – millinery.

Dressmakers of the time would often value the opportunity to fit dresses for formal occasions with suitable hats, as the proportions usually had to be carefully considered for balance as well as style.

This was not a practice that could be incorporated with the queen's fittings though, because she had her own established milliner and it was a long time before Hardy was able to exert much influence over the hats Her Majesty wore with an Amies dress or outfit. He found it easier once the queen employed a second milliner because the role was taken by a hat designer called Aage Thaarup, with whom Hardy was friendly. Later on, after the retirement of Thaarup and the sad death of Her Majesty's original milliner Kate Day, Hardy was actually asked who he would recommend for the position. He put forward the name of Frederick Fox, with whom he subsequently had a close working relationship in which the queen's hats and clothing were fitted together, enhancing the compatibility and harmony of the outfits.

For the royal tour of France in 1957, Hardy felt confident enough to ask if he could design a dress for a specific occasion, a practice not usually encouraged as the itinerary of a royal tour is usually kept fairly flexible to allow for vagaries of climate, weather, and any other factors which might unexpectedly come into play. Hardy had discovered that the tour's itinerary included a visit to the Opera House at Versailles, the history and architecture of which he knew well.

The Opera House had been built on behalf of Louis XV for the marriage of Marie Antoinette to the Dauphin, later to become Louis XVI. Hardy knew that it had recently been restored to its original glory and he was consequently able to design some dresses to complement the building's opulent decor.

A pale blue embroidered dress and matching coat were duly chosen and these were worn on the day as planned. Hardy was able to fully enjoy the occasion as he and Norman Hartnell had both been given invitations to the event, and were seated together in a box at the Opera House. Although Hardy regretted not being more flamboyant in the design of the dress, he was immensely gratified when his fellow designer complimented him on its appearance. Hardy acknowledged that it was Hartnell's other designs for the tour which were the most memorable, but graciously said in *Still Here*: 'it was a very pleasant experience for me to have shared the visit with him'.

Hardy's primary moment of joy on the tour came after he was invited to meet with the queen before she left for a reception at the Louvre. When the dresses and outfits were being planned he had been struck by the fact that Her Majesty had acknowledged that the time had come for her to become more visible by wearing brighter colours and perhaps even more flamboyant jewellery at all times of the day. This reflected Hardy's view that a member of the monarchy such as, for example, Queen Mary, the queen's grandmother, was almost above fashion and did not feel it her duty to follow the etiquette of dressing that other members of society observed.

Due to the greater access of the public via the press and photography, it was perhaps harder for the new queen to depart from the accepted fashions of the day, whereas Queen Mary continued to dress in clothes which could unequivocally be described as regal, even when the current styles were transitioning to simpler, more practical models. As Gyles Brandreth notes in *Philip and Elizabeth* 'Queen Mary wore long Edwardian dresses long after they went out of fashion. The diarist Henry 'Chips' Channon said meeting her was "like talking to St Paul's Cathedral".'[2]

This marked the older queen out and Hardy remembers 'seeing Queen Mary driving through the East End of London in the morning in pale-green lamé, wearing emeralds. The queen today is too much in the public eye and her wardrobe too much the subject of fashion comment for her to do this.' Today, this quote seems to say as much about Hardy as a teenage boy as it does about Queen's Mary's uniqueness.

The dress Queen Elizabeth II was to wear that evening at the Louvre, however, was eye-catching and luxurious and drew on her acceptance of dressing in a more opulent way. It was peacock-blue thick taffeta and was accessorised with stunning jewellery. She told Hardy that she hoped the dress would glow in the rather gloomy decor of the Louvre, and he notes that that is exactly what it did.

The teenage boy who had watched Queen Mary all those years before must have felt a great deal of pride gazing at the glamorous new young queen outshining all the other ladies present in one of his own spectacular creations. It was a feeling he maintained over the five decades during which he and his company worked with Her Majesty.

After being granted his Royal Warrant in 1955, Hardy's position was firmly established and the effect of royal patronage was working wonders on his business around the world. The press were by this time taking an even greater interest in clothing worn by the most high-ranking members of the royal family and their outfits were subjected to great scrutiny in the pages of magazines and newspapers.

Hardy sometimes found this very irksome, especially when things were not necessarily 'worn' in the way he had envisaged them. Although he eventually had more input in the pairing of hats with dresses and collaborated to some extent with those milliners with whom he had previously worked or was acquainted with, he was to discover that the last word often went to the dresser or presumably even the wearer of the clothes on the day.

Thus, when photographs appeared and he was subsequently interviewed about certain outfits he had to try to contain his dissatisfaction, which could come across as petulance and eventually became a source of apprehension for his press and public relations staff. It was as though he felt he had lost some control of his original vision for the clothes.

Hardy obviously had extremely high standards and would never have countenanced compromise where the queen was concerned. As he wrote in *Still Here*: 'I can count the garments on the fingers of one hand that have been rejected … and more than half of these were withdrawn at my request.'

Despite greatly enjoying working for the queen and considering it an enormous privilege, the restrictions naturally imposed by her duties, public image, and commitments must have caused some frustration for all of her designers. For Hardy, who hated the mini-skirt and did not find it at all relatable to the work of a couturier, the advent of the 1960s was probably the most difficult era in which to be clothing the monarch. Not only was it more problematic, having to consider skirt lengths in terms of decorum and ensuring that the queen always projected an aura of gravitas, but also factoring in the practicalities of her day-to-day public life.

The growth in press attention, together with more worldwide television coverage, meant that every outfit needed to withstand scrutiny during activities ranging from sitting on platforms or climbing up airline steps, to gracefully emerging from cars and bending to accept bouquets from small children. Preserving Her Majesty's dignity was obviously paramount.

What Hardy found particularly disappointing was that the proportions of the styles from the early 1960s onwards were much smaller, with narrow or A-line skirts and straight-cut tops which did not really lend themselves to the previously accepted image of sensuous glamour of previous decades.

This also led to a problem with hats; only the most simple, close-fitting or pillbox styles, as sported by the American First Lady, Jackie Kennedy, really complemented the slim shift dresses and column shaped gowns that were then fashionable. Mrs Kennedy was a fashion icon and a pioneer of these styles, but her position as First Lady allowed her more freedom than the British queen and Head of the Commonwealth enjoyed so, while Jackie would happily wear a dress or suit without a hat, for the queen to do the same would almost be seen as her missing out her 'crown'. All in all it was a difficult time to be a couturier to Her Majesty.

Nevertheless, the simple pared-down designs that Hardy and Ken Fleetwood provided to Her Majesty during that era probably encapsulate his most signature look, and in some ways came to represent the style Her

Majesty took forward into the following decades. Ironic really, as another period which Hardy had found challenging was the era of clothes rationing and utility styling once it became too focused on using the least amount of material, thus not allowing for the level of creativity he most enjoyed. However, the slim silhouette had one advantage in practical terms, as it avoided the risk of a gust of wind catching a hem and subsequently revealing too much of the royal limbs, as well as spoiling the line of a dress in a cheekily snapped photograph!

A rather comical weather-related story which Hardy recalls in *Still Here* involves rain as well as the dreaded wind, and although he seems to see the humour in it in the retelling, it must have been very frustrating and disappointing for him at the time.

The queen was to visit Mexico in 1975 and Hardy was asked to produce designs for various events, one of which was to be held on the top of a mountain. He describes producing a silk gown of opulent colours with a matching shawl to counteract the potential strength of the wind at high altitude. He and his team waited excitedly for television or newspaper coverage of the event and were most crestfallen to finally see a photograph of Her Majesty huddled under an umbrella with somebody else's mackintosh hastily thrown across her shoulders! The beautiful dress was obviously considerably obscured.

'We subsequently learnt,' he explains, 'that the entertainment offered to the queen had been a Mexican dance invoking the rain god to open the heavens.' This could of course be an apocryphal story, but if true, perhaps some punishment was meted out to the obviously very effective traditional dancer, as he could perhaps have chosen a less damaging way of demonstrating his mystical dance skills!

By this time Ken Fleetwood was also experienced in designing for the queen and in many cases he, Hardy, and other members of the design team would collaborate on the royal wardrobe. Ken's artistic leanings meant that his designs often had a romantic flair, and he produced some beautiful and extravagant evening dresses which Her Majesty would wear for formal occasions, as well as in portraits, when her regal glamour was expected to take centre stage.

Ken's undoubted talent for illustration greatly enhanced the initial appeal of the sumptuous gowns, and Hardy always fully acknowledged Ken's valuable role in dressing the monarch. By the early 1970s, Norman

Hartnell was slowly stepping back from his high-profile position as the queen's principal dressmaker and Hardy Amies, together with Hartnell protégé Ian Thomas, were moving up the ranks.

In fact, on the occasion of the queen's visit to Paris in 1972, Hardy was to receive a misplaced accolade, but one which he found entertaining and which also obviously gave him a scintilla of pride in himself and the house. Both he and Ken were in Paris staying at the Ritz, and Hardy had been invited to several of the grand occasions which the queen would be gracing with her presence. He had provided several outfits for the French tour and these were largely well received, although Hardy always harboured a slightly cynical view of the fashion press.

In *Still Here*, he gives his translation of a review published in *Paris Match* in 1972: 'A young English couturier of the new generation, Hardy Amies, is gradually taking the place of the celebrated Norman Hartnell, principal dressmaker to the queen since the start of her reign.'

Since Hardy was by then 62 years old, a mere eleven years younger than Hartnell, he believed that the publication had muddled him up with Ian Thomas, and found the fact that *Paris Match* referred to Hardy himself as a *'jeune couturier'* rather amusing.

Royal tours were, of course, always an exercise in diplomacy with meticulous planning on every front. The queen would always be fully informed about customs, etiquette and expectations in every country she visited and her clothes, and those of other members of the royal family were, and are still to this day, chosen with an eye to the message they will give out to the host nation.

Floral embroidery or embellishment was a way of conveying respect to a particular country or region, and this was something that Hartnell and Hardy Amies often used as a way of allowing the queen to pay tribute to the location she happened to be in. Hartnell had famously incorporated the national flowers of the countries of Her Majesty's realm in the queen's coronation gown, an inspired idea, which seems to have influenced the slightly younger Hardy.

One particularly spectacular example of Hardy replicating this initiative was the dress the queen wore in Hollywood during a visit to America's West Coast in 1983. Shining from a pure white bodice were beautifully embroidered vivid red poppies delicately linked with a network of dark green stems and foliage, in tribute to the state flower of California.

An earlier outfit designed for a 1975 visit to Japan turned out to be a tribute to the visited nation more by chance than intention on Hardy's part. The fact that he happened to be in Japan himself on business at the time meant that Hardy was able to witness at first hand the effect the queen's displays of flattery had on her welcoming and enchanted hosts.

He tells the story of how he was in a boardroom discussing a licensing arrangement for his men's and womenswear to be reproduced and sold in Japan, when they were interrupted by an alert to view the queen's arrival in Tokyo on the television. Hardy did not at the time realise that Her Majesty was going to be wearing one of his creations, but to his delight she was 'looking young, fashionable and regal in a pretty mauve silk coat of ours'. His Japanese business partners were enraptured, 'Imperial colours', they apparently declared. 'How flattering to us!' Hardy goes on to admit: 'I had no idea that mauve was an imperial colour, but I shouldn't be surprised if the queen had known.' The favourable impact this would have had on Hardy's business negotiations is not noted.

An extremely memorable royal tour for Hardy took place in 1965. The queen was to visit West Germany and Hardy was intensely interested in it due to his travels there in his youth. A state banquet given by the president in the queen's honour was planned at Schloss Augustusburg, Brühl, a palace with which Hardy was familiar from his time on the Rhine during the 1920s. Built in the mid-eighteenth century, it was a suitably lavish venue which was preserved for formal state occasions, and Hardy had specific memories of its lavish interior, with a predominance of blue and white, which he was to discover were the official colours of Prince Clemenze August, a member of the Wittelsbach dynasty of Bavaria, who had ordered the building of the palace.

Hardy settled on those colours for the dress he was to submit for the queen to wear at the banquet. In keeping with the era, it was a simple yet spectacular, slim gown in pale blue soft satin for the skirt and with a richly embroidered bodice covered in 'white beads and pearls in a rococo design which reflected the influence of the stucco decoration', as he described it in *Still Here*. The embroidery was executed by the skilled craftspeople of S. Lock and Co of London, a company which was established in the eighteenth century and is now known by the name Hand and Lock.

Hardy had total admiration for the embroidery skills of Mr Lock and his staff. Established in 1767, the company holds the Royal Warrant as

Embroiderers to the queen. Knowing the monarch was so pleased with the design made the fact that Hardy himself was invited to the reception before the event even more thrilling. He devotes three full pages of his second autobiography to the German trip, such was his fascination for the country where he had spent such memorable times during his youth, and he was obviously extremely gratified that the clothing he had submitted was a triumph.

There is a beautiful photograph of the queen in the Schloss Augustusburg dress taken by Cecil Beaton in the White Drawing Room at Buckingham Palace, in the collection at the Victoria and Albert Museum. It is a sublime photograph of Her Majesty, looking at once regal and relaxed, at the height of her beauty, and her happiness and comfort in the dress radiates from her. At the time of writing the image takes pride of place on the Hand and Lock website – with a credit to Hardy Amies, of course.

Hardy was accompanied on his trip to the Federal Republic of Germany by his sister, Rosemary and his loyal public relations man, Peter Hope Lumley. On this occasion Peter was instrumental in a great PR triumph for the House of Hardy Amies. There was always an embargo on images of what the queen was to wear on formal occasions until she had actually been seen in the garments. Peter arranged for the *Daily Express* staff artist, Robb, to send over his copy of the designer's sketch of the queen's dress as soon as they knew she was definitely wearing it. Hardy and the team were able to confirm this by arranging to view the queen driving through the streets of Bonn to the event. Thus the paper was able to print the sketch in its full glory on the front page of the newspaper back in England the next day. The headline read 'The Queen Dazzles Them' and the caption stated, 'Robb captures the brilliance of a gown that stunned a nation.' Peter Hope Lumley's instincts and talent for highlighting the skill and creative vision of Hardy Amies was invaluable.

More than a thousand people gathered for the reception which followed the banquet and Hardy was among them. He found the whole thing a profoundly moving experience and was particularly pleased to reconnect with some of the people from the worlds of both industry and the arts that he had met during his days in the area before the war.

The assembled throng awaited the VIPs' arrival and Hardy had a superb vantage point at the top of a vast elaborate staircase. He describes the scene in *Still Here*: 'the royal party duly appeared and inexorably wound its way upwards and towards us. It was a stunning and unforgettable sight.'

The queen was travelling with a wardrobe which included the designs of Norman Hartnell as well as Hardy Amies, but she wore several of Hardy's outfits on the West German tour. The Amies team were both pleased and surprised when Her Majesty arrived at a performance at the opera wearing a dress they had not even realised she was taking with her!

However, the most emotional event for Hardy and perhaps one which was even more moving than the glittering evening at Schloss Augustusburg was the visit to Coblenz, the scene of some of Hardy's most cherished memories of his youthful sojourn in the town.

In fact, one of the grandest hotels in the area, the Riesenfürstenhof, had been the scene of a farewell party thrown by his friends and colleagues for the 21-year-old Hardy when he returned to England after his two-and-half years spent there. It was with a mixture of nostalgia and pride that he pondered how, on that day in August 1930, he could never have dreamt that he would one day be back at the invitation of the town's mayor to welcome the queen of his home country on her first visit to Germany and the Rhineland.

The young man who had at that time been a trainee in a tile factory was now awaiting the arrival of his monarch, who would be wearing a dress he had designed under the auspices of a fashion house bearing his name! The cherry-red and white coat and dress ensemble was a simple outfit suitable for a daytime cruise up the River Rhine and a subsequent meeting with dignitaries. However, despite the relatively low-key occasion, Hardy described it as a moving experience; this was undoubtedly due to his feelings of affection for the region and its people, and his soul-searching during the war years.

Another extremely proud moment in his tenure as the queen's dressmaker, came at the Silver Jubilee Celebration in 1977. Hardy recounts in *Still Here* that the queen seemed to have an unprecedented calendar of engagements that year, including multiple foreign trips, and scheduling fittings for outfits was a logistical conundrum.

For 7 June, the actual day of celebration, Hardy, and in particular the vendeuse Sheila Ogden, were quite convinced that a pale green dress in chiffon had been selected. As so often happened, the weather played havoc with the plans that had been put in place, and the temperature dropped to such an unseasonal low that it became apparent that the lightweight dress would be unsuitable. This would therefore mean that a different outfit and, more disappointingly, one by a different designer, would likely be called in as a replacement. However, joy rang out at the fashion house when the Gold Coach emerged from under the arches of Buckingham Palace and the queen could be glimpsed in a striking bright-pink silk dress and coat which Amies had submitted for an event during Her Majesty's tour of the United States the previous year.

On that occasion, disappointment had followed as the temperatures in New York at the height of summer precluded Her Majesty from wearing the outfit. However, it was eventually seen to great effect as the queen wore it to open the Olympic Games in Montreal shortly afterwards. It was a perfect choice then as the vibrant colour meant that Her Majesty was highly visible to the crowd in the vast Olympic stadium, and it proved to be similarly appropriate for the Jubilee Day service at St Paul's Cathedral. 'I gave myself a pat on the back,' Hardy says in *Still Here*, 'for having insisted that the loose coat be lined with the same material as that of the dress.' This was an extravagant and costly decision but most pragmatic, as it meant that the weight of the material stood up well to the buffeting of the summer winds on the steps of the cathedral, as well as protecting the queen from the decidedly unseasonal temperatures!

Often emotional, Hardy recounts another moving moment during the jubilee celebrations, when he also no doubt felt he deserved another small 'pat on the back'. He tells of how he made an additional piece for the coat and dress ensemble when he was originally planning the design for the US tour – a matching scarf. Having been aware of the force of the air conditioning in some American buildings, he had decided to add the extra item to the outfit in case the queen felt the chill around her shoulders once she had taken off her coat indoors.

He was touched when he realised that the queen must have been carrying the small scarf in her bag during the cathedral service and on her return to Buckingham Palace in the carriage, decided to slip it over her shoulders. 'There is no doubt from our point of view,' he declared in *Still Here*, 'that this pink outfit is the most important that we have ever made for the queen.'[3] Its significance would be enhanced by the fact that Her Majesty appointed him Commander of the Royal Victorian Order (CVO) that same year.

One of Hardy's most disappointing experiences in his time dressing Her Majesty took place in October 1981 when she visited Italy and was to have an audience with Pope John XXIII at the Vatican. 'I have always thought it would be a joy to dress the queen in black with all the jewels and the garter', he is quoted as saying in Michael Pick's book *Hardy Amies*.[4] He was therefore understandably delighted to be asked to submit sketches for a dress for Her Majesty to wear on the great occasion. However, it was perhaps injudicious of the designer to veer away from the traditionally expected fabrics of velvet or heavy lace, and decide to experiment with creating more of an ethereal, diaphanous, shaded look, rather than one which could be described as 'the dead funereal black'.

His resultant concept was to create a cloud of very dark charcoal grey with a combination of fine Chantilly lace, combined with white and grey tulle. The design seemed to meet with approval from the monarch at the dress fittings, and the idea that the slightly more adaptable design would also serve at a later date as a dark dinner dress seemed to bode well.

In a paragraph which seems to highlight some regret on Hardy's behalf in *Still Here*, he recalls how he was precluded from attending the final fitting with the queen due to being called to an essential business planning meeting in New York which necessitated him being away at the time. He talks about the quandary of whether to 'put the queen's commands first', or to prioritise keeping a business thriving which was an economic asset to Britain and one which the queen herself patronised. That was probably an overly analytical assessment of the situation, but the fact that the queen subsequently failed to wear his carefully conceived dress obviously disappointed and, to some extent, irked him.

With the perceived 'snub' still weighing on his mind, when another visit to fit for a tour came up, Hardy asked Bobo if she thought the queen would like them to make some alterations to the dark dress with a view to it being wearable for another occasion.

He recalled in a subsequent letter that the queen's response to his staff was: 'I can't think why Mr Amies wants to alter my black dress, it's very pretty. Not dark enough for Rome. I'm saving it.'[5]

Thus Hardy realised that although the dress was not 'black enough' for the Vatican, it was popular with the queen and would potentially be worn on other occasions. He must have been greatly relieved considering the anxiety he seems to have felt over the non-appearance of the gown in Rome.

It was shortly after this in 1982 that Hardy's protégé, Kenneth, was rewarded with the opportunity of representing him at a Buckingham Palace fitting. A request from the queen for a visit was suddenly brought forward and, once again, clashed with an overseas visit of Hardy's. Ken was duly dispatched and it turned out to be a highly successful first meeting, resulting in a happy note from the queen about what an enjoyable time she had spent with Ken, as well as a substantial order for outfits being placed for the Caribbean and North American tour of November 1982.

Hardy was delighted by the fact that Ken had got on so well with the queen, and on subsequent occasions the two men were able to attend Her Majesty together. Hardy personally witnessed how his potential successor was 'beguiled by the queen's personality' and did not miss any of her frequent 'tiny shafts of humour'. Thus began a new and equally successful stage of the partnership of the House of Hardy Amies and the Monarchy, which was only halted by Ken's untimely death in 1996. This sad event was marked by Her Majesty in a warm-hearted, handwritten letter sent to Hardy, in which she writes: 'I have just read the sad news of Ken Fleetwood's death and I would like to offer you my sympathy. There will be many people who will miss him, not least myself.'

The US business trip which meant Hardy had been unable to attend the meeting about the queen's North American tour was to prove fortuitous in that during his travels he visited San Francisco and gained some insight about the queen's planned itinerary through his business contacts and from the British Consulate. Not only that, but he returned with an invitation to attend the cocktail party at the consulate which was planned to take place during the trip.

Once the outfits were made and dispatched to the palace, Hardy was off again on another visit of his own to the United States, and as the queen and her party made their way to California, he was already in New York at the start of a month-long visit.

He was now, to his great delight, in possession of another prized invitation – to a glittering evening party in Hollywood. This came about due to the fact that one of Hardy's old friends had introduced him to Nancy Reagan a few years earlier and they had got on well. This same friend, Jerry Zipkin, had spoken to Mrs Reagan, who was now the First Lady, and she had insisted Hardy be invited to the event. This turned out to be an occasion of great pride for Hardy as, despite the weather being the worst that California had seen for over twenty years, the queen chose to wear his spectacular 'California Poppy' dress to the party.

Up until that point of the tour the queen had not worn any outfits by the house, but this could be seen as a fortunate turn of fate. Almost all the ensembles she had worn when having to appear outdoors had had to be compromised in some way due to the inclement weather conditions. This had led to some disparaging reports in the fashion press, which did not seem to understand that the queen had needed to improvise, suddenly changing coats and hats and having to contend with umbrellas. All of this put the queen, and consequently her designers, at a great disadvantage with the press, but Hardy's luck was in, as his glorious dress was unveiled in an indoor setting. 'Suddenly there it was: the happy, glistening white and youthful-looking party dress that I had always hoped the queen would choose to wear,' he recounted in *Still Here*. 'I swallowed a lump in the throat and heaved a sigh of pride and relief.'

In relation to the North American tour, Hardy paid tribute to the whole royal enterprise and how, despite outside forces causing all sorts of decisions, not least those connected with the queen's wardrobe, to be thrown into disarray, things still went smoothly. To the watching public and the dignitaries involved in all Her Majesty's engagements, things would invariably go according to plan, with rarely a hitch or delay, while behind the scenes courtiers and staff were no doubt pedalling furiously beneath the surface.

The queen was due to be immersed in preparations for her next tour, which was to Sweden, on her return from the United States plus, as always, hosting visits, banquets, and other events for visiting Heads of State. The staff at Amies were pretty sure that they would not be called upon to make any clothes for the 1983 season as so many things had gone unworn in California: 'We concluded that the queen must have had enough clothes to see her through the London season as well as other occasions, such as Ascot.'

While expressing how impertinent it would be of him to put thoughts into the queen's head, Hardy says: 'I may risk suggesting that, on her return from California, the queen must have been relieved at the thought that for the rest of the year she would not have her privacy invaded by a gaggle of dressmakers.' He was quite possibly right, but from the way he describes the queen's relationship with the aforementioned 'gaggle', if they had needed to come together, it would most likely have been a gracious and cordial gathering.

Hardy's greatest honour came after the publication of *Still Here* in 1984. In 1989, the year of his 80th birthday, the queen bestowed upon him the honour of Knight Commander of the Royal Victorian Order. As Michael Pick recounts in his illustrated biography, *Hardy Amies*: 'He said, "When the letter came, I was alone, and I just sat down and burst into tears. It's a personal gift. Other people who got it are more important than just a dressmaker."' He is even more humble in a quote from his interview with Naim Attallah, saying, 'I still think it's the biggest stroke of luck. Queen Victoria founded the Royal Victorian Order for services to the sovereign. I don't think she ever intended it for dressmakers.'[6]

Hardy was too modest. His work for the queen over four decades had been valuable and greatly appreciated. He stopped dressing her personally in the late 1980s, saying, 'she doesn't want an octogenarian crawling about her feet', although he did continue to sit in on final fittings even as he approached his 90th year.

Hardy's association with Her Majesty had brought him worldwide fame and helped him to establish one of the great British success stories of the time, and he became an ambassador for the nation in the world of business and commerce. His former role in the Special Operations Executive during the Second World War had already been rewarded. He could never really be described as 'just a dressmaker', and it is clear that the queen almost certainly did not think of him as such.

Part Four

People

Chapter 18

Changing Faces

Hardy continued his work for the queen and other members of the royal family including Princess Anne, Princess Alexandra, Princess Michael of Kent and Diana, Princess of Wales, for five decades. However he was steadfastly true and loyal to his original clients, the older established members of the royal family, and apparently his head was not inordinately turned by the charms of the new young Princess of Wales, in the same way that those of most of the nation were.

During this time his colleagues, including Ken Fleetwood and later his assistant Jon Moore, who took over a lot of the design work from the 1980s onwards, would run the studio while Hardy was engaged abroad on the business side of the company. In 1974 Ken became Design Director, having played a vital role at the house for around two decades, and designing for the queen for much of that time. Jon Moore was appointed as his assistant in 1979 having just completed his training at Kingston School of Art, which is now part of Kingston University and still producing talented and creative fashion graduates.

Moore was considered a great asset to the house, being considerably younger than Hardy, who was by then 70, as well as also being much younger than Ken Fleetwood, his effective 'manager'. Jon had been trained in all aspects of design and dressmaking as part of the new style of educating emerging designers. Jon could, 'cut a toile and sew it with his own very nimble fingers,' Hardy recalled,[1] and 'His considerable charm is of great value in dealing with the customers.' This does sound like high praise, although, according to David Freeman, both Hardy and Ken mainly admired Moore's skills as 'a great stitcher'.

His acquisition was a shrewd move on the part of Hardy Amies Ltd because, despite being the most important couture house continuing to survive in London at a time when the world of fashion was substantially changing, it was full of very traditional staff with long-established practices which could probably do with something of a shake-up.

Not everyone would have agreed with that approach however, and Jon Moore's new ideas did not go down well with some of the staff. Roy Allen found Jon Moore difficult to work with and cites the fact that Moore took over from Ken's assistant when she left to have a baby, as one of the reasons that he himself decided to leave the house. Roy and Ken had been contemporaries and had enjoyed a very cordial relationship. 'Ken used to ask for my advice and Jon Moore didn't really like that,' he said. 'He was unpleasant and I decided I wasn't going to put up with it.'

Jon Moore was one of a new breed of textiles and fashion graduates and as such was fully trained in pattern cutting and sewing, skills which many designers before him were not accomplished at, the tradition being to have separate staff who were skilled at those tasks. This shift in the culture of couture operations also appears to have initiated an unfortunate disparity in pay scales and the longer-serving staff were soon to become aware that the incoming contingent were being paid considerably more than the old guard.

Roy Allen recalls a rather shocking incident during the latter part of his time at 14 Savile Row, when he had approached Hardy for a rise but none was forthcoming, despite him explaining that he was in fact struggling to make ends meet.

'I was cutting down on a lot of things,' he explains, 'even food. One day I actually passed out at work due to the fact that I hadn't eaten. Ken came along and I told him what was wrong and he took me to lunch at the Westbury.' This act of kindness did not, however, lead to a change of heart at the top of the firm. 'You would think they would have done something about it, wouldn't you?' Roy continues. 'But they didn't.' His disillusionment with the hierarchy at the house continued to grow, until he was approached by actress turned couturier Anouska Hempel, Lady Weinberg.

'When Anouska Hempel came along, she offered me what I should have been earning which was four times what I was getting at Hardy Amies', he reveals. Roy decided he had no choice but to make the move. 'Ken did try to persuade me to stay but Mr Amies did nothing whatsoever, until my last day and an hour before I was due to leave.' Hardy then approached Roy at this eleventh hour with an offer to match his new salary at Anouska

Hempel, as well as covering the cost of his tickets for his annual trip to visit family in Canada.

However, by this time 'I was so annoyed that it had come so late that I said No.' Roy reveals with some regret. Part of his grievance was to do with the fact that he had always been on the lookout for injustices in the workplace and was happy to stand up for others when things seemed unfair for the staff. 'There was a canteen when I started so we would always be able to get lunch, but later that was changed and we were only given teas and coffees,' he explained.

After a protest by the girls in the workrooms, they were given luncheon vouchers instead but, according to Roy, these were also withdrawn a couple of years later.

'I thought that wasn't fair at all, as that money was part of their wages,' he continued. A delegation marched off to see Stanley Cox, Hardy's business manager at the time, but by the end of negotiations the only representatives left from the workforce were Roy and one of the other fitters, Miss Lilian.

The two stood their ground and the luncheon vouchers were duly reinstated. 'I was always prepared to stand up for things that weren't right,' Roy said. Summing up his career, he says reflectively, 'I've never really made any money, but I have had an interesting life.'

In the mid-1980s another Kingston College graduate joined the Amies ranks. Ian Garlant joined as an assistant in the womenswear department, but when a position opened up to move over to the burgeoning menswear operation, he accepted it and the trio of Ken, Jon Moore, and Ian Garlant took the business forward for the next ten years until Ken's tragically early death from AIDS in 1996.

Ian Garlant appears to have had more in common with Hardy than Jon Moore did. In Michael Pick's illustrated biography, we discover that Garlant came to be referred to by Hardy as 'a grandson' and due to the fact that he got on famously with Ken, was often invited for weekend trips to Hardy's country home in Langford.

They bonded over literature, music, and opera, although the future of the business once Hardy died grew to be a point of contention, and ultimately disillusionment, for both Garlant and Moore, who kept it afloat through stormy financial times during the founder's later years. According to David Freeman, both Moore and Garlant thought of Hardy as 'a bit of a silly old man and could be unkind and thoughtless towards him', while still assuming that they were much valued and in line for eventual rewards. 'Jon Moore didn't come to the funeral,' said David. 'He, Ian Garlant and Roger Whiteman were all miffed because I got everything.'

Garlant eventually left the fashion industry, returned to his native Norway and took up a career as an artist and sculptor. According to Nicholas Worth, who worked at the house during the latter years of Hardy's life, this was his real calling. 'Ian was a true artist,' he said. 'His illustrations for the menswear collections were a joy to behold.'

Hardy's position as the titular head of the firm diminished more and more as time went on. He never officially retired, and his driver would often bring him in after a stroll through Hyde Park and he would, according to Nicholas Worth, 'sit down in front of my desk, which was just inside the front door, and discuss anything relevant that had appeared in the papers. The journalists often talked about things in a way that he didn't agree with and he would complain about it.' Apparently a writer once gave a description of what they referred to as 'an afternoon gown', and Hardy irritably remarked: 'What's an afternoon gown? That's a bloody stupid name to give it!' Hardy's input into the operations of the company and his influence on its public image were volatile and at times unpredictable. Another member of staff whose loyalty and skill became invaluable was Peter Hope Lumley. Once Hardy reached the autumn of his years he did not have the sensitivity or level of discretion which would have allowed for gaffe-free interviews with the press, and Hope Lumley was often called upon to exert a moderating influence to avoid damaging and ill-advised quotes finding their way into the newspapers.

'The mistake was to ever leave Hardy alone with the press, especially after a good lunch where he had had too much to drink,' Chris Stratmann laughs. Chris recalls a rather indiscreet interview Hardy once gave to *The Sunday Times Magazine*. 'He "outed" his sister in the 'Relative Values' column of the magazine,' Chris reveals (although it is unclear whether Hardy categorically stated that his sister was gay), 'He was talking to an attractive young man who was egging him on, and he also managed to say something very inappropriate about Princess Michael of Kent!'

'The company decided to make an appeasing phone call to the press office at the palace and fortunately their attitude was just to say nothing about it and wait for it to pass.' Luckily there seemed to be no reprisals after Hardy's indiscretion.

Considering the irascible Miss Cammie had once been in charge of 'press' for the house, the experienced and equable Peter Hope Lumley must have been a monumental improvement. As Hardy said in *Still Here*: 'Peter interprets to me the point of view of the man in the street,' and this was in the early days of their association. He must have been even more invaluable during Hardy's indiscreet and unpredictable later years. Roy Allen remembers Peter Hope Lumley, who was said to have been 'the inventor of Public Relations' as 'A lovely man'.

Some time after Roy left Hardy Amies, he happened to be in a Kensington restaurant which was one of Hardy's favourites. Lo and behold Hardy was dining there with Peter, and Roy was called over. 'Hardy chatted to me and then Peter said: "If you ever need any help please come to me."' Hardy, perhaps on realising the loss Roy had been to the company, then felt the need to say: 'I have to say Roy, it was one of the worst things I ever did, letting you go.'

In some ways Roy does regret leaving the man who had obviously set him on his path through a great career in couture. He still works as a couturier now, numbering the Queen Consort, Camilla, as one of his clients. In Angela Levin's 2022 book, *Camilla: From Outcast to Future Queen Consort*, his name appears at the head of a list of the Queen Consort's favourite clothing makers.

'Maybe I should have stayed at Hardy Amies,' he muses, 'but, if I had, I wouldn't have got my own Royal Warrant.' As head of his own business, Roy dressed Queen Elizabeth the Queen Mother for the last eleven years of her life and, due to the fact that she sadly died while he was still working for her, he retains the Warrant to this day.

Honours such as this are obviously a great source of pride for those who receive them, although this can sometimes tip over into what could be considered a sense of superiority and elevation. According to Michael Pick, Ian Garlant said that once he received his knighthood, Sir Hardy could be terribly outspoken and insensitive, believing that his way was invariably right and that he was entitled to tell everybody else so.

In mitigation, it is believed that the death of Ken in 1996, and also that of his sister Rosemary in 2001, left a huge gap in Hardy's life. This led him into despondent and introspective periods during which he revisited many distressing episodes from the past, and this psychological tendency could have led to some of his uncensored outbursts.

Chapter 19

A Sibling Bond

Hardy's sister, Rosemary was obviously his strongest link to the past and his parents, in particular his mother, who could of course be seen as the conduit for his whole path through life due to her own career in London's couture houses. Rosemary was, however, in some ways her brother's complete opposite and was much more in tune with their father than their mother. He describes Rosemary in *Still Here* as having great common sense and 'good application to practical problems', and says that the two of them 'complement each other'.

Rosemary herself summed this up in a quote used in her obituary, when talking of her time living with Hardy at Eldon Road: 'It was far too much like hard work. I had to spend all my time going round with the *Black and Decker* while Hardy lay on his bed eating chocolates and reading *Vogue*.'

David Freeman confirms this, saying: 'She was self-taught and probably learned it all during the war. [...] She was very self-reliant and actually left Liverpool where she had been based, travelled to Italy and followed the advancing force, driving three-ton canteen trucks dispensing tea and sympathy to the troops.'

When Rosemary died, David had the idea of getting an obituary written and submitted to the *Daily Telegraph*. 'I asked the biographer Selina Hastings to write it as Hardy and Selina were great gossips together,' he says. 'When the piece was published the caption on the photo of Rosemary, which was of her in her WVS days, said: "Preferred mending tractors to decorating hats"!' This was a reference to Rosemary's unhappy period working for a milliner just after the war.

Shortly after Rosemary's death, one of the Hardy Amies' vendeuses, Valerie Scobie, was discussing her funeral with the queen, who said: 'I didn't realise he had a sister. I think she and I would have got on.' That is probably very true, as the young Princess Elizabeth spent the last months of the Second World War as a Second Subaltern in the

Auxiliary Territorial Service. Even though her service did not amount to much more than completing the training, the young princess did emerge as an expert driver and with a good knowledge of 'the workings of the combustion engine', subjects which herself and Rosemary could no doubt have enthusiastically discussed. That would not have been an area of conversation that her brother could easily have shared with Her Majesty. According to Christopher Stratmann, the drivers could always tell when Hardy had taken his car out himself. 'If he had been in the car there would always be scratches or mirrors off,' he laughs. 'He wasn't a competent driver.' David was even more critical: 'If he did ever drive around the countryside people would have to dive into hedges for safety.'

Rosemary had lived a challenging and eventful life in her own right, having served with the National Fire Service during the Second World War, as well as subsequently in the Women's Voluntary Service in Italy, Germany, Greece, Malaya, and Hong Kong.

Unlike Hardy, she showed no interest as a child in her mother's skills and pastimes in the world of needlework, clothing and craft, instead much preferring active, outdoor pursuits. Following her time at school she was, like Hardy, sent to Germany to study, and became a fluent German speaker.

Hardy takes credit for encouraging his sister to widen her horizons in this way, thus creating a bond between the siblings which continued on her return from Europe, when she assisted Alexis ffrench in his antiques business. However, after returning home shortly before her mother's death in 1938, primarily to take care of her father, she moved away when it became clear that Mr Amies was likely to remarry, and worked in a milliner's in Reigate, Surrey. This was actually a rare occasion in which her mother's career had converged with hers, as the owner of the business was a friend of her late mother and obviously the connection with dressmaking and hats was a close one.

Rosemary, however, did not share either Mary's or her brother's interest in fashion and it was with great relief that the declaration of war gave her the chance to swap the frivolity of frocks and bonnets for motor vehicle engines in the transport section of the National Fire Service.

After her wartime adventures abroad Rosemary returned to London and, presumably through experience as well as fortuitous contacts, began work in another clothing company, Jacqmar of Bond Street. This quickly bored her and she went off to sell agricultural vehicles and machinery instead.

It was her undoubted head for business rather than any attraction to couture that eventually saw Rosemary join Hardy in Savile Row, and she ended up running his office for him for fourteen years with a staff of, at times, as many as 100. She got on well with Hardy's highly dependable company secretary, Stanley Cox, and was obviously able to relate well to the staff, who at the time were mostly women. Her solid, pragmatic and down to earth character proved to be a good counterpoint to her brother's rather more flamboyant, and at times extravagant, ideas.

This was all very good while it lasted, even when the two siblings, separated in age by six years, lived together in Hardy's handsome five-storey house in South Kensington, but Rosemary always longed to return to the countryside with its opportunities for active rather than creative and cerebral pursuits.

With the sale of part of Hardy Amies Ltd to Debenhams in the early 1970s, Hardy was able to give Rosemary a sum of money which enabled her to buy a cottage in Oxfordshire. Her decision was originally a disappointment to him, but it cannot really have been a surprise that Rosemary decided to purchase a rural rather than a London property for herself.

Hardy looks back happily over his childhood in North London and Essex with his parents and Rosemary. However, he describes their latter home as being located in 'an ugly suburb' from which he was glad to escape, first to boarding school and later to France and Germany. Even at that early age, he had created a persona which craved freedom and adventure rather than the constraints of suburbia, and he appears to have been fearless in pursuing it. When he started work at Lachasse in 1934, he soon began to tire of the commute in and out of London from Essex, and at this point he left the family home and moved into the flat of Alexis ffrench – the first of his many residences in the capital.

The next move was into the larger flat, which Alexis quickly acquired above his own new antique shop premises in Pont Street, Chelsea. This effectively became a London home for the two men, with Alexis and his wife Anne having already agreed to maintain separate apartments in London for their individual use during the week.

Weekends were spent in Kent and, once again in what may seem a rather curious arrangement to the more conventional observer, each of the married partners had their own property very close to each other. Hardy was, of course, allocated his own room in Alexis's weekend retreat. The arrangement seemed to work well for the whole family however, and Hardy was welcomed lovingly by everyone involved.

At the onset of war the flat in Pont Street was vacated and Alexis decided to move out of London, while Hardy took on a flat of his own in nearby Chesham Place. Alexis continued their mutual living arrangement by making use of it as a *pied-a-terre*. The family links continued too, with Hardy having a room of his own at Alexis's new country home and describing the situation succinctly as 'a family life, with the members all having a great deal of independence'.

Hardy's next move on his own account was back to Kensington, to the house at number 22 Eldon Road, which had five floors and a garden, and was situated on what he describes then as being a 'remarkably quiet street'. Once again Alexis had his own quarters, this time amounting to a whole floor, and in return the decor and furnishings seem to have been his creation, with his opulent themes pushing Hardy's bank balance to the limit.

A further move, to the larger 17b Eldon Road, followed Alexis's untimely death in 1956, and although the premises must have offered comfort and space internally, Hardy appears to have been growing increasingly frustrated at the limitations put on his gardening efforts by the spatial restraints of London. In *Still Here*, he bemoans the difficulty of nurturing a herb garden in Kensington, declaring that such plants need 'a lot of space and sunlight'. It was not until he bought his own country house in Oxfordshire in 1972 that he was able to give free rein to his green-fingered aspirations.

Nonetheless, he appears to have thrown himself wholeheartedly into the decoration of the second London house, this time without the influence of his erstwhile design gurus, ffrench and Fowler. He seems to have taken a more minimalist approach to the interiors of what was a considerably larger house, although nevertheless referencing the work of Felix Harbord, an extravagant designer, decorator, and collector who was heavily influenced by the grandeur and opulence of Versailles.

Hardy also loved to entertain. This was partly because it gave him the opportunity to display his interior design choices to his friends, contacts, and even his workforce from the time he owned the Eldon Road houses until he expanded his property empire with The Old School, his home in the Oxfordshire village of Langford.

Roy Allen remembers:

> He used to celebrate his birthday as well as the end of the show season in July, with a big party. He once covered the entire garden at Eldon Road in a huge tent and filled it with white lilies. You could smell their scent as you moved around it.

Roy enjoyed many trips to the homes of his employer during his near forty years of loyal service. However, Hardy was not always so unreservedly generous and hospitable. He remembers that on a few occasions when he happened to be in Langford staying with an erstwhile colleague, Miss Eileen, who had also moved out there, Hardy had no compunction about taking advantage and setting him to work, once he realised he was temporarily in the village. In the countryside, this work took on a more manual form than it would have done in the highly skilled confines of the tailors' workrooms at Savile Row. 'I was staying at Miss Eileen's house over the road from Hardy, but he would ask me to come over and mow the lawn for him.' Roy was, of course, happy to oblige and was occasionally rewarded with plants from the garden at Langford.

The first foray out into the Oxfordshire countryside had been made, of course, by Rosemary, who spent every weekend at her cottage in Langford, while initially still returning to London during the week for work commitments. She took up residence with a dear friend, Gwyn Owen, a colleague from her days in the WVS. The two women lived there happily together until their deaths.

Hardy describes Rosemary's relationships with other women in the interview with Naim Attallah: 'she is, I think, sexless, in the sense of not really being interested in sex,' he explains, 'although she has had sentimental attachments to women.' Since Rosemary shared her home with Gwyn for around thirty years, it is fair to say that their attachment must have been strong, although these comments appear to contradict the statement Hardy is said to have made in the earlier interview in *The Sunday Times*.

At the time Rosemary bought her cottage in Langford, Hardy does not seem to have imagined that he would commit to buying a country home of his own, preferring, as he said, to take up invitations to enjoy others' weekend hospitality when offered. This was partly because he had witnessed the burden of responsibility which a second home brought with it, through the life he shared with the ffrench family. It was easier to be able to pack a case and arrive in the established comfort of someone else's retreat and not have to worry about maintaining one of his own on a permanent basis. This was to change in 1972 when The Old School became available and, with circumstances surrounding the business being fortuitous, he purchased it.

The house at 17b Eldon Road was owned by Hardy Amies Ltd and, as Hardy sold off part, and later the whole, of the business to Debenhams, the fact that he still lived there made him uneasy, as he did not 'officially own' the property. The deal with Debenhams does not appear to have been entirely beneficial to Hardy, although according to David Freeman, the enabler, Hardy's then financial adviser, Eric Crabtree, ended up owning a yacht bought with his dividend.

'Crabtree was a nasty piece of work,' says David. 'He persuaded Hardy to sell to Debenhams. Hardy should have been a multi-millionaire but instead others made money out of him.' At this point, Hardy was advised to put a third of the proceeds from the sale respectively into property, art, and stocks and shares.

Because Hardy was only entitled to carry on using the London house for seven years after the sale, and that his Rolls Royce, chauffeur, and valet would also be withdrawn after that, Hardy decided to buy his own London flat in Cornwall Gardens, Kensington. By this time both he and Rosemary were getting on in years and Hardy increasingly came to value their strong family connection. This led him into a new lifestyle choice which resulted in the acquisition of The Old School.

Hardy purchased the quirky building, which had not been adapted since it ceased to be used as a school in 1933, for the knockdown price of just £4,000; ironically, approximately the price of a designer handbag today! He subsequently spent a great deal more on renovations and remodelling, summing the venture up in his own words as more than a domestic relocation, but rather 'an act of importance to me. A statement of personal taste'.[1]

Hardy had many friends from the world of interior design and decoration, from his long-term friends Alexis ffrench and John Fowler, through David Hicks of the renowned artistic family and also including the American-born designer and decorator Billy Baldwin. He set great store by the knowledge and influence of designers when refurbishing properties and despite the extra cost, was of the opinion that it would ultimately save money by causing fewer mistakes to be made which would subsequently need to be rectified.

He loved seventeenth- and eighteenth-century interiors and furnishings and had concentrated on this style for the houses at Eldon Road and his own business premises and to some extent he continued this, albeit with different parameters and proportions at The Old School.

One feature he was able to introduce without incurring the disapproval of the late Alexis, was oak furniture. He declares his love for it in *Still Here*, describing it very extravagantly as a mixture of 'black, dark brown, olive green and honey', a colour combination which apparently 'entranced' him. Perhaps because it has rather 'tweedy' connotations.

Rosemary's proximity, living almost next door, meant that he could still comfortably combine town and city life, as she and Gwyn were on hand to help with the running of the house, cultivation of the garden, and organisation of Hardy's many gatherings and parties.

Although he kept the flat in Kensington, a stone's throw from Eldon Road, Hardy's home was now in Oxfordshire and he embraced the concept of country living with no less style than he had maintained in the city. He quickly acquired a nearby barn which was extended and adapted to provide very comfortable guest accommodation, with what he described as 'a really rather elegantly proportioned living room' with a large log fire.

To his great delight he was able to obtain land for his own hard tennis court, and tennis became a regular and immensely enjoyable activity for him until his twilight years. He was never humble or modest about his skill at tennis, rather seeing the fact that he was able to tell others of his accomplishment, as encouragement to them to take up what he saw as an entertaining, worthwhile, and health-promoting activity.

Hardy also loved to watch tennis, and was a debenture holder at Wimbledon, which meant he and his guests could attend each day of the tournament if they wished. One of his regular escorts with whom he attended the championships was a lady with a pedigree that would certainly have impressed Hardy. Born Jane Armyne Sheffield in 1937, she was the daughter of John Vincent Sheffield and Anne Margaret Faudel-Phillips, both the offspring of baronets. An earlier ancestor had been the Duke of Buckingham who built Buckingham House, later to become Buckingham Palace. Known as Janie, she and her husband, the publishing heir Jocelyn Stevens, were leading lights of the 'Chelsea Set' of trendsetters in the 1950s, along with the photographer Tony Armstrong-Jones, who married Princess Margaret in 1960.

Once she became Jane Stevens, she had a column called 'Serendipity' in British *Vogue*, in which she highlighted fashionable and prestigious items to purchase as well as giving general advice to London debutantes. Around this time Jane was regularly dressed by Hardy Amies and they became friends. Her relationship with Princess Margaret and Tony Armstrong-Jones, who had by now been given the title Lord Snowdon, led to her being made godmother to their daughter, Lady Sarah. Officially taken on as the princess's lady in waiting in 1970, such was their friendship that after her divorce in 1979, the princess gave Janie use of an apartment at Kensington Palace as a London base. Her main residence was by then in Oxfordshire, and her friendship with Hardy continued for the rest of his life, particularly through their love of tennis.

The superior access which Wimbledon debenture ticket holders have, allows them priority parking and Chris Stratmann recalls how, even though Hardy was a fit man up until very late in life, he was not averse to using his age to achieve even more privilege:

> When we arrived in the car he would always tell the attendant he could not walk very far so we would get a space really close to the courts. Actually he was perfectly capable of walking, but liked to use his age as a way of getting better service.

> He kept really fit for most of his life. Number 14 Savile Row was part of that. The rear area was very unforgiving with steep stone staircases which they all ran up and down every day. It was only the front which had the sweeping grand staircases with the elegant landings, so all the important visitors would get the full effect!

Hardy had great stamina, especially where socialising was concerned, and this was something he also seems to have maintained until very late in life. Chris Stratmann again:

I remember when the Duke of Northumberland's daughter was getting married in the early 1990s at Syon House in London, and Hardy Amies were responsible for all the important dresses. Hardy was invited to the afternoon and evening receptions. We left the venue, Syon Park in West London, at about 8 pm because he wanted to drive down to the country as he had two other parties to go to. I think we got back to Langford at about two in the morning, and Hardy was around 80 years old by then.

After dropping Hardy off on another such occasion, Chris made the mistake of setting out to drive back to London along the M40 in the early hours of the morning.

It was summertime and the sun started to come up, so going eastwards it was rising right in my eyes and sort of blinding me, so I must have closed my eyes briefly and nearly fallen asleep. I slightly veered off the road, but started to bump along the ribble strip which jerked me awake and the shock carried me all the way back to London. Luckily at that hour there was nothing else on the road, but I decided after that to stay overnight if it was that late when I finished, and Hardy was always happy for me to stay in the house or the barn.

Apart from tennis and general fitness, Hardy's other main hobby – and one which he also continued to pursue throughout his life – was embroidery and needlepoint. He was a proficient and meticulous exponent of the craft and produced many beautiful pieces of work over the years, which were used as cushion covers, rugs, on chair backs and seats, and even an entire rug, depicting his favourite flowers, which was ultimately used to cover his coffin when he died.

He also maintained a flat overlooking Central Park in New York and on his trips over there, latterly on the British Airways Concorde aircraft, he would take out his needlework as soon as he was settled on board. He spoke of the contrast in his two favourite pastimes in *Still Here*: 'I often smile at myself getting on a plane to Tokyo or Sydney with two tennis rackets under one arm and with a travel bag containing a piece of needlepoint on the other.'

Hardy loved going to New York, and said: 'I cannot imagine living in New York and not being near Central Park', as he loved to walk there and always found himself giving thanks to 'the city fathers' for preserving the huge piece of land in the heart of the metropolis which brings a sense of fresh air, space, and well-being to all who live and work there.

He felt that the flat was located in 'his spiritual home', as not only did he have access to the city's principal wide open space, but he was located twenty-four storeys above the area centred around Fifth Avenue, where many of the iconic fashion stores and businesses of New York were situated.

Chapter 20

Friends in Foreign Places

Hardy felt that New York was a hub of fashion and that maintaining a presence there gave him access to business centres all over the world. Although he did not refer to the apartment as in any way an office, Hardy acknowledged that it was a necessity for his commercial operations, as it allowed him to meet and conduct his operations in America while still feeling as if he was somehow on 'home ground', with all the obvious advantages that brought with it. Although he visited between four and six times a year throughout the peak of his career, he was astute enough to realise that the fickle nature of fashion could easily mean that a name would soon be forgotten if a regular presence in New York was not maintained.

It was as a result of his wartime work with the Board of Trade that Hardy's name began to be known across the Atlantic and became synonymous with haute couture in the US. Up until 1959, Hardy's work was almost totally concentrated on womenswear, with just a small presence in the men's necktie market. But that year saw him form an association with the British menswear brand Hepworth's, and this was formalised in the early 1960s. Soon the runway shows for this collaboration began to attract the attention of overseas buyers, including representatives of the American market.

The most important of these was the organisation Genesco, a large corporation which included several top US and Canadian department stores, as well as a chain of menswear shops and a number of factories producing male clothing. Once Hardy discovered that there were many highly skilled tailors working for the company, he happily joined forces and launched a partnership which thrived for many years and gave him access to many of the perks of being involved in such a large and prestigious organisation. Not least of these was the use of the company private jet to travel around the United States to monitor the operation, a privilege he was very happy to take advantage of.

Hardy's approach to becoming a well-known and respected name in America was to put himself front and centre and become a familiar presence, rather than rely on advertising and company promotion. His description of himself in his books as 'a living label', evokes his personal image of the quintessential Englishman who could be trusted by American 'guys' to bestow upon them the style, elegance and good taste that the name 'Hardy Amies' evoked.

Companies such as the Greif clothing factory, the Hudson Neckwear Company and Berkley Shirts, entered into licensing contracts with Hardy Amies Ltd. They produced clothing which, although aimed at, and sold in, the American market, still maintained the standards of fabric and workmanship that the British customer had come to expect. The licensing arrangement allowed American retail firms to sell all forms of menswear bearing the Hardy Amies label, having started out with just a simple line of suits.

Hardy employed a female public relations agent, Anne Taylor Davis, and was more than happy to give interviews to television, radio, and the press, particularly the hugely influential *Womenswear Daily*, for which he had the utmost respect. He considered John Fairchild, the president of the overseeing company of the magazine *W* as well as *Womenswear Daily*, to be 'the arbiter' of the US fashion industry as a whole and a force of disruption within it, which kept those who wanted to stay at the top, on their toes.

The menswear business in the US began to grow and soon incorporated casualwear, knitwear, and accessories. The market for British design in menswear far outstripped the demand for womenswear during the sixties and seventies, with the demand for less formal outfits. However, once Hardy Amies began designing for the more casual menswear market including companies such as Pebble Beach in the early 1980s, the lines between men's and womenswear became more blurred and a crossover of sorts was developed. In *Still Here*, Hardy describes his ventures in New York as 'a pleasant but tough struggle', but one that he considered worthwhile and ultimately satisfying.

At around the same time as the menswear business in the States was becoming established, a link was forming with clothing firms in Canada, helped in no small way by the fact that as a patriotic Commonwealth country, they were eager to amalgamate with a design house with such strong ties to the queen.

Shirt makers T. Lipson and Sons, together with clothing firm Coppley, Noyes, and Randall, became the mainstays of the business in Canada, and Hardy fostered happy relationships both professionally and personally with the companies, which lead to a long-lasting and harmonious enterprise. Hardy's image as an immaculately dressed English businessman crossed with a movie matinee idol, was a breath of fresh air to the staid and predictable menswear market in North America generally. This certainly helped to generate lucrative sales for the Genesco company, and in 1982 over $15 million of sales of men's clothing were generated under the Hardy Amies label.[1]

A similar bond was forged with Australia, a country Hardy first visited in 1959, the year he began his working partnership with menswear brand Hepworth's. Hardy regarded Australia as a country with an undeniably brusque and macho image, and he talked of the less than 'tactful' approach of their media, when he was asked very personal questions about how close his relationship was to the queen. Being a gentleman, he was of course easily able to deflect any indiscreet and indelicate questioning, saying: 'Sir, I get as close as any professional man in whom the queen has confidence.'

Of the Australian capital Sydney he said: 'I don't know what Sydney thinks of me, but I am in love with him. Sydney is a chap. Sydney's most famous lady is Dame Edna Everage. And he's a chap.'[2] The ladies of the capital may consider that representation as rather unfair. There was a distinctly stylish atmosphere in the centre of Sydney, and some of the wealthy women from the suburbs around the northern beaches would most certainly have been customers of any high-end fashion brand that cared to sell its wares in the capital's upmarket stores.

Hardy describes Sydney in glowing terms and compliments the harbour as 'one of the most beautiful sights in the world'. The city's most famous department store, David Jones, eventually stocked Hardy Amies' men's and womenswear, and the designer enjoyed annual visits, staying at a succession of hotels, both traditional and modern.

As much as he enjoyed the conventional and old-school comforts of the upmarket Australia Hotel, The Menzies, and The Wentworth, he reserves some of his most appreciative words for an establishment which occupied a position in what could be described as bordering the rougher end of town. Hardy's interest in everything *outre* and creative, which ran alongside his highly publicised obsession with everything being 'just so', meant that he never squandered an opportunity to take in the vibrant and rather edgy atmosphere of Sydney's notorious Kings Cross District.

Even today this area is seen as the slightly downmarket part of town, attracting those on the margins of society, although as with many such neighbourhoods across the globe, some parts are now being increasingly gentrified. As Hardy put it, it was 'never really squalid, often funny, and always pulsating with life'. He used his walks in the area to observe the street fashion of the youth of the day, whose rebellious and disruptive sense of style he found stimulating and at times inspiring. With his own scarcely suppressed sexual orientation, and friends from all echelons of society, it is doubtful that he would have found any of this at all challenging or confronting.

New Zealand also beckoned Hardy and his licensing enterprise, not least because the New Zealand dollar was performing more favourably for them than its Aussie counterpart, so eventually suits were manufactured there instead of in Australia. Fabrics were imported from the UK, but with such a prolific sheep-farming industry, it soon became apparent that it would make sense to use the native wool to supplement the British imports.

New Zealand, both then and probably still today, does not have a reputation for being at the forefront of fashion, and nowhere is that more apparent than in the menswear sector. In *Still Here*, Hardy talks of attending a Rotary Club lunch where, to his probable horror, all the male attendees were in their shirtsleeves and each of these shirts were without exception 'dead white', which he described as being the white of 'the drip-dry variety'. Hardly Savile Row style!

He declares in the book that it took twenty years, but eventually, on his periodic visits, he would start to notice the odd pale blue or discreetly checked or striped shirt, the influence for which he felt had arisen from the Hardy Amies Menswear line! Despite his obvious affection for the country and the gratitude he had for the hospitality he was offered there, he observed that New Zealanders are 'a notoriously conservative race', an opinion that would probably still be held by many in the world of fashion today.

Indeed, it was rather later in Hardy Amies' relationship with New Zealand that womenswear crept into the licensing agreement alongside the menswear collections. With such a small population, the quantities were always going to be insignificant and were concentrated largely on occasion wear in conjunction with a native fashion house which specialised in that market.

Another country with which Hardy Amies Ltd made a substantial alliance and ultimately influenced the native modes of dressing, was Japan. In menswear especially, the house oversaw a marked input of colour and style over the first few years of their association with the company Daitobo, which had a close link to one of the country's largest organisations, Mitsui and Co.

The Japanese affection for tradition which stands alongside innovation in colour and design, made for a highly successful partnership with the British company, and Hardy had nothing but admiration for the 'refinement of taste in living and clothes', which he grew to love on his visits.

What was also greatly appreciated by himself and Ken Fleetwood was Japanese cuisine, and they delighted in visiting certain restaurants which excelled in both their food and their decor and ambience. As part of their contract with the licensing company in Tokyo, Hardy and his team would visit every eighteen months as their guests, travel first class, stay in top hotels, and be taken to many beautiful and exclusive locations.

This hospitality was reciprocated to some extent when a contingent of no fewer than thirty-five representatives came over to Savile Row to get an idea of what a classic London fashion house stood for. They were also treated to visits to The Old School at Langford. The visitors' book contains many pages of lists of names of Japanese delegates who would no doubt have been completely overwhelmed with joy at being among the honey-coloured Cotswold enclaves of Oxfordshire.

On 30 September 1983 no fewer than thirty-two Japanese business people appear to have visited The Old School, and in 1995 a smaller contingent is listed under the heading of *Japanese Lady's Magazine* The arrival of all these foreign visitors must have caused quite a stir in what was actually a very small and sleepy village.

Hardy was extremely confident about the image he presented to these visitors, declaring in *Still Here*: 'What they saw was a business that was classic but not old-fashioned, and modern but not aggressive.' He continues: 'Such a calm attitude to the business of clothes designing appeals very much to the Japanese.' He was extremely gratified, and in no small way surprised, when another aspect of the Hardy Amies business was adopted by the Japanese market.

At the time of publishing his second autobiography it was customary for young Japanese women to be married in a traditional kimono, which was often constructed from extremely expensive silks and therefore usually hired rather than purchased. By this time the House of Hardy Amies was well known for its wedding dresses, and it was with great delight that they began to receive orders for these from Daitobo. In the tradition of the country, however, they quickly realised that they were hiring the dresses out rather than selling them. This cannot have been a great surprise because, after all, the craftsmanship that went into them would almost certainly have meant the cost would be on a par with traditional Japanese ceremonial outfits.

Hardy Amies' stellar reputation quickly saw him diversifying into designing clothing for many purposes as well as simply for his own collections and licensing enterprises. His International connections provided a natural progression into creating uniforms and corporate wear for those in various sectors of the hospitality and travel industries. Being a frequent flyer, he was delighted when, in 1968, Hardy Amies Ltd was invited to submit designs for new uniforms for the female crew of British European Airways, as it was then known. The first designs that were adopted continued to be worn for three years, and after that a second set was taken up. However, the sister airline, the British Overseas Airways Corporation, considered themselves superior to BEA by virtue of operating long haul flights and, on their eventual merger with that airline to form British Airways, declined to take on the uniform across the newly formed company. Obviously this disappointed Hardy and he was even more crestfallen when, on suggesting he be allowed to update the uniform, he was told that the budget would not allow for this.

Yet more dissatisfaction was to follow in connection with the revolutionary supersonic aircraft, Concorde. As a regular transatlantic traveller himself, Hardy was surprised to learn that this prestigious plane was to be operated with staff sporting the same uniform as the crew on the conventional planes. This was even more disappointing to him when he discovered that one of his rival Paris couture houses had been commissioned to design special uniforms for the French staff on the supersonic jet! This realisation was too much for Hardy and he volunteered his services to the then Chairman of British Airways, Sir Henry Marking, free of charge. This offer was understandably accepted with Hardy declaring: 'National

Pride was my first interest, the second was the hope of gaining a contract.'
He submitted the designs shortly before Concorde's maiden passenger-
carrying flight was due to take place in 1976, so the preparation time was
minimal.

The designer largely blamed the trade unions for what happened next.
His designs met with a mixed response from the airline crew representatives
and he later discovered that the unions had allegedly instructed them to
turn down the designs 'at all costs'. This could have been due to concerns
about separate uniforms fostering feelings of elitism among the airline's
workforce, although Hardy was likely to have disregarded any notion that
the staff simply did not like the designs! Despite stating that he would
be happy to revamp the outfits taking into consideration any suggestions
from the employees themselves, the designs were rejected and, as Hardy
states with an element of melodrama in *Still Here*: 'This was all in vain.
Concorde flew into the future with its crew dressed in the past.'

The fact that Hardy had formulated the designs for the Concorde
uniforms with unusual speed came back to haunt him as, shortly after
the debacle of the rejection, it was decided that the airline wished to have
new uniforms for all staff across the whole fleet, including those working
on Concorde.

British Airways persuaded Hardy Amies to resubmit their Concorde
designs, despite Hardy having reservations about the speed at which they
had been produced. Inevitably they were turned down again, and a new
design team taken on. The fact that the goodwill he felt he had generated
with the company did not hold weight with the powers that be, left a bitter
taste for him.

He sums it up when he says that designing for a large corporation was
always going to be fraught with problems, as so many opinions were involved
and there would also inevitably be someone in the background with the
ear of the man at the top, who often had a major influence over the final
decision – and usually they were 'invisible', so could not be argued with!

Despite this setback, uniforms continued to be a major part of the
business at the House of Hardy Amies, and a collaboration was made with
a Bristol-based workwear firm, the prosaically named Alexandra Overalls,
for which Ken diverted from his couture work to design up-to-date
uniforms for many employees in the service industries. Quite a contrast
of products!

This burst of diversification during the 1970s and 1980s also led to interiors-based projects, with the Hardy Amies label being one of the first in the UK to be represented on bed linen and household goods. This trend, extensive today, grew out of the United States and appealed to Hardy, who felt that had he not been a couturier, he could equally probably have been an interior designer, especially after his immense learning experiences with Alexis ffrench and John Fowler.

Despite this he did not find any particular financial or personal sense of achievement during the time he ventured into housewares, and talks about it with a certain sense of regret in *Still Here*. The satisfaction he got from designing, remodelling, and furnishing his own homes far outweighed any professional achievements on that front. From his needlepoint for upholstery and soft furnishings, to the design of the tiles in his kitchen at Langford, he personalised his own homes with great individuality and flair.

Kitchen textiles were very important to him and may have been more of a success than the bedroom ranges that appeared during the 1980s. He spoke of how he believed in eating in the kitchen and how that room should therefore be designed with 'elegance and comfort' in mind. Beyond the kitchen, he also had an eye to the future with an interest in making useful yet attractive items for the garden, and functional yet pretty pots for the plants that may be brought in from outside. The vast availability of such ranges now proves that he could perhaps have made inroads there given more opportunity.

The main focus of the business was always going to be the clothing; both men's and women's, and it is on this that Hardy continued to concentrate his primary efforts. Around the world and at home, in the rarefied world of couture or in the diffusion of the boutique line and the collaborations with stores such as Hepworth's, he aimed to be the best. He acknowledged that exemplary standards of quality and workmanship were easier to achieve with the high investment and marketing of the couture range, but also welcomed the democratisation of fashion. He believed in accessibility and was unable to see why high standards could not be more widely achieved in more reasonably priced ranges.

He summed up this approach in *Still Here*: 'I will continue to design and be associated with the marketing of any product which is cheap in price, providing we aim at being the best article on the market at that price.'

Chapter 21

The Silver Screen and More

Seeing into the future was a talent Hardy and Ken Fleetwood needed in 1965, when they were called upon to design 'space-age' clothes for the 1968 film *2001: A space Odyssey*, which was to become a cult classic. The director, Stanley Kubrick, chose Hardy Amies as he had such a high profile through working with the queen and had also built up a growing reputation for excellent menswear. Coincidentally, he and his family had recently become neighbours of Hardy in Oxfordshire.

Hardy remembers the time he spent working with Stanley Kubrick as 'wonderful', but goes on to explain how ostensibly difficult it was to interpret what was required for the costumes. The date in the film's title was thirty-three years ahead of the time that he and Ken were creating the clothes, but he took an interesting path towards working out how fashions could have changed by then. Hardy chose to look backwards at the revolution made in fashion from thirty-three years prior to the present day, in order to see how much styles had changed in that particular number of years.

To his retrospective eye it did not seem as if there had been a drastic change in the way people dressed, and apparently Stanley Kubrick accepted this as a way to interpret the clothes of the future. Hardy does reveal that the famous director was very quick to let them know when they presented any ideas that did not appeal to him, which is not surprising in someone who had risen to the top of their profession. The working relationship between the two men who were obviously each exemplary in their own genre, appears to have been cordial, and the film that resulted has become a classic both for its storytelling and its visual imagery.

As Hardy envisaged, the general day-to-day outfits worn by the characters did not stray very far from contemporary clothing, and the menswear in particular drew inspiration from the actual Amies gentlemen's collections of the day, which were now under the direction of Mr Michael

Bentley. Bentley was specifically consulted by Hardy and Ken about the details and colours used for the costumes.

Hardy also considered the zero-gravity situation the characters would be experiencing, when designing the clothes and choosing the fabrics. The latter could obviously not be too flimsy or floaty, so he stuck to heavier, clean, narrow lines, which also had the beneficial characteristic of photographing and appearing distinctive and visually appealing on screen. Accessories were also crucial to the costumes and Hardy collaborated with the Rayne footwear company, coincidentally favourites of the queen, as well as Frederick Fox on the headwear, which certainly made an impact as part of the uniforms of the female characters.

Overall the film, which came to be considered one of the most innovative ever made, was a major success, and Hardy describes working on it as 'a wonderful time' for himself and Ken. Although it appears rather dated now – it can easily be pinpointed as having been made in the 1960s – its cult status firmly maintains its position in the league of the most viewed films ever made.

Although Hardy did not create any particularly influential position for himself in the world of film costume in the way that someone like Hubert Givenchy did with his association with Audrey Hepburn, his designs were used in many productions, either by the choice of the actress or the director. Many stage productions saw Hardy Amies' designs onstage and also in the audience, as a visit to the theatre was seen as a major evening out and most of the ladies who attended provincial theatres as well as the West End, would always dress up for the occasion.

Marlene Dietrich, Hedy Lemarr, and Ginger Rogers were among the many foreign actresses who were regulars in the audience at Hardy Amies' fashion shows, buying for their personal wardrobes. Major British stars of the forties, fifties, and sixties such as Vivien Leigh, Phyllis Calvert, and Margaret Lockwood, were established Amies' clients, and in 1955 the costume designer for the film *Cast a Dark Shadow*, in which Margaret Lockwood was to star with Dirk Bogarde, utilised Hardy's workrooms for the creation of her own designs. Such a privilege was not often bestowed. Once Hardy's reputation for menswear became established, his designs were used for the actors in several films, as well as initially being worn by Patrick MacNee as the suave John Steed in *The Avengers* television series. He also dressed the actor Albert Finney in the 1967 film *Two for the Road*.

Hardy's own good looks and urbane and cultured demeanour saw him in high demand as an escort for glamorous ladies from the worlds of stage and screen. In addition to movie stars, he counted many theatre and television actresses among his clientele. Despite reports of Hardy considering the beautiful film star Vivien Leigh rather demanding, he was often to be seen out on the town with her. No doubt the relationship was mutually beneficial, however fractious, as she was one of the biggest superstars of the 1940s and 1950s. He also dressed British actresses including Dame Edith Evans and Moira Lister and, of course, Virginia Cherrill, who went on to marry Lord Jersey after divorcing Cary Grant. The ballerina Dame Margot Fonteyn was another client, as were the opera singers Dame Joan Sutherland and Kerstin Meyer.

One lady whom it seems did not make it onto Hardy Amies client list, though not through lack of desire, was the famous socialite and novelist (and member of the notorious family of six sisters and one brother) Nancy Mitford. In the book *Letters Between Six Sisters* by Charlotte Mosely, daughter-in-law to Nancy's sister Diana, we glimpse a winsome vignette of the relationship between Nancy and her younger sister Deborah, later the Duchess of Devonshire. In a letter written on 4 August 1959, during Hardy's halcyon days of dressing the queen, Deborah writes to Nancy: 'No, you can't have a suit from Hardy Amies, you would have to make it yourself as well as design it and this might be beyond even your talent. Forget it.'[1] This was an example of the way the Mitford sisters would tease and provoke each other with their idiosyncratic wit. Deborah was a practical person, and probably considered Nancy rather frivolous and extravagant. It is likely that Nancy could have afforded the suit, but Deborah felt that she should urge restraint upon her sister by implying that she would have to make it herself and sew a Hardy Amies label into it. Obviously even the aristocracy had to think carefully about engaging the services of Hardy Amies at the height of his powers! This particular story is even more interesting because "Debo" Devonshire would later become a friend of Hardy and gave a reading at his memorial service in 2003.

Chapter 22

A Living Label

Hardy attributed his self-proclaimed title of *Living Label*, the name he also gave to one of the chapters in *Still Here*, to his admirers in the United States. He declares: 'If I am successful enough in my licensee operations my name will become that of a brand', and, despite citing his foreign enterprises in conjunction with that entity, he also hoped: 'that this will always be based on the present high level of quality so closely monitored by me and my team at Savile Row.'

As is the case with many eponymous businesses, especially in the creative industries, Hardy certainly exemplified the appearance, quality, and attributes which, over the years, grew to be associated with Hardy Amies Ltd. He personified the image both of the charming couturier who had entranced the ladies who frequented Lachasse back in the 1930s, and also the debonair man-about-town who aspired to owning a Hardy Amies gentleman's suit. He was a handsome man, possessing the proportions to look good in clothes, and was possessed of the social skills and cultured demeanour to project the image of a high-end company, both personally and in the business world. Describing his own physical attributes in *Still Here*, written when he was in his mid-seventies, he devotes at least a full page to the structure of his body, his fitness regime, and even his grooming habits.

He sums up his approach to his image thus: 'I am vain in the sense that I take care to look as well as I can.' He stresses that, despite his fairly advanced years, he strives to keep his weight down. He managed to maintain a waist size of 33 inches – though he would have preferred 32 – which, combined with his chest measurement, meant that he could 'try on a Hardy Amies man's suit anywhere in the world and judge its fit, finish and quality.'[1]

His admiration for the tailoring side of couture transitioned easily from Hardy's origins in womenswear, to the establishment of the menswear label, upon which in many ways his reputation today may be largely centred. He does not hesitate to give credit to the man from whom he took over at Lachasse in 1934, saying that Digby Morton left behind many examples of his prowess, which the aspiring young designer could effectively deconstruct, thus absorbing the skills, techniques, and practices that were to be the bedrock of Hardy Amies Ltd.

Thinking about that youthful ex-tile salesman coming into what was a reputable couture house, one can only imagine the confidence both in himself and the team he was brought in to lead, which would have been needed to facilitate such an ultimately smooth and successful transition. The intuitive way in which Hardy talked about the fabrics, colours, and structure of the clothes which Lachasse had built its reputation upon, shows that he was certainly in tune with the business and had the self-assurance to be able to learn on the job at Lachasse and beyond.

He credited Alexis ffrench with teaching him 'how a gentleman should dress and where he should order his clothes', as well as being an exemplary arbiter of good taste in interior design and antiques. His other simultaneous influence, John Fowler, was also a mentor, despite the fact that Hardy had more experience of foreign travel under his belt. 'It made me feel almost sophisticated,' he said, 'compared with his simple country upbringing,' continuing modestly, 'but I was always the pupil.'

One of Hardy's greatest strengths appears to have been his eagerness and ability to learn from those around him, and he humbly admits that at the time of his launch into the realm of couture, his 'knowledge of the world' was 'very slight'.

His friendship with the ffrench family gave him access to a great resource and, due to his mastery of French and German, one of which he was able to take full advantage. Alexis's sister Yvonne and her companion, the Italian Countess May Voss, had a vast and international library at their London flat. The shelves were of perpetual interest to him and, because of his skill at languages, he was able not only to read most of the books, but also to discuss them with the two women and their cosmopolitan friends. In the last chapter of *Still Here*, Hardy recounts how he had recently finished reading Marcel Proust's enormous seven-volume novel *A La Recherche du Temps Perdu*, a work that is high up on many people's 'The book I was Unable to Finish' lists. He goes on to reveal that it was not the first time he had read the book, but the fourth!

Hardy replicated his friends' library in later life. The sitting room at The Old School is lined with copies of the bookshelves Samuel Pepys had at Cambridge University. Hardy had them replicated by Thomas Parr of Colefax and Fowler, and even today they house an enormous collection of Hardy's books, as well as many belonging to Freeman. 'The barn was full of books too', David revealed.

As Bill Howat said: 'He never allowed himself a wasted moment. He was always educating himself by reading more. He just loved finding out about things. [...] He always told me to help myself to something to read while I was waiting at whichever house for him.' However, Hardy's saucy sense of humour was evident one day when he recommended that Bill borrow a book about the early days of telegram delivery boys. 'It was about how a telegram boy was delivering to a Lord in a grand house somewhere and this gentleman took a fancy to the young man,' Bill explains, 'He propositioned him and then began paying him for his services.' It turned out that this arrangement backfired on the aristocrat somewhat, as the young man started to recruit a group of his fellow workers who were also prepared to take cash from willing men, and he set up a rather seedy business. The situation inevitably imploded and a vice ring was exposed involving MPs and other supposedly upstanding society gentlemen. Whether it was Hardy's intention to shock his chauffeur by recommending he read this rather tawdry tale, or just felt that it was a rip-roaring read, is hard to tell.

The Italian Countess Voss had been married twice to German aristocrats, and the knowledge and ease with which she moved around Europe, both physically and metaphorically, was enjoyable and educational to Hardy. Her influence upon him reverberated through the years and he always remembered her recollection of the skills and good taste of the ladies of Florence and their discernment when buying for their homes as well as their wardrobes, while on his travels later.

Yvonne ffrench herself was a respected author and biographer, and yet another influential member of the family that Hardy almost came to call his own, such was their keenness to take him under their wing. Alexis and Yvonne had a rather unusual upbringing in that he and his brother were brought up as Catholics by their father in Rome after he left their mother, but Yvonne was retained in England and, presumably raised as a Protestant.

Despite Alexis being the primary presence in Hardy's early adulthood, John Fowler's influence through his professional skills as a decorator, designer, and general arbiter of good taste in one's surroundings was also significant. A particular area in which Hardy appears to have bowed to

Fowler's superior knowledge was the garden. In *Still Here*, he refers to John Fowler as having 'shocked me into readjusting my standards'.

He remembered how, in the days of his parents' suburban garden in Essex, colour was valued for its own sake and the bolder, the brighter, and the more of it, the better! To some extent, Alexis apparently shared this horticultural approach, and it was interpreted in his own country house garden through a multitude of rose bushes and herbaceous borders which Hardy enjoyed choosing and planting with him.

John Fowler's ethos, however, was to design 'passages' and 'rooms' in the garden of Odiham, his Hampshire home, through the use of hedging and bushes, creating structure rather than simple seasonal displays of colour for its own sake, which he considered rather vulgar. From him, Hardy learned to appreciate more delicate plants for their subtle colouring and intricacy of design.

However, in summing up the influences he had drawn on for his garden he declared: 'The great pleasure I get today from the clumps of old-fashioned pinks and violas in my own garden is full of grateful memories of John and of Alexis.'

Despite this more colourful and bounteous aspect of the garden, an anecdote from Bill Howat suggests another interpretation of its character and that of its creator: 'Hardy's housekeeper at Langford, Helen, once told me she overheard a psychiatrist friend of Hardy's say to another houseguest while observing the regimented and geometric layout of the garden, "That is the work of a very selfish man."' An interesting interpretation!

Some of Hardy's friends' emphasis on style and good taste could also easily tip over into the realm of snobbery and harsh judgement. A generic quote by Alexis, that Hardy often used in the mid-1980s but, to his credit, seemed actually to disagree with, was: 'Quite nice people but, I'm afraid, no taste.'

Richard Martin of the Cotswold Woollen Weavers remembers an amusing incident involving both men's gardens in Oxfordshire:

Hardy was a bit of a confection. He portrayed a particular view of the world and of himself. We all do it, but he did it in a very unashamed way. [...] He once came to my garden and I had one of those tall plants growing that looked like a cabbage or a large Brussels sprout and Hardy pronounced, 'Richard, that is so vulgar. You really shouldn't have that in your garden – it's horrible.' Then, about a week later I was in his garden and I noticed he had a row of these things and I said, 'Hardy, you've got a whole line of those plants you told me were vulgar', and he replied, 'Oh, but mine came from Chatsworth – they were a present from the Duchess.' As if that made it all right!

He was a curious chap! Some people in the village thought he was a bit pushy, but he was entertaining and always talked to everyone, and local people liked being associated with someone so well known.

Despite becoming more outspoken, Hardy appears in some ways to have developed a slightly more forgiving attitude, or at least came to modify some of his opinions, with his advancing age.

During an interview with the writer and designer Simon Doonan, he was asked why he did not dress the queen with more 'chic'. 'My dear,' he drawled, 'there is an unkindness to chic and the queen must always appear kind.' He felt that Her Majesty wished to both dress for the occasion and to appear friendly and accessible to her subjects, who would invariably flock to see her on her relentless round of royal visits.

Doonan's partner, American interior designer Jonathan Adler, subsequently said: 'It made me try to design things that were chic enough to make me happy, while at the same time being friendly and inclusive.' Adler interpreted Hardy's response as suggesting that elitist design and expensive style could naturally appear somewhat exclusive and marginalising, and showed that he understood the need not to alienate people by shutting them off from the beautiful things in life.

Perhaps another way that Hardy put this approach into action was to be uncompromising and intransigent about his taste in his surroundings, wardrobe, and the inanimate objects that he possessed, while at the same time trying not to be snobbish or superior in his dealings with people.

He appears to have been quite democratic in his relationships with some employees. Chris Stratmann remembers that whenever he was driving Hardy around he would invariably sit in the front with the chauffeur, 'except when he was escorting a lady to an event. Although that could have been because he loved to talk!'

Hardy seems to have been fairly generous to auxiliary staff members such as his chauffeurs. 'He gave me three or four suits as well as a dinner suit,' Chris reveals. 'But I would never wear a Hardy Amies suit for work. As the man himself said: 'You must never be better dressed than the clients or it looks as if you are charging too much!'

In the interview with Naim Attallah, Hardy is asked if he has any qualms about describing himself as 'a self-confessed snob.' 'No,' he replies, 'I am a staunch supporter of the class system. The London upper class is like a club and I am always amazed that I am admitted as a member. And I am very pleased, because one meets much more interesting people.' In a veiled dismissal of some of his peers he continues: 'Sometimes I see others in the same business and I think, how naff you are. I am not naff, but I easily could have been.' As the writer Selina Hastings said in the eulogy: 'naff' was known to be one of Hardy Amies' favourite words!

Roy Allen spoke of Hardy as being very caring, but occasionally 'not very diplomatic' in his dealings with people. As mentioned in Chapter 18, in the early 1980s Roy discovered that the assistants brought in by the new chief designer, Jon Moore, were being paid significantly more than the original workforce. What is more, Roy had been led to believe that when Mr Ernest left the company, he would be promoted to being fitter to the queen. He explains:

It had always been the case that, at that time, it always had to be a British person who fitted the queen. Then Mr Michael, who was Polish, came in and apparently he said he would only come if he was given the queen. But the thing was, nobody came to me and said 'Oh, sorry Roy, but we have had to do this.'

It was at this point that Roy began to seek out a new position and ultimately left to join the up-and-coming fashion house of the former actress Anouska Hempel, Lady Weinberg. Hoping that Hardy might wonder about his reasons for the decision and perhaps to attempt to get him to change his mind, Mr Roy let it be known that his salary was a factor in his decision to move on. As we know, Hardy left it to the eleventh hour to finally approach Roy, who felt that his thirty-eight years of devotion to the business had gone unrecognised; of course, he told Hardy he would not reconsider. Sadly, their long and successful working relationship came to an end that day, with an unfortunate feeling of lack of appreciation on the part of Roy.

Looking back, he recalls how impressed he was by his boss's talent for design. 'Mr Amies was amazing. He had that touch where a dress would come out and it looked lovely but he would say, "If you just do this or just do that" – and it would make all the difference.' He also recalls with affection the way that Hardy took an interest in his family:

I once took my sister to one of the House Christmas parties in the early days. Mr Amies came up to us and chatted and at the time my sister was expecting her first baby. After that he would often come up to me and say 'Roy, how is your sister and how's the baby doing?' In general, he was very nice to me. He even gave me plants from the garden at Langford when I was down there.

Chapter 23

Brides and Their Mothers

oyalty among his clientele did not seem to be something Hardy found difficult to inspire despite the vagaries of his temperament. His 'man-about-town' persona and the fortuitous close friendship with the ffrench family went a long way towards forging relationships with many society ladies and their debutante daughters. Designing evening wear as well as daytime suits for these women naturally led on to being asked to create wedding dresses when the time arose.

Hardy had been involved in the designing of wedding dresses from the beginning of his career but, once the House of Hardy Amies Ltd was established, one of its bespoke wedding gowns became something to aspire to. However, in the early part of the twentieth century even the landed gentry were not inclined to squander money on a dress about which they apparently were quite happy to declare to the designer: 'After all, it is only for one day.'

Perhaps the growth of interest in the dresses of royalty and even Hollywood 'royalty', helped to encourage families to invest large sums into their daughter's finery. Hardy also believed that once the number of couture houses began to diminish, the demand for the services of those remaining would grow, and therefore they would be able to charge higher prices while obviously not 'stinting on time, labour and cloth. He was at pains to point out that 'it is very difficult to work out the cost of a dress that has never been made before'. In other words, a Hardy Amies wedding dress would always be unique, as would the price tag.

In a quote from *Still Here* he says: 'What makes the House – from the seamstresses, fitter, vendeuses, to the designers in the studio – very happy, is the large quantity of wedding dresses we are now being asked to make.' These were of course largely requested by members of the aristocracy, or indeed families with considerable wealth, as they were probably the only people likely to be able to afford a bespoke design by a house of the calibre of Hardy Amies.

The couture Houses of London craved society weddings, as the bride's mother was highly likely to be an established customer and thus would draw in her friends and relatives to purchase their wedding outfits, not to mention the added income from producing the bridesmaids' and attendants' dresses. The resultant spectacle was a very valuable piece of advertising for the house and would also often lead to new clients drawn from the wedding guests, as well as the new bride herself.

The sleek, column-like style of the 1930s was represented in Hardy's wedding dress designs at Lachasse, but once the war was over and society weddings were able to resume being planned on a grand scale, the beautiful, fitted bodices and crinoline style full skirts of the *Golden Age of Glamour* of the fifties and early sixties took over at Hardy Amies.

The house was never short of eager brides and their mothers keen for a Hardy Amies design for the family's big day. The ladies who gave Hardy their custom on a regular basis were invariably totally confident in entrusting him to produce a gown worthy of the grandest occasion, be it in town or country for their daughter's or future daughter-in-law's wedding.

One such client, the Duchess of Buccleuch, brought all her daughters to Hardy for their special dress, and also introduced him to the young lady who was to marry her son, the Earl of Dalkeith, in Scotland in 1953. The earl was a most eligible young man, who had actually been spoken of as a potential beau for Princess Elizabeth herself, according to Lady Pamela Hicks, Earl Mountbatten's daughter.

As it turned out, his fiancée was to become one of Hardy's favourite clients and an unrivalled model for one of his early wedding gowns. Described by Hardy in *Still Here* as 'the very beautiful Miss Jane McNeill', she could not have been a better ambassador for the design and construction skills of the House of Hardy Amies, and her dress epitomised the heyday of couture with its mystical glamour and classic elegance. It was at once figure-enhancing and modest but above all made a statement while showcasing the delicate and feminine features of the bride.

With its long sleeves and simple bodice, the silver lace dress was described by Hardy as 'very plain in detail, very bold in outline', which does not do it justice. Later he perhaps sums it up with more adulation, saying: 'It was magnificently simple and simply magnificent – helped of course by the bride's beauty and elegance of figure.'

Despite the obvious likelihood of him never having a family of his own in the traditional sense, when talking of customers like the Buccleuch clan, Hardy obviously relishes the opportunity of becoming immersed in the family lives of those with whom he made strong connections in the course of his life and work. As he said: 'One of the pleasures of working as a designer for fifty years … is that of seeing the families of your customers burgeon.'

Following on from the wedding of the Dalkeiths, their son grew up to marry Lady Elizabeth Kerr, daughter of the Marquess and Marchioness of Lothian, herself a 'much-loved patroness' of Hardy Amies Ltd. It was therefore inevitable that the wedding dress for Lady Elizabeth would be commissioned from the house. By this time Ken had taken over responsibility for all womenswear at the business, a change which was finalised in 1974, and he was therefore put in charge of designing Lady Elizabeth's wedding dress. He was often known to sketch out ideas in front of the bride herself, in order to involve her in the design, an idea which his successor Jon Moore also took up. On this occasion, rather than reference the beautiful gown that Hardy had made for the bride's future mother-in-law, Ken took inspiration from even further back in time, creating a dress which was apparently based on a design from the late nineteenth century, which featured drapery and a bustle!

Part of the reward for the making of the dress was the allocation of two seats in the family chapel for the service, which Hardy seemed to be very pleased with, as they were 'just behind the family'. Ken jokingly remarked: 'It's a bit like *Upstairs, Downstairs* [a television series of the day]. Can't think what we are, not upstairs and not downstairs; I think we're *entresol*.' Translated that means they were on the mezzanine floor just up from the ground floor, but not the top storey! I think that perhaps the fact that this humorous exchange is reported in his own book belies Hardy's much vaunted reputation as a snob. An enthusiastic social climber is perhaps a better description.

Another of his wedding dress clients was Princess Michael of Kent who was also a regular attendee at the fashion shows in Savile Row, and who ordered a cream silk suit for her civil wedding ceremony to Prince Michael in 1978. So pleased was she with the outfit that it came out again for the validation service in London in 1983 and Hardy noted that the princess regularly reused his clothes and was often to be found leading the applause at the end of his catwalk shows. According to David Freeman, however: 'I understood from Hardy and Ken that she hardly ever paid for any of the clothes he designed for her, including, I think, her wedding dress.'

In *Still Here* Hardy acknowledges how democratic fashion was becoming in the latter half of the twentieth century. Despite being known for his elegance and appropriateness of dress for whatever occasion or location he was situated in, he understood the loosening of social mores, the androgynous nature of modern clothing and the element of informality which was inveigling its way into day-to-day life. His emergence as a menswear designer left him under no illusion that the suit would ever be ousted from its position as 'the most important status garment', and that 'status dressing will remain with us'.

He portentously saw that womenswear and menswear would not be greatly different in the future, as was obviously becoming apparent by the time he was writing in the early 1980s, but he declared of women: 'At night I believe that she will always want to be dressed like a princess.' And that, obviously, was what the House of Hardy Amies excelled at.

Chapter 24

Collaborations

The Hardy Amies name is probably best remembered now firstly for his work with the queen, but also perhaps for his menswear collections both in-house and through companies such as Hepworth's and Debenhams.

With Hardy himself being such a connoisseur of clothing, a wonderfully well-presented man – if not a *dandy* – and also an expert in the attributes of tailoring, it was perhaps inevitable that his menswear output would eventually come to equal the reputation he achieved among his female clientele.

By the early 1960s Hardy was in his mid-fifties, and Ken Fleetwood and his assistants had taken over a great deal of the designing from him. His role as ambassador for the brand, otherwise known as the 'living label', had virtually eclipsed his hands-on designing work, as he spent more and more time travelling to oversee the licensing operations. Nevertheless, he always kept a keen eye on whatever was going on at the house.

After diversifying from couture into boutique ready-to-wear for women in the early 1950s, Hardy's next natural progression was into the realms of menswear and this was well-established by the mid-1960s, his reputation gaining a considerable boost when he was chosen to design the off the pitch clothing for the ultimately successful English soccer team for the 1966 World Cup.

His first foray into menswear sales had been the tentative introduction of ties in his boutiques around the world but, once this took off during the 1950s, he was well on his way to expansion with the collaboration of various overseas menswear firms.

The ties were brought into the boutiques initially as potential gifts for lady clients to purchase for their husbands while they were selecting their own clothing on a shopping spree. This was a trend that Hardy had noted was burgeoning in Paris, not least in the houses of such eminent designers as Jacques Fath and Pierre Cardin. Having had the ties made for a number of years by the well-respected tie-making company of Michelsons, Hardy eventually formed an association with the firm's director, Hans Wallach.

He describes in *Still Here* his near ecstasy at visiting the tie-silk weavers on Lake Como and watching the whole process from production to presentation: 'Alternatives to designs and to colours can be discussed in the morning and new samples woven during luncheon in a lakeside *albergo*, ready for further examination in the afternoon'.

It was 1959 when the embarkation began from the exquisite yet obviously rather limited world of the gentlemen's tie to the full launch into menswear for Hardy Amies. By this time the enterprises of couture and boutique were both flourishing and prospering, and the reputation of the label had risen to new heights with the gifting of the Royal Warrant. Hardy was supremely comfortable and secure in himself and his operations and he even states in *Still Here*: 'I had no other ambitions at the time than to see that this was the case.'

However, a telephone call from Prince Yurka 'Yuri' Galitzine, who managed public relations for the British menswear brand Hepworth's, was set to change all that. The call was to put forward an invitation to Hardy to meet with the directors of Hepworth's to discuss a potential collaboration with a company that was based in the north of England but had hundreds of retail outlets throughout the country, along with another northern competitor Montague Burton.

These companies had cornered the market in non-bespoke men's tailoring, transforming the wardrobes of the average man in the street from the 1930s onwards. Hardy would have been fascinated by the intervention from Prince Yuri, not just because of the business opportunity, but for another reason that he does not really allude to in his autobiography, *Still Here*.

Prince Yuri, as well as being of estimable family connections and lineage, had had a distinguished war as an intelligence officer, a backstory which would of course have sparked Hardy's interest. Born in 1919 in Japan, Yuri's lineage can be traced back to the middle ages in Lithuania, with a family member, Boris, being chosen as a Tsar of Russia 200 years later in the sixteenth century. Almost all of the living family members were exiled during the Russian revolution.

Yuri's grandfather escaped to Paris and Yuri spent his early years in France and Austria before being brought over to England at the age of seven to be educated. After a brief foray into business, at the outbreak of the Second World War, Prince Yuri was commissioned into the Middlesex Regiment and subsequently the Royal Northumberland Fusiliers. During his war years he witnessed cruelty towards prisoners, a group which included SOE agents, male and female, and was part of the liberation of the death camps when the Allies were finally victorious. Such was his commitment to bringing the perpetrators to justice, he continued working with the SAS Tracking Unit, even after it was officially closed in 1945.

After his work in the area of war crimes investigations was finished, the prince moved back to the business world, establishing his own public relations firm in 1954, and eventually becoming head of an enterprise which represented over eighty companies.

The telephone call in 1959 was therefore the catalyst for a momentous new step in Hardy's design career. The call itself had a very significant effect on Hardy, and the way he talks about it in *Still Here* gives a thinly veiled hint of an implied empathy, perhaps because of the similarity of their wartime experiences. 'He said he had a business proposition to make,' Hardy recalled, 'and he asked me to lunch with him at Brook's in such a charming way that, although he was a stranger, I remember having no hesitation in accepting.'[1]

The invitation the prince put forward was for Hardy to travel to Leeds to meet with the directors of the Hepworth's Menswear company, with a view to him designing a collection of men's clothing for the brand, which had many retail outlets throughout the United Kingdom.

Hardy's enthusiastic agreement to the meeting was on the condition that, rather sensibly, he did not go alone. He stipulated that he would be accompanied on the visit by his highly capable and astute financial adviser of the time, a man who, coincidentally, hailed from the north of England. The estimable Eric Crabtree was well respected and totally trusted with the financial running of operations by Hardy. True to form, Eric mounted an investigation into the finances of the Hepworth's group and, being suitably satisfied and actually rather impressed with their performance on the Stock Exchange, gave the green light to the proposed meeting.

Eric had been with Hardy Amies since the end of the war and, like Hardy, had a distinguished service record in the Royal Army Service Corps and later founded the Royal Military College of Science. Apparently the subject up for discussion was considered quite revolutionary so the two visiting gentlemen were invited to a private room at the Queens Hotel in Leeds, rather than a boardroom at the Hepworth headquarters.

Things went according to plan and both sides were happy with an arrangement for Hardy to produce a maiden collection within the subsequent two months, and Hardy was obviously excited about the venture to the point of being almost oblivious to the customer profile of the company. As he said in *Still Here*: 'I knew exactly what I wanted to do. I gave no thought to the fact that Hepworth's clientele were not rich and that the greater part of their chain of over 300 shops was situated out of London, mainly in the midlands and the north.'

This comment implies that Hardy viewed good taste and fashion as being the preserve of London and the south of England, and he does indeed continue on this theme: 'The style of their clothes could be described as more middle-of-the road than fashionable.' He seems to view his role as a saviour and inspirational leader who is making a foray beyond the boundaries of the Home Counties in order to help the gentlemen of the north of England to broaden their horizons and thus become better dressed!

'It has never been my policy to play down,' he declared. 'In clothes you must make men and women look up.' Writing in 1984 he continues: 'In those days fashion's job was to make a man or a woman look and feel richer and younger than they were, and more attractive.' An admirable and somewhat democratising aim, and one which the deal with Hepworth's seemed destined to help fulfil.

Being a Yorkshireman, Eric Crabtree no doubt felt a sense of destiny in his return to his home territory with the Hardy Amies venture. His down to earth northern pragmatism obviously found favour with Hardy, but his *de facto* deputy Ken Fleetwood does not seem to have shared the same affinity or affection for him.

With the Hepworth's deal Ken appeared to fear the blurring of the demarcation lines, as Eric perhaps delved into areas other than those where his financial and business accomplishments usually lay. In Michael Pick's biography, *Hardy Amies*, he reports that 'he [Eric] was mistrusted by Ken Fleetwood, who found the cosy life at Amies being rocked'. He goes on to quote from a letter written to Hardy by Ken in 1966: 'Eric is on the phone to nag, because business is down, doesn't help, how can a man with a voice like that get on so well.'[2] Obviously Mr Crabtree's Yorkshire tones were not well received by the more sensitive, yet also northern-born, Ken – although hailing from Lancashire he perhaps would have considered Eric to be from 'the other side'. The Wars of the Roses lived on within the rarefied world of Hardy Amies Ltd.

In order to produce the best products he possibly could for the collaboration with Hepworth's, Hardy consulted his own tailor, Mr Wyser of Wyser and Bryant Ltd, who had made Hardy's first 'London suit' in 1934. Once the collection was ready to be shown to the directors of the company there was another hurdle to overcome. Hardy was quite determined that the best way to display the clothes was to emulate the procedure he would employ for womenswear, and put on a catwalk show, but this idea was quite shocking to the traditional, staid, and masculine directors of Hepworth's. 'They thought that the sight of a group of male models parading up and down would make them a laughing stock,' Hardy recalls in *Still Here*.

All worked out well however, when Hardy persuaded Prince Yuri to host the show at his house, after which the high praise of: 'By gum, we could sell these!' rang out from the mouth of one of the managers and was swiftly concurred with by the other executives present.

Later that year, September 1961, the first public airing of the Hepworth collection took place at London's Savoy Hotel with a second catwalk show, causing a sensation in the world of British menswear. The great benefit of this show was the attention that it attracted from overseas companies. The Genesco group from the United States was represented at the showing and this resulted in what Hardy describes in *Still Here* as 'the beginnings of what was to be a major diversification of my business'.

The collaboration between Hardy Amies and Hepworth's resulted in a financial boost for the house, due to the fact that its name became so woven into the image of Hepworth's, that the directors were persuaded by Eric to put money into the business and to take up a seat on the board.

A most fortuitous liaison developed from that partnership as Eric became a director at Hepworth's after selling another company he had taken over, Cresta Silks, to Debenhams. This formed a link between Hardy Amies, Hepworth's, and Debenhams which was to become pivotal in later years.

It was to be a trip to Israel that brought about this next step on the business ladder for the Hardy Amies label. Eric Crabtree had made an arrangement for the womenswear side of the company to partner with a textiles firm called Selincourt, which was run by a Jewish man by the name of Louis Mintz. Mr Mintz invited Hardy and Eric to Israel to consult with him on his business and, as luck would have it, Eric also happened to be a friend of the British Ambassador of Israel who was happy to give the two gentlemen guided tours when they were not engaged in the machinations of fashion.

This event had a great impact on the future of Hardy's business via a chance meeting at the airport with a former favourite customer of Hardy's back in the days of Lachasse. The previous Mrs Parr was now, through a second marriage, Lady Burney, the wife of Sir Anthony Burney, who had recently retired from a position in an eminent firm of accountants. While Hardy renewed his acquaintance with Lady Burney, Eric took the opportunity of having a most interesting exchange with her husband on the subject of finance and company business.

This was the point at which Hardy Amies' association with Debenhams began to develop; quite soon after the airport meeting, Sir Anthony became the chairman of Debenhams. Eric was appointed vice-chairman soon after and, in 1973, Debenhams bought the whole of the Hardy Amies company.

This resulted in Hepworth's being paid off for the funds they had put into the business and Debenhams, the former Debenham and Freebody department store of Wigmore Street in London, playing a major role in Hardy's business life.

Hardy describes the years in partnership with Debenhams as 'not unhappy', but he obviously felt that their mantra of bigger being better may not have chimed so well with the ethos his company had perpetuated for so long. The store's penchant for buying up other businesses inevitably led to a corporate structure and atmosphere which, though it obviously alleviated much of his administrative and financial responsibility, did not allow for Hardy to retain much control over the image and characteristics which, up until that point, had been closely bound up with his own persona.

By this time the company had had a very positive and profitable fourteen-year relationship with Hepworth's and had happily run this alongside the couture and boutique operations in Savile Row. The acquisitive nature of the board of Debenhams, led at that time by Sir Anthony Burney, meant that what was now Hardy Amies' parent company was perhaps too large and diverse an organisation to be able to operate a business of that nature in an appropriate manner. To compound the problem Hardy talks of the period as being at the beginning of an economic recession when 'money was getting scarcer'.

This did not seem to have concerned Hardy too much previously, apart from with hindsight as he says in *Still Here*: 'I was, however, encouraged to take but a little part in the running of the financial side of the business.' However, he continues: 'This was not an uncomfortable arrangement, for our licensee business overseas was growing rapidly and required a great deal of my time.'

Towards the end of the 1960s Hardy personally took the decision to expand, but seems to have regretted it to some extent. A concession was opened within the department store Harvey Nichols, as well as a stand-alone shop in Hans Crescent, London SW1, just around the corner from the iconic Harrods store.

Manufacturing ready-to-wear clothes for the three of these outlets proved challenging, although Hardy shoulders the responsibility for the decision himself saying: 'I badgered Debenhams to let me do so.' He states that he wanted to sell clothes with 'a modern and athletic British look', but that the suppliers were unable to fulfil this remit and the clothes ended up being sourced from France and Italy and became 'indistinguishable from what could be bought in other shops'.

The fact that the alliance between Hardy Amies and Debenhams appears to have veered off course inevitably led to a breakdown in the professional relationship between the two sides in early 1980 after a seven-year association. Hardy felt that Debenhams had grown so quickly that they had difficulty in settling on their own company image and that did not help them to portray his business with the type of characteristics he would have desired for it. The Hardy Amies and Debenhams relationship was now seriously in the balance.

During the interview he gave to Naim Attallah some ten years after the Debenhams episode, Hardy was more critical of the firm than he had been when writing *Still Here* in 1984. Although he conceded that they had not tried to control his creative output, he refers to there having been 'blatant jealousy' towards him. In a rather scathing attack he states that 'it always comes down to personalities, and the personalities at Debenhams were inferior'.

He claimed that the two promises made by the company were never kept. One was to launch a perfume business, which never transpired, and the second – and probably the more crucial – was to set up *Hardy Amies Ready-to-Wear*, thus showcasing it on the platform of Debenhams' sixty stores, another venture which never got off the ground, according to Hardy.

He summed up the animosity by referring once again to the fact that it was his image and his name which was the attraction in the marketplace, and that Debenhams came to realise that overseas licence holders, for instance, would never give a contract to Debenhams but would bestow one on Hardy Amies. In other words, without a compliant Hardy they really did not have a profitable operation. It was this friction that really heralded the breakdown of the association between the two establishments.

On linking himself with Debenhams at the outset of the merger, Hardy had signed a Contract of Service and this was to come up for reassessment in 1979 at the time of his 70th birthday. That spring the manager of Hardy Amies Ltd, who had been appointed by Debenhams, was asked by the company to negotiate with Hardy for a Contract for Life. Hardy initially agreed to this and the administration of the new contract began, but during the course of the negotiations disagreements between the two sides began to emerge.

It had been observed that Debenhams' retail sales had been declining and, as part of restructuring and addressing the resulting losses, it was suggested that the Hardy Amies label should close its stand-alone store in Knightsbridge, as well as the menswear concession in Harvey Nichols.

Hardy considered this negative approach and concluded that it was Debenhams' own practices and running of the ready-to-wear business that was causing the downturn, and felt that it was not a fair reflection of the potential success of the Hardy Amies brand. After all, their couture operations and licensing arrangements overseas were simultaneously thriving. He decided that the best course of action would be to break free. He put this forward diplomatically to the then Debenhams Chairman Robert Thornton, suggesting that rather than see the potential constriction of the company, he could be given the opportunity to organise the finance to buy back the name and the business. This idea was apparently eagerly accepted.

At this point the obvious person to approach appeared to be Charles, Lord Chelsea, who had purchased the Michelson tie brand, which held the licence to use the Hardy Amies name. Hardy had also become aware of the fact that Lord Chelsea, who headed the Cadogan Real Estate business, wished to expand and diversify his empire by moving into the wider area of menswear. Thus, more negotiations began.

Initially Hardy had stated that he would be prepared to sign any 'reasonable' contract put forward by Lord Chelsea, but as he pondered on the nature of the Hardy Amies business at that time he realised something which gave him pause for thought. 'The only real asset that the company possessed was me,' he concluded. The licensee arrangements which brought in revenue amounting to 'many hundreds of thousands of pounds', were all in his name and were drawn up with the requirement that they would become null and void in the event of Hardy's retirement or death. He concluded: 'the idea came to me that perhaps I should buy back the company myself'.

Hardy spent many a restless night pondering all the positive aspects of the business. He thought about all of his harmonious and profitable associations around the world, the cordial relationship the company had with Hepworth's Menswear, his Royal Warrant and the CVO which had been awarded to him by the queen during her Silver Jubilee year, 1977, and decided that he 'ought to be able to stand on [his] own two feet'.

Together with his accountant and tax adviser, Hardy approached the bank, and to his great satisfaction, a ten-year loan was put into place making it possible for him to buy back the business. As a result of this epiphany, in February 1980 the seven-year hiatus of Hardy Amies Ltd being owned by the department store giant Debenhams came to an end. During the administration and instigation of the deal it became apparent that what Debenhams had actually owned could not in any way be viewed as the substance of the business as, without Hardy himself, it was really just a shell, of which all the component parts were operating separately.

For instance, Debenhams had had no control over the couture and dressmaking business at Savile Row, or the overseas licensees, and Hardy's flat in New York was not part of the deal, so the price he eventually had to pay for the reacquisition turned out to be fairly modest. Once the arrangement was in place, a clean break was effected and Debenhams were no longer permitted to trade in any way under the Hardy Amies name. However, Hardy and his team's delight at their resumed sole ownership was somewhat tempered by the realisation that they were once again responsible for all the behind-the-scenes operations that go with running a successful business. Additionally, the years during which all this had been run by the administrative arm of the Debenhams group had left them quite unprepared for the challenges that lay ahead.

Some of the changes that had been implemented during the years of Debenham's ownership had benefited the company financially, but Hardy himself could not be described as being particularly well off personally at any period of his life.

Hardy appears to have been selflessly open and honest about his approach to the administration and finance of running a couture house. He admits that at the time of launching the business, as well as when he bought it back from Debenhams, he 'did not want to listen to planning schemes'. Back in 1945 he 'just knew it had to be a success and that self-belief and willpower were enough to see me through'. However, he acknowledged that this feeling of optimistic invincibility was part of the general aura of relief and positivity which was part of the post-war euphoria of the time.

Having been under the Debenhams umbrella for so many years, the company as a whole was not used to the practices of what was then known as the 'counting-house' and would now be referred to as 'accounting' or the finance department. So many things had changed; from business overheads and bank interest rates, to the complicated costings involved in the production of a couture garment, and this was now suddenly once again under the auspices of Hardy and his autonomous operation. One of the processes that had to be addressed in the short-term was the system of billing and the resultant cash-flow issues. Although the changes of practice impacted on the customers it was a move that had to be made, and seems to have been graciously accepted by Hardy's customers, along with the realisation that this was the only way forward in order to keep such a business afloat.

However, the cachet of having a couture wardrobe was still something which certain echelons of society were quite prepared to invest in at the time. Reading the autobiographies now, Hardy's lofty opinions and sense of self-belief may come across as rather fanciful and aloof, but it is possible to see how this would be interpreted in a positive way by his potential client base, and exert a magnetic force over it. However, one of his rather dismissive pronouncements in *Still Here* would probably have a counter-intuitive effect on the ladies who bought from the couture house.

He speaks of the difference in attitude to the amount of money a customer might expect to pay for a tailored coat in France or Italy compared with that paid by an Englishwoman. Furthermore he goes on to say that his prices were 'half or sometimes even a third, of what can be asked in Paris or New York'. He concludes, 'I feel very strongly that to pay for a garment made in an establishment such as mine is a very good investment if you can afford it.' Even in those days, what better incentive could there be for the English lady than to be seen to equal her European cousins in the world of aspirational fashion?

Notwithstanding the aura and cachet of being in the fortunate position of having a dress created by Hardy Amies Ltd, by the late twentieth century the haute couture business was experiencing a decline, and changing attitudes to fashion were having an impact on such businesses just as Hardy was taking back the reins. The team he had behind him at Savile Row was the firm foundation that he needed to keep things on track and look towards the future.

Part Five

Coming to a Close

Chapter 25

The House in its Later Years

The long-serving design team and construction staff in the house, in addition to the introduction of carefully chosen new employees such as Jon Moore and Ian Garlant, was obviously a crucial part of maintaining a loyal clientele as well as opening the doors to new customers. Behind the scenes, by the late 1960s Hardy had also introduced a highly significant member of the administration and business team. In *Still Here* he refers to Roger Whiteman as a close friend and, together with Ken Fleetwood, a 'most loyal supporter'. Indeed, David Freeman reveals that Hardy and the handsome Roger Whiteman, an accountant who became his business manager and finance director, had a brief affair when he joined the firm.

When talking about the duo of Fleetwood and Whiteman, Hardy invokes his self-selected motto, which, translated from the Latin means, 'Less than art, more than trade'. Although he does not allude to any conflict between the pair, he does concede that there is 'a struggle between the desire to achieve perfection in the clothes and a wish to make a profit'.

Hardy generously devotes several pages to referencing and describing the roles of what seems to be just about everyone in the workrooms and offices at Savile Row in *Still Here*. He credits young and old equally and, citing himself, Ken Fleetwood and Roger Whiteman as the 'chief gardeners' cultivating the growth of the house, declares that 'there is no room for old people in the dress trade. Some members are mature in years, but all have to be young in heart.'

He goes on to say: 'We are all reborn twice a year with the showing of our collections. As the winter orders get finished in November and December, so we have to gear ourselves to work and plan ahead for the following spring and summer designs. Life never stops.'

Indeed, the business prospered after the reacquisition and, under Roger Whiteman, the licensing operations worldwide, featuring both men's and womenswear, were thriving. Roger and Hardy made many overseas trips to licensees and foreign buyers. Hardy acknowledges that both he and Roger were 'good and tidy travellers', but that Roger had the added skill of being able 'to read a complicated timetable better than some experienced travel agents'.

Top hotels and first-class travel were justified by 'the necessity to keep up good appearances'. No expense was spared when the two men travelled overseas. Jon Moore, the designer who succeeded Ken in the womenswear studio, recalls that at the height of their success, Hardy's manservant would be sent on ahead to prepare his New York apartment. 'Once Hardy and Whiteman arrived on Concorde, he would be dispatched to the nearby Plaza Hotel where he slept, as there were only two bedrooms available at the flat.'

'Mr Whiteman seemed to be in charge,' said Bill Howat, Hardy's chauffeur for much of the last twenty years before the business was sold. 'The business never appeared to be short of money and Hardy had the brains to get over any problems by finding someone who could sort things out if he couldn't do it himself.' Bill's recollections of working for Hardy are generally positive: 'It was a relaxed atmosphere compared with anywhere else I worked,' he said. 'Although he wasn't a particularly generous employer.' According to Bill, another employee once overheard Hardy talking about the high status that a job for him would enviably bestow on operatives. 'People should pay me for the chance to work for me', the couturier supposedly proclaimed.

As finance director of the company, Roger Whiteman spent much of his time travelling to all the licensee locations both with and without his boss. 'The licensee trade was bringing in millions every year, which is what kept the Couture House going,' Bill continues. However, both Bill and Chris Stratmann had their doubts about Roger Whiteman's capabilities. Chris explains:

One of the problems was cash flow. I was a fill-in freelance driver so I had to submit my invoices in order to get paid. Often the accounts department would ask me if I could wait a bit as there was no cash available. Usually it was because Hardy or Ken had cashed a cheque and taken out all the ready cash. I always got paid eventually, and luckily I had my income from my other contracts to keep me ticking over, but I did not really think Roger Whiteman was any good as a Financial Director. In fact Hardy didn't like confrontation, and that sometimes led to him not making good decisions – like not getting rid of Roger Whiteman.

Bill raises a rather sinister theory about the operations of the Hardy Amies' licensing business under Mr Whiteman. He talks about a representative of the company Cardingtons, who were negotiating to purchase the company in 2001, coming to him and asking surreptitious questions about the financial arrangements of the overseas businesses.

> One day a director of the company which was in line to buy the business telephoned and asked me what I did while I was hanging around waiting for Hardy in the London flat in the mornings. He asked if I used to see the post arriving and, if so, were there ever any letters which looked like statements from banks?

Bill told them that he had not seen any recognisable letters but concluded that the reason for the question was that apparently they could find no evidence, during their due diligence, of where much of the money from the overseas operations was going.

> They said they only ever saw the accounts from the Japanese operation, which coincidentally was just about the exact amount which kept the couture house going. The worldwide operation was bringing in millions of pounds at its height, and the implication was that the money was disappearing somewhere and could Roger Whiteman have been involved in that?

> I'd had dealings with another company whose director had asked me to go and collect a suitcase from 'a relative' and bring it back to them, but I had refused, because I suspected it could have been part of a money laundering operation. I told the Cardingtons director about the story, but whether they ever investigated Mr Whiteman, who was always travelling overseas, and whether he had been bringing money back and putting it straight into a safe deposit box, I don't know.

Obviously this would have been a way of avoiding paying tax on the money when it was brought into the country, although there is no evidence that that was what was going on at the company. Hardy's own personal financial status would certainly imply that he was never involved in any such activity.

As fashion became more democratised, a process which gathered momentum in the 1960s, the post-war boom years gave way to recession in the 1970s. Haute couture would inevitably diminish and lose its high status, not just in Britain but around the world. Hardy, however, maintained his belief that in cash-strapped times consumers would buy more wisely, therefore affecting the lower end of the market more than the high-quality names, because people would invest in long-term pieces. This is an underlying principle of the present-day drive towards more sustainable fashion. 'Buy better but buy less' is a theory which is currently being promoted by the ethical clothing industry.

Recently, the popular and most common way of dressing, particularly among the younger demographic, is to indulge in fast-fashion, with all its detrimental effects not only on the planet through excessive consumption and greenhouse gas emissions, but on style itself. Back in the early days of Hardy's business and all through the 1940s and '50s, the alternative for those who could not afford high-end clothing was to buy second-hand. Nowadays, to do that can be refocused as dressing in 'vintage' style, and this approach can lead to a highly personal and unique image for the wearer. In the twenty-first century there are also more and more fashion brands that are putting their emphasis on sustainability, better working conditions for clothing technicians around the world, and cutting out emissions from mass-production techniques.

However, then as well as now, these conscious methods of buying fashion are only attainable by those who can afford it, and on an even more extreme scale, there were not that many women in society who could prioritise expenditure on haute couture pieces. The post-war recession would filter down through society's different strata, and this is what led to the many different layers of consumer spending and the opening-up of more options to buyers.

Of course, by the time of its alliance with Hepworth's, Hardy Amies Ltd had a foot in both camps, and Hardy felt that the way they had managed this diversification stood them in good stead whatever the economic climate. He was pragmatic enough to have a democratic view of the world and was not frightened of dabbling in the slightly lower end of the market.

In *Still Here* he says: 'I never for one moment thought that our trade in expensive haute couture clothes at Savile Row stood to be endangered by our move into the market of cheap clothes for men, and I have since been proved right.' He had of course introduced the boutique at the couture house many years earlier, and the production of the diffusion lines which were sold through the boutique propped up the more expensive design business. Hardy's policy was to design as well as he could to fit the price-point of the market at which the garment was aimed, so that everyone could dress with style within their own budget.

When asked about style in his interview with Naim Attallah, Hardy said: 'The main characteristic of the English style is that it has to have something to do with the country. A well-dressed, well-bred Englishwoman is at her best when she looks as though she has just come up from the country or is just going back there.'[1] This is perhaps a rather outmoded statement which does not really relate to today's lifestyles, but it could be interpreted as having parallels with today's casual to formal look. Thinking particularly of the fashion for 'athleisure' wear, which blends sportswear with casual clothing and is a staple of the wardrobes of today's younger consumers, Hardy was perhaps quite the visionary.

At the time he seemed to think that town or city clothes were better produced by French designers and the English market was geared more towards what he referred to as 'country' clothing. Obviously time has moved on and now many people take a very informal approach when in town and would probably shock the likes of Hardy with the casualness of their attire in either town or the countryside!

Hardy once declared that his studio invented the word 'nonchalance' in relation to dress. He claimed to 'abhor the dressed-up look', although his clothes could not possibly have been described as just thrown on, and would be seen as the ultimate in structured formality nowadays. However, one famous quote sums up what he feels should be a person's approach to dressing, even if there has been more going on with the preparation than might meet the eye of the casual observer.

In *The ABC of Men's Fashion*, which was first published in 1964, he declares, 'A man should look as if he had bought his clothes with intelligence, put them on with care, and then forgotten all about them.'[2]

A look which actually takes a great deal of personal style and flair to pull off. Hardy himself, of course, managed it with ease and aplomb. He penned a letter to the *Daily Telegraph* in 1993 saying: 'It is clear that the man's suit – an English invention, I must add – is still worn by men at all times when respect for tradition and hope for an ordered future prevail. [...] The suit is the uniform of the gentleman.'

Obviously a traditionalist, he somewhat surprisingly did not take sartorial matters too seriously. Referring to the attitude of some of his fellow countrymen, an increasing number as time goes on, he appears to relate to their indifference to matters of dressing. 'Even though it defeats me as a dressmaker, I admire the British attitude. Clothes are not really as important as all that.'

To read the book he published a year on from that letter to the newspaper, one would get a slightly different view, as over a hundred pages on one specific aspect of men's dress is hardly showing scant regard for it. He produced the book *The Englishman's Suit* in 1994, a subject about which, it cannot be denied, he was eminently knowledgeable. According to Richard Martin, Hardy 'tended to lord it a bit, and he had a certain infatuation with things like collar-shapes such as the Ghillie collar.' This was a style of collar which was done up to the neck and would be seen on men's tweed suits used for shooting in the mid- to late 1800s.

Hardy refers to an illustration of King Edward VII wearing a Ghillie coat, which he specifies as 'the most important illustration in the book'. In a paragraph in which he sounds as if he has unearthed a crucial facet of British history, he explains 'the new coat with the collar pressed open to reveal the shirt and the tie. It clearly shows the origin of the single-breasted revers of the soon-to-appear and still-very-much-with us lounge suit.'

Hardy's attention to detail was something he obviously felt that other people should be educated in, if they were to be able to dress in an acceptable way. Bill Howat was once spotted by Hardy hanging around at Savile Row, seemingly at a loose end.

He asked me to come and sit next to him and watch a run-through of one of the fashion shows. As the show went on he said, 'I hope I'm not boring you, but you see the crease coming from the buttonhole on that model's jacket', and he went on to explain how a small adjustment would rectify the situation immediately!

He had learned that the French designers would always place the first button on a suit jacket directly over the belly-button and in that way, as long as all the buttons were equally spaced, none of them would ever pull.

The chauffeur was undoubtedly most impressed! However, when his employer very kindly had a suit made for him, Bill was slightly disappointed to find that he had had it made up as a double-breasted style despite the fact that the younger man favoured single-breasted. Surely Hardy was not trying to impose his own preferences on his subordinate?

According to Nicholas Worth, Hardy's vision for menswear also came into its own in the 1970s:

He was an innovator and the first to put men into two-button suits and jackets without vents – that was Hardy. He was a huge influence on the 70s, had a great eye on menswear and was ahead of his time. Once he started working with Hepworth's it became mainstream.

Hardy always looked stylish, neat and perfectly turned out, and had the slim, well-maintained good looks that not every man sustains into their ninth decade. This was partly due to genetics, but also to a lifestyle which certainly encompassed luxury and indulgence, but was also disciplined and focused on presenting the very best image of oneself to the outside world. He was, after all, a living label, and much like the glamorous actresses or models of his era, he considered it his duty to represent his eponymous 'brand' in a positive way at all times.

During the interview with Naim Attallah, he stated: 'tennis is a very good cosmetic. I play an hour's tennis on Saturday and Sunday and for the rest of the week people tell me how well I look.' Interestingly, he eschewed sun lotion and espoused the theory that 'constant contact with fresh air and sunlight keeps the skin of my face youthful'. This is not an approach that is endorsed by current dermatologists, who would say that, without protection, UV rays can have a very detrimental effect on skin over time. However, Hardy does have another skincare technique. In *Still Here*, he declares: 'I no longer lie in the sun: I take exercise in it. Sweat is a good moisturiser.' Chris Stratmann thinks that sometime during the latter part of Hardy's life a doctor must have warned him of the potential dangers of sun damage to the skin. 'He always used to insist on the sun-roof of the car being open,' Chris said, 'but he suddenly changed his mind and asked me to leave it closed, and I think that the doctor must have had a word with him and warned him about possible skin-cancer.'

Hardy claimed that he maintained his health largely through the use of homeopathic remedies, which is quite remarkable considering he lived until the age of 93. In the later years of his working life he was assisted in his day-to-day life by his manservant James, who shared the flat in Cornwall Gardens with him from Monday to Friday. James also travelled with Hardy to the apartment in New York, acting as valet as well as chef for the dinner parties Hardy gave there for his licensee operators and members of the fashion press.

Apparently selected by one of Hardy's secretaries in the late 1970s, Hardy was delighted to discover that James had trained at Buckingham Palace. Unsurprisingly, James was indispensable to Hardy on his travels and he declared in *Still Here*: 'Naturally he packs and polishes to perfection.'

Bill helped to fill in the gap left when Hardy's valet was let go. 'He didn't replace James, so I would step in and do various jobs for him,' said Bill, although the designer Jon Moore goes further:

Bill was much more than a driver. He went above and beyond, especially when Ken Fleetwood was so ill. Bill did so much to help Ken and when it came to the end they allowed Bill to go for a holiday in the New York flat, as it had all been so traumatic.

Chris also feels that the tragedy of Ken Fleetwood's death in 1996 was not just a personal loss to Hardy, but also to the future of the business, claiming that 'Ken would have kept the business on track'.

Bill reveals that after giving up his Rolls Royce, Hardy opted for a Mercedes estate car which appears to have often been utilised to bring down the weekend supplies of wine for his house parties from his favoured wine merchant in central London. 'I used to check the cellar before we left on a Monday morning so he knew how much we needed to bring down the following weekend.' explains Bill, 'I could never understand why he didn't just buy the wine more locally – it would have been simpler!' Chris concluded, however, that the reason for this was that any entertaining that Hardy did in Langford would be passed off as an expense against the business for tax purposes, so it was a calculated move to buy the provisions in London!

Hardy also used his country residence to facilitate other thrifty operations. Chris remembers that he was a member of The Royal Academy and registered The Old School as his main home, rather than the London flat, when joining, so that he could pay the cheaper rate for out of town membership. 'He didn't like to throw money around,' laughed Chris.

Hardy's devoted sister Rosemary was his greatest supporter and constant companion in Langford and the two had a loving yet often irreverent relationship, mainly due to their very different characters. Hardy had intended to leave his personal assets to Rosemary. She was six years his junior and as a consequence had always been thought likely to outlive him. He had to alter his will in October 2001 as Rosemary sadly died in June of that year at the age of 85. His other companion and sidekick in the business Ken, also predeceased him and mutual friend David Freeman, who had cared for both Rosemary and Hardy, inherited the bulk of Hardy's estate.

When asked about death by Naim Attallah, Hardy confirmed that he was not in the least afraid of it. 'No, You're just going into nothing, so why should you be frightened of nothing?', as he pragmatically put it. He believed in the existence of God but said: 'it could have any other name – nature, for example, or order ... but the order is gone when you're dead, totally gone'. He concluded: 'And I don't mind it. I was meant to have a life, not a death.'

Hardy supposedly did not fully step down from his work until the year before he died and was always compelled by a great desire to keep going. To quote from his 2012 biographer Michael Pick: 'The decline was inevitable, but managed with great style by David Freeman.'[3]

David, a fellow of the Royal Society of Arts and former curator of Tredegar House in South Wales, met Hardy in November 1986. A mutual friend, Allan Pryce-Jones, invited David, then aged 30, to a lunch at the Garrick Club in London where Hardy would be present as he 'thought they may amuse each other'. David recalls that although Hardy was at that time 77 years old, he could have passed for twenty years younger and was full of energy. 'I remember seeing him running for a taxi afterwards,' David said later. 'Soon after the lunch I sent him a copy of my latest guide to Tredegar House, because he had bought The Old School some years before and was passionate about the seventeenth century.' Shortly after that Hardy went to Tredegar for lunch with David, and was no doubt impressed by the younger man's comprehensive knowledge of the historic collection at the house, having been the curator since 1979 and completely rewriting the guidebook.

Indeed, such was Hardy's love of the English country house style of interior design that David remembers visiting Hardy's apartment in New York and being confronted with the fact that he had changed the mid-century decor to that of an English stately home, which did not seem entirely appropriate for a high rise flat in a block which towered above the streets of Manhattan.

On meeting David, Hardy was eternally surprised at how well-connected he was. Often if he was excited to introduce him to an eminent friend, David would already know them, much to Hardy's disappointment. The apex of this competitiveness was exposed in the late 1980s when David revealed that a member of the royal family had been his personal guest. Her Royal Highness, Princess Margaret, had decided to visit Tredegar House and, due to security concerns at the time, ended up having lunch in his private cottage on the estate. As David remembers, this high-status social engagement caused the upwardly mobile Hardy to be 'beside himself' with envy!

David came from Usk in the Welsh county of Monmouthshire, and continued to maintain a property there throughout the time he was associated with Hardy. After leaving his position at Tredegar House he became a freelance art consultant, later working for Lord and Lady Faringdon of Buscot Park near Hardy's home in Langford. By coincidence, Lady Faringdon's mother, Lady Susan Askew, had been instrumental in Her Majesty the Queen becoming aware of the work of the couture house of Hardy Amies.

Hardy always had a cohort of younger male friends and admirers, but according to Richard Martin, Rosemary wholeheartedly approved of David. The feeling was mutual, and David became indispensable to both Hardy and Rosemary, eventually arranging care for them both in their last years and organising their obituaries, funerals, and other necessary arrangements at the end of their lives. Many of the siblings' friends acknowledge the kindness and care he showed them. In his diaries *Scenes and Apparitions, 1988–2003*, Sir Roy Strong notes that David 'did everything for him during the final years'.[4]

Sir Roy has his own personal reason to be grateful to David. When Sir Roy's wife, the theatre, ballet, and opera set designer Julia Trevelyan, was diagnosed with terminal cancer in June 2003, three months after Sir Hardy's death, he remembered David once saying, 'I'm an expert on carers.' Sir Roy got in touch with David and this resulted in a team of exemplary people being put in place to care for his beloved wife in her final months of life.

David would be invited down to Langford most weekends as Hardy had the barn with its guest accommodation as well as Ken's room and a spare at The Old School, there was always the potential for lively house parties. 'I loved coming here,' said David. 'It was like a mini-Tredegar.' This is in fact how many of Hardy's friends characterised his purchase of The Old School. With its large double height drawing room, one entire wall of which he would cover with a historic tapestry, imposing stone fireplace, and huge oak doors, not to mention the formal garden, The Old School gave the impression of being a true country mansion, although in fact it is on a much smaller scale.

Hardy did in fact build on to the house during 1972/3 after he made the purchase, adding quite considerable extra space and substantially increasing the size of the property. However, at least a couple of the neighbouring properties in Langford are much more imposing, though despite this Hardy saw fit to employ a retinue of staff to keep the property in tip-top condition and ready for his weekend visits.

The attention to detail in the renovation was comprehensive and exquisitely applied with the help of a litany of influential designers and builders. According to David Freeman, the ever resourceful Rosemary, or 'Miss A' as she was always known to friends, colleagues, and Hardy's workforce, even arranged for a local quarry to be reopened so that the appropriate stone could be used for an authentic renovation.

With his eye for status and prestige, Hardy even managed to lure a lady by the name of Helen, the cook and housekeeper of the Lord Mayor of London, away from the capital to work for him at The Old School. This arrangement was soon terminated however, because Helen would smoke in the kitchen and, as she did not meet with Rosemary's approval anyway, this soon became one of the reasons for her departure. According to David: 'They didn't get on, and once she realised Hardy and Rosemary didn't approve of her smoking, she left.'

He goes on to explain that, like many ex-smokers, both Hardy and Rosemary were vehemently opposed to smoking and were militant in their disapproval of others indulging in the habit. Rosemary's office in Langford was accessed via Helen's accommodation, so this must also have proved an irritation for the pair, and set their relationship on a delicate footing. The invasion of Hardy's whole retinue over the years must have felt like rather a takeover for some of the established residents of Langford, and David recalls that one villager had been heard to comment: 'He seems to think he owns the village.'

On visiting The Old School, the playwright Alan Bennett said: 'It's a country house in miniature', and was even tempted to buy his own property nearby, so taken was he with the rural idyll which Langford seemed to offer.

According to Richard Martin:

Hardy's barn was a very important part of life in Langford, as entertaining was crucial to him. He wanted a place with a big reception room and also lots of cupboard space and that's what the Old School had, and so did the barn. The Old School has an air of grandeur even though it is not a particularly big house, but it has a certain look about it and that's why he bought it.

Hardy would still manage to preside over his house parties with a continuing aura of patronage and propriety and enlisted the help of others during his later years when became unable to circulate to his desired extent. Sir Roy recalls:

He had a great sense of occasion. I went to several of his drinks parties and, towards the end of his life, he used to sit in a chair to greet people just back from the front door. As the room began to fill up he'd have his acolytes move him around in the chair because otherwise he'd start to be crushed at the back and people wouldn't be able to see him! He was also a stickler for convention. I remember turning up at one of his lunch parties and I had an open-neck shirt on. I recall a poor Australian chap telling me he had been sent upstairs on arrival to put a tie on, so he was most put out when I turned up not wearing one!

It is fascinating to consider how Rosemary, and subsequently Hardy, were viewed by the locals when they bought their various properties in the village back in the 1970s. Richard feels that that particular area of the Oxfordshire and Gloucestershire confluence had an artistic and slightly unconventional aura about it which was, in part, the legacy of the Arts and Crafts movement, which had included William Morris and the artist Edward Burne-Jones:

> If you think about why certain people gravitate towards particular places you have to remember that there is still a faint aura of the Arts and Crafts movement around the area. A sort of acceptance of the innovative and unconventional, and maybe Hardy latched onto that.

> Although there is this idea that villages are stuffy and that the people don't like incomers, actually they've always been full of quite bizarre goings-on and stuff seems to happen in villages. Villages are surprisingly tolerant of peculiarities.

The atmosphere created by artists and other rather unconventional individuals and communities, prevailed in the area where Hardy and Rosemary and many of their cohort chose to live.

Richard became aware of a sort of magnetism that emanated from Hardy:

> There would have been memories formed in the not too distant past of frivolity, people coming down from London and being gay ... there was an acceptance of unorthodoxy down here.

> Certain people were accepted here because of historical precedent and Hardy was carrying on a tradition of slightly flamboyant Londoners coming out to the country. He had a talent for pulling people in to him and most people in Langford were always happy to help him, especially when he got older. For all his braggadocio, he was very self-deprecating.

> I think he revelled in creating an image and setting up situations in the same way as he created clothing, and in that sense he was quite an endearing chap.

Referring to Hardy in his later years, Richard seems to have had quite an insight into the way he conducted himself in his life at home, and how that probably reflected the way he had functioned as a businessman:

> Hardy bought cloth from me and we got on reasonably well. He had a good way – I wouldn't say of getting other people to do his work – but he had a very good network of people on whom he relied to get things done and to keep the wheels turning.

> I don't think he really liked business and, if things got too 'businessy' he would just delegate it, and I think that's partly why the business side slipped rather. He seemed to think that his friends all ought to do 'a turn' as chairman of the firm, and one of those was Lord Faringdon of Buscot Park.

Lord and Lady Faringdon are not mentioned in *Still Here*, but their friendship with Hardy was strong enough for them to host his eightieth birthday party at their stately home, Buscot, just down the road from his Langford property. Their names also appear in the Langford visitors book on several occasions. To look through Hardy's visitors books is fascinating, with the signatures of people ranging from Sir Roy Strong and Rosemary Verey, who helped Hardy to design The Old School garden, through James Bond author Ian Fleming, actress Vivien Leigh, Princess Michael of Kent, and the television presenter Anneka Rice, a one-time neighbour in Langford. Weekend gatherings at The Old School would have been made up of rounds of drinks parties, tennis, and scintillating conversation among scholars, politicians, celebrities, and luminaries from all walks of life. As Freeman explained: 'Hardy was a life-enhancing person. He kept introducing me to extraordinary people.'

Hardy did not officially retire until 2001, two years before his death, by which time life at Langford had become the main focus of his diminishing energies. Still maintaining the Hardy Amies image and epitomising the label, it had sadly become apparent that in order to maintain the lifestyle he needed, the business would have to be sold.

Chapter 26

The Final Years of Hardy Amies –
The Man and The Brand

In the later years of Hardy's life, the business was better known for its menswear than its ladies' collections and this may have partly been due to the collaboration with the more accessible Hepworth label and the gentlemen's accessory range, which still seemed to keep the brand name in the public eye overseas. In terms of womenswear, Hardy's vision had been diluted and subsumed by Jon Moore and Ian Garlant and the collection seemed no longer to epitomise his personal look. This must have disappointed him, although Sir Roy Strong believes that he should have embraced modern style in a more inclusive way and maybe that would have helped the label appear more relevant and cohesive.

In the 1950s there was still this idea of 'the Season' and mothers being dressed by someone and then the daughters following on and being presented at court, and Hardy was part of all that, but it was all dying out. He moved among the upper classes and was always at Glyndebourne and Wimbledon, but he was a minor figure really and he didn't seem to recognise how society had changed [...] I don't think he got out soon enough.

This view is somewhat borne out by a comment from David Freeman: 'Hardy couldn't stand the way Jon Moore dressed and the music he chose to play at the shows,' he reveals. The formality and glamour of the heyday of couture was becoming a distant memory. As Nicholas Worth said:

One day he came into my office and threw down a copy of *Vogue* which had a picture of a Ralph Lauren dress which was being advertised at £10,000 and said, 'What do you think of that? People just don't understand that they could come here and have one made for that.'

It was starting to become a struggle as people just didn't understand the world of couture by then.

Nicholas Worth recalls the Victoria and Albert Couture show which was mounted in the early twenty-first century:

They showed a beautiful coat by Ian Garlant and it was absolutely stunning – so wearable, but it was displayed next to a *pantomime* outfit by Galliano and the effect was totally lost. The pieces that were made at the House were so memorable and unique to the client, once they had been tweaked by the fitters. It was really the last 'whole house' devoted to couture and truly was a *temple to clothing.*

It had long been Hardy's aim to be able to bequeath his business to his workforce in a healthy state. This was an admirable plan but, in the light of the deaths of his sister and his erstwhile partner, Ken Fleetwood, it did not seem a practical or economically viable possibility.

According to David, Hardy had to sell his flats in London and New York by 2001 in order to balance the company accounts. By now an integral part of the Amies family life, David had tasked himself with working out how much it would theoretically cost per year to keep Hardy in Langford, having reached the age of 90. With bills, staffing costs, and generally upholding the lifestyle Hardy expected, this worked out at about £120,000 a year and it became obvious at that point that a serious reassessment of the business needed to take place.

Under the advice of Phyllis Newall who was now overseeing the business and accounting side of Hardy Amies Ltd, it was decided that the sale of the company was the most appropriate way forward. Cardingtons, which later became The Luxury Brands Group, sent representatives to Langford to speak to the then 91-year-old Hardy. Mrs Newall, Rosemary and David were also in attendance and David recalls:

Miss Amies looked at me and said, 'David, what's your opinion?' She clearly felt that Hardy had to be given time to consider such a major decision. Miss A went on, 'I don't think it's fair to expect him to sign today', although they were obviously pushing for it. 'I think he needs time to think.'

David explains that part of the agreement that was finally settled, which resulted in the whole business being priced at £240,000, was that Hardy would be paid the £120,000 per year for the first two years and after that be paid as a director. However, he died before that could be put into practice.

Hardy had been awarded a Royal Warrant in July 1955 for his service as Dressmaker to Queen Elizabeth II. This honour was given to the company, but under the leadership of Hardy himself. This was a fact that would cause some controversy at the time the business was sold in 2001. According to David, Angela Kelly, the queen's personal dresser, was very keen to have the Royal Warrant passed on from Hardy himself to the new owners of the business, one of whom she appeared to have been on very good terms with. David recalls:

> I had seen Angela Kelly at an exhibition of Bryan Adams' photographs at Savile Row with Simon Petherick of Cardington's, and it was obvious she was trying to influence him. They were getting very excited about securing the Royal Warrant for the new owners. Kelly wanted to remove the Warrant from Hardy, who remained a director of the new company, owners of Hardy Amies, until whenever he died, but the Warrant had been awarded to him personally. Kelly wanted to give it to Petherick. This was not going to happen while Hardy remained alive. Both of Hardy's executors and I made sure of that. I suspect Kelly could be a bit of a bully.

Shortly after Rosemary died, David took Hardy to London for lunch at one of his favourite venues, Launceston Place. Also present was Phyllis Newall, then finance manager for Hardy: 'During the course of the lunch Phyll and I decided that the best thing to do would be to hand the Warrant back, as Hardy was at that point no longer working for the queen. And this would stop the new firm from getting it.

The Warrant was eventually returned after Hardy's death in March 2003, causing some consternation at Buckingham Palace. 'We asked the Lord Chancellor's office about how to proceed, and the court had to set up a protocol for it because it had never been done before,' David explained. 'The court Warrants Officer then rang me and said that the queen would be happy to get it back.'

David then sent the certificate for the Warrant back to Buckingham Palace and it was returned afterwards, having been voided. It still hangs in The Old School but with a stamp in the bottom right-hand corner containing the words: 'Cancelled, Lord Chamberlain's Office, Buckingham Palace, 1st August 2003'.

This unusual turn of events did not go down well with Cardington/ Luxury Brands, the new owners of the business, who had possibly been led to believe – by no less than the queen's dresser – that they would naturally be able to keep the Warrant. 'The directors of Hardy Amies and their shareholders were apoplectic when we returned the Warrant after his memorial service,' David Freeman reveals with a hint of triumph! And he credits the redoubtable Mrs Newall for her role in the episode, revealing that she was known as 'The Exocet' in business circles, such was her fierce approach in negotiations. The business was later sold on to the Chinese firm Fung Capital in 2008 for £1 million according to David. 'They should have made more from the original sale,' David said. Coincidentally, the Fungs had also previously purchased the House of Norman Hartnell as part of an expansive London fashion portfolio.

Hardy's sister Rosemary had died in June 2001, a month after the sale of Hardy Amies Ltd. David recalls: 'Rosemary had a massive stroke at the age of 88 and was moved into a hospice. I think she knew I would continue to look after Hardy, who was by then 90, so she gave herself permission to go.'

By this time Rosemary had given David her own bank cards and ensured that he had access to Hardy's financial arrangements, such was the trust that the siblings had by now placed in David. Having been spending a great deal of time in Langford, David had actually gone back to his home in Wales briefly when Rosemary died. There was obviously some concern about safety and security, with the potential for the elderly Hardy to have been taken advantage of in his time of grief.

'Phyll Newall was at the Old School and she was aware that Hardy had someone staying at the time whom she considered was acting a little suspiciously, so she asked me to come back quickly,' he recalls. Apparently Hardy was still fairly well in control of his faculties at this time, but he was walking with a stick and obviously becoming more and more frail. The prospect of any visitors or houseguests who may not have had his best interests at heart was a cause for concern.

Some time before her death, Hardy's PR man Peter Hope Lumley, had encouraged Rosemary to write down her life story, and this is what David used as the basis for the address at her funeral. He also submitted a version to the *Daily Telegraph* to draw from for the obituary. Hardy was quite surprised when his sister's obituary was published in the newspaper, but considering not just her connection to one of the most famous couturiers Britain had produced, but also Rosemary's own highly eventful life, it was well-deserved. Her intelligence and wit were certainly on a par with those of her eminent brother.

Rosemary had applied for Officer Training in the National Fire Service during the war and was always convinced that it was the answer to the final question at her interview that secured her place. To quote from the obituary, which was written by biographer, historian, and friend of Hardy, Selina Hastings: 'Can you remember the number of the railway carriage you were in this morning?' the interviewer asked. '726497' came the reply. 'How do you know that?' 'I don't,' she said, 'But, with respect, nor do you.' The obituary goes on to sum up the fairly typical feisty, yet loving relationship between brother and sister. Describing Hardy's customary dandyish posturing in one of his latest beloved Ghillie collar coats, Rosemary was heard to say; 'I don't know why he's showing off so much. He looks perfectly ridiculous.'

A congregation of 250 attended Rosemary's funeral in June 2001, at St Matthew's Church, Langford, which is just a short stroll from The Old School. At this point Hardy was still managing to get around fairly independently, despite needing to use his walking-stick. However, David recalls the moment he entered the church with David on one side of him and Lord Faringdon of Buscot Park on the other.

'Just inside the church door he let all of his weight go, and everyone was wondering whether he was all right,' said David. 'But it was all a performance!' Hardy's sense of theatre and his desire to make a grand entrance were ever at the forefront of his mind. In an affectionate yet barbed aside, perhaps due to slight irritation at his older friend's mischievousness, David went on to reveal: 'Afterwards we held a wake at the barn and we parked him out in the marquee with a whisky!'

Hardy soldiered on after Rosemary's demise with a selection of carers living at The Old School in addition to David, who had contacts within the care industry and who oversaw the help that both siblings received in their final years. According to David, Hardy deteriorated physically once

Rosemary died, but retained his mental faculties. Several villagers were involved in his day-to-day care, with one local man, Patrick, happy to push him around the lanes in his wheelchair. David explains that Hardy never really succumbed to any form of dementia or Alzheimer's, although he became more provocative and cantankerous with age, as many elderly people do.

Sir Roy Strong recalls in his diaries, *Scenes and Apparitions*, that Hardy did, frequently, seem to be pushing the boundaries of propriety during his later years. Speaking of a lunch at a fete in the gardens of the famous horticulturist, Rosemary Verey in 1998, he writes, 'One on from me was Hardy Amies, complaining about everybody and everything. If I live to that age, pray God that I never go that way.'[1]

According to David, Hardy 'had had several TIAs by then and was using a wheelchair,' (Transient Ischaemic Attacks are otherwise known as 'mini-strokes' but do not necessarily lead on to a full stroke). At the time of his death in March 2003, he had been suffering from a cold but did not seem to be in a particularly serious condition, although 'by then he did used to stay in bed a lot.'

'He had a South African carer at the time who was not particularly experienced', remembers David, 'I had gone into Faringdon one day and came back and there was a baby monitor kept in the kitchen and I could hear gasping on it.' David could tell that Sir Hardy was distressed and he decided to call the doctor in the nearby village of Carterton. The doctor went to the house straight away.

'He was having a seizure,' David explains, 'Hardy had given instructions for no intervention.' Taking this into consideration and being satisfied that Hardy was obviously coming to the end of his life, the doctor decided to administer a morphine injection to prevent him being in too much pain.

Hardy calmed down after that, but the situation was obviously terminal, and David was advised not to leave the house for a planned imminent trip back to Wales. 'A friend came around a bit later and we were talking, then she decided to go up to see Hardy at about 1.45 pm.'

David continues, 'It was obvious that he was fading so I went up to sit with him and I talked to him about his garden and things that we'd done together and he died peacefully at 2.20 pm.' Once David had come to terms with what had happened he realised he had to take control of certain practical matters.

There was no press release ready so I decided to phone Phyll Newall. I knew she was a friend of the newsreader Anna Ford, who was by then reading daytime news on BBC radio, and we got in touch with her and she announced it on the 3 o Clock News. I hadn't wanted Hardy to be moved during the day, as then it would have been all round the village, but after the announcement the phone started ringing and that carried on for five days. I was concerned about what to say, but the doctor said, 'I'd describe Hardy's death as 'peaceful'.

Every newspaper carried the story the next day. It was great that, despite his sexuality and all of that, he never had any trouble with the press. They knew he was always good for a quote and would always be open and honest with them.

Neither Hardy nor Rosemary had left any instructions for their own funerals.

Hardy had always said that if he died in London he wanted to be brought back to Langford. And he also said he didn't want a memorial service, but Rosemary and I had told him we didn't think that was a good idea as a lot of his friends who were busy might not be able to come to a funeral in the country. We decided he should have a funeral here and a memorial service in London, which is what we did.

David's planning of both the funeral and the memorial service for his dear friend was exemplary and greatly admired by everyone who attended the events. The funeral address itself took a great deal of organisation, as David could not initially find anyone to take responsibility and step forward to do it.

'I had asked Selina Hastings, then Debo, the Duchess of Devonshire,' David explains. Although the Duchess of Devonshire, formerly Deborah Mitford, declined to read the funeral address she did subsequently read the address at the London memorial service four months later. 'Debo suggested I ask Lady Faringdon, which could have been appropriate as it was Lady Faringdon's mother who introduced Hardy to the queen. However, she couldn't do it and nor could Lord Faringdon.'

David's next request went out to Lord Snowdon, an admirer of Hardy's who had been thrilled to find himself one day lunching at Launceston Place at the same time as the ageing couturier. 'When I passed him in the restaurant he asked me if it was indeed Hardy on the next table, and would I ask him if he would mind if he came and said hello? Hardy was very pleased.'

'Lord Snowdon actually agreed to read the address, but it turned out he would be out of the country, so I asked Roy.' Sir Roy gave a typically acerbic response, according to David: 'He said "Oh, so I'm the last ditch before the vicar!" and I said, "Basically, yes." He said he would think about it until the next day, but he rang me back two minutes later and said he would do it.'

Sir Roy obviously had something of a love/hate relationship with Hardy, summed up when he told me the couturier was 'the master of the *put-down*'. Though in all fairness, Sir Roy was no slacker in that department and is not beyond a scathing remark or two himself. Perhaps that is what made him so capable of interpreting the character of Hardy, in whom he may, in a small way, have recognised a kindred spirit! In his recollections of the occasion of the fiftieth anniversary of the coronation in 2003, he invades Sir Hardy's territory by writing: 'the queen, who stepped out in pale yellow with a better hat than of late.'

At that ceremony and on the same sartorial subject, he comments on other members of the assembled royal family, 'Princess Michael ... wore a ridiculously over-large hat.' and 'the Edward Kents ... she looking quite weird, her face ashen.'

Referring in his diaries to a call he received from Hardy in 1999 after the publication of his book *Spirit of Britain*, he says: 'He wanted to tell me how much he loved the book. What a strange man he is. One minute he's an old bitch and then, quite suddenly, genuinely thoughtful and kind. It made me feel guilty at having been so down on him.'

In Sir Roy's diaries, *Scenes and Apparitions 1988–2003*, he devotes a whole section to Sir Hardy's funeral, calling it 'Farewell to Hardy Amies'.[2] His rather cutting view of the location heralds a perceptive summary of the day. 'Langford is one of those dream Cotswold villages where no peasants exist', it read, 'everyone has a large bank balance and lives in a rose-embowered house or cottage.' Sir Roy does, however, go on to say that 'David Freeman had organised everything perfectly.'

Thus, on 15 March 2003, Sir Hardy's funeral took place in St Matthew's Church, Langford, where the remains of his sister Rosemary, and collaborator and partner Ken Fleetwood are also interred. Ken's funeral had been in London, but his ashes subsequently returned to Langford.

Surprisingly, Sir Hardy, the great arbiter of dressing, had left no instructions about what clothing he should be buried in. David chose a suit for him and the cloth it was made from was, significantly, supplied by the Cotswold Woollen weavers in Langford's neighbouring village, the quaintly named Filkins, of whom Richard Martin is director.

A rug with an embroidery by Hardy of several of his favourite flowers was sent to Savile Row to be backed with cloth in order to make it an appropriate weight to be placed over the coffin. On top of this was Hardy's KCVO award on a cushion surrounded by sprays of the flowers he loved. Inside the coffin had been placed two sprigs of rosemary, one plucked from his own garden and the other from his sister Rosemary's garden down the road in Langford.

The funeral was a simple, traditional English country ceremony with a choir, readings, and communal hymns. The church was packed and a gathering of press reporters and photographers was outside. Ian Garlant, at that point the head of menswear at the couture house, read out a piece that Hardy had been asked to write for the magazine *World of Interiors*, which described The Old School and Hardy's rural idyll in Langford, but as David reveals: 'Rupert Thomas, the boyfriend of Alan Bennett, the playwright, asked Hardy to contribute a piece for a series of features about famous people and their favourite places.' This was in 2002 however, when Hardy was already 92 years of age. 'I offered to write it in Hardy's style and then get his approval, which I did.'

Referring to the piece of needlepoint which adorned the coffin, Hardy (via David) had written: 'The rug is one of my favourite pieces of needlepoint. I made it for my bedroom in my flat in Cornwall Gardens. It depicts my favourite flowers; among them auriculas, hellebores, Rosa mundi, tobacco and tulips.'

The article was read out at both the funeral and the memorial service and was described by Sir Roy as 'charming'. Sir Roy then gave his address and 'made them laugh, for he was a wonder and a wicked old thing. He ended up a country gent in mock Jacobean and made his exit via the parish church.'

Sir Roy also raised the humour quotient with his riposte to Hardy's old friend, the writer, television producer, and critic Derek Granger, when he asked him whether Hardy had ever visited Sir Roy's renowned garden at The Laskett in Herefordshire. 'Yes, he did,' Sir Roy replied. 'He was wickedly scathing about it. He described it as *Mr Pooter Goes to Versailles*, but I never cared. When I left, I gave it to the Royal Perennial Fund for Gardeners, as it was recognised as being so important.' The Versailles comment was credited to Hardy but, according to David, was not actually a 'Hardyism'.

'It was originally said by John Harris, the architectural historian,' David explained. Harris had been a co-curator of *The Destruction of the Country House* exhibition in 1974, alongside Sir Roy, but the memorable quote has become part of the legend of Hardy's critical epithets among the distinguished circles he moved in during the ensuing years.

The memorial service for Sir Hardy was held at St James's Church, Piccadilly in London on what would have been his 94th birthday, 17 July 2003. This was to be a much grander affair, once again curated to perfection by his loyal stalwart, David Freeman. The total cost was around £10.000, with attention to detail being paramount.

One of the major feats David pulled off was to get the choir of Magdalen College, Oxford, to come together out of term time to sing at the service. 'They all agreed to do it and I bussed the whole choir up to London,' he recalls. David particularly wanted one of Hardy's favourite Schubert sonatas to be played by a soloist: 'I rang a musician I know in Wales and he recommended a Japanese final year student at the Royal Welsh College of Music and Drama. He told me she would only be able to play the first movement, but that was all I wanted, so it was fine,' he explained. The student, Miyuki Kato, was apparently delighted, and said her parents would be thrilled as the Hardy Amies name was still well known and 'big' in Japan!

The service was attended by a congregation of several hundred, ranging from members of Hardy's staff to the aristocracy. Hardy's friend Lady Selina Hastings gave the eulogy, and also in attendance were Mrs Pamela Powell, the widow of the MP Enoch Powell, whom Hardy had met during his military service; Lord Hurd the former foreign secretary and his wife Judy, who were Oxfordshire neighbours; the Duchess of Devonshire, who read the address; and the writer and television producer Derek Granger, who, with his partner Kenneth Partridge, had been a frequent guest at Langford. Another guest, whom David remembers turning up in an eye-catching white suit, was Phillip Vigo Norman, a maverick character who had lived an itinerant life since being let go from his position of design consultant at the Garden and Horticulture Museum. He had since been working occasionally on a freelance basis but spent a great deal of his time volunteering at the London Lighthouse, a hospice for AIDS patients in the capital. He was a source of great comfort to Ken Fleetwood when he was dying as, according to David, he visited him there very frequently, often spending all night at his bedside. This was at a time when, such was the culture of fear and ignorance surrounding AIDS, even family members were unable to visit their dying loved ones. David strongly encouraged Hardy to remember Phillip in his will and this he duly did, leaving Phillip a £1,000 bequest.

Her Majesty the Queen was represented at the memorial service by Lord Faringdon, and Princess Michael of Kent by Emma, Lady Fellowes, the wife of the Downton Abbey writer, Julian Fellowes. Princess Michael had been a customer of Hardy, and was pictured in a photograph by Norman Parkinson in *Still Here*, wearing a pale lilac ball gown. Interestingly, according to Nicholas Worth, the princess and Hardy spoke to each other in German and she told Nicholas that Hardy's German 'was perfect'.

The order of service for the memorial was beautifully printed on ivory parchment which David had chosen to be bound with the same white satin ribbon that Hardy Amies clothing parcels had been fastened with at Savile Row. This was of course the same ribbon that Hardy had designed in his suite at the Hyde Park Hotel half a century previously, when he was formulating the dream of his own company.

The wording in the order of service was printed in the same style of font as the name on the ribbon and there were quotes and well-remembered sayings by Hardy throughout the document. His cypher, used as his bookplate, and self-penned motto: 'Less than art, more than trade' appear on the back and inside front covers respectively and the text of Sir Roy Strong's address from the Langford funeral is printed in full. The final paragraph contains these words: 'Let us give thanks today for all the creativity, wit, delight and service which he gave not only to his sovereign but to so many others…'

Selina Hasting's eulogy, reproduced in the book *Well-remembered Friends* by Angela Huth, contained many reminiscences which would have caused mirth among the congregation. 'The first time he came to dinner at my house he looked round my kitchen/dining room and said with a kindly smile, "It's so *amusing* how people live nowadays, I find!"', was one such memory.[3]

Today, David lives in the stately Old School in Langford, which of course, contains a most tasteful kitchen! To visit is to feel the presence of the previous inhabitant and his enormous strength of character. The furnishings are much the same, and pride of place in the sitting room is taken by the portrait of the much-loved Alexis ffrench, which adorns the cover of Hardy's book, *The Englishman's Suit*. The atmosphere is one of faded grandeur, but ultimately of a greatly loved home rather than a mausoleum. At the time of writing David has a little dachshund, Treacle, a breed of which Hardy owned many examples in his lifetime.

The garden, still in the formal Tudor knot-garden style, is striking with its background of well-established mature cottage garden roses. Small in scale, like the house itself in comparison to some of its neighbours, it is nonetheless impressive, representing as it does, the good taste and sense of style of the man who created it.

David is a mainstay of the Langford community and on Queen Elizabeth's platinum jubilee in 2022 he mounted a small exhibition in tribute to Hardy and his connection to the monarch in the spacious front window of a nearby house. The display of memorabilia and appropriate photographs of the queen in Hardy's clothes was just a small collection of Hardy's possessions from over the years, which David has managed to retain through all the ups and downs of the company since Hardy's demise. No doubt the departed couturier and patriarch would have looked down favourably on the gathering his heir held to mark the seventieth year of Her Majesty's reign, which was sadly followed by her death that September.

Villagers and friends milled around the house and garden and were presented with printed sheets of the words of the full National Anthem, which was then rousingly sung after an entertaining speech by David, recounting some of Sir Hardy's more memorable moments. The party invitation card was a fitting tribute with a stunning photograph of Her Majesty in a Hardy Amies dress with the famous classical lettering which had been the corporate style for all those years. In a tongue in cheek gesture, David had erected a sign in the adjacent field, which was used for car parking, pointing towards the house with the words 'The Queen's Party'. A *double entendre* which would have undoubtedly met with the sparklingly witty and charismatic couturier's total approval.

The Company's Demise and Hardy's Legacy

After being sold in 2001 and subsequently for a second time in 2008, Hardy Amies Ltd seemed to lose its way, and for many reasons the highly respected name and heritage of skilled tailoring that was synonymous with the label was dissipated.

Cardingtons, which became The Luxury Brands Group, took the business forward but are not considered to have honoured Hardy's legacy by those closest to him. David Freeman, who initiated the return of the Royal Warrant, describes the company as 'spendthrift, inexperienced and incompetent. After Hardy died the business went belly up.'

Nicholas Worth notes that: 'After the sale the people who were in charge initially did not know what they were doing and a lot of money was wasted. When I saw the collection they produced I thought it was hideous and I wasn't impressed at all.'

Chris Stratmann remembers a technique used by the new operation which was highly questionable in terms of keeping costs down in the company:

When Hardy designed ready-to-wear, the instruction was to only ever sew in a label at the top of the garment. The new people were as stupid as anything as they had all the clothes lined in Hardy Amies printed lining.

The point of Hardy's instruction was so that the label could be removed if the garment didn't sell well, and then it would be sold on to a man in Petticoat Lane who would buy things for cost and sell them himself. If they had the full Hardy Amies lining in them, he couldn't do that, so you wouldn't make any money back on them.'

Obviously not as astute as one would expect a high-end fashion operation to be, the business did not thrive under the new ownership and, after being sold on again in 2018, went into administration for the second time. The label is now owned by the Australian brand Austico, and a small collection of formal menswear is sold online and through outlets such as the iconic Sydney department store David Jones.

Hardy first visited Sydney in 1959, so it is interesting to reflect over sixty years later, how Hardy would have felt about his eponymous label living on in that setting. In *Still Here*, he writes: 'Sydney Harbour is one of the most beautiful sights in the world and it is always a pleasure to go there.' He also states that the story of the David Jones department store is 'the story of Sydney itself', going on to say that 'The 'Queen of Sydney' at the time was Lady Lloyd-Jones, the widow of the son of the store's founder.'[4]

It would no doubt be a source of great comfort and self-satisfaction to him to know that clothing bearing his name was to this day being offered in a setting he described at the time as having 'the vitality and range of products of any great shop which dominates a city. Nothing of quality was ever missed.'

Those words are perhaps a fitting legacy for a man of taste and a designer of such great talent.

Notes

Introduction
1. H. Amies, *Just So Far*, p.140.
2. Ibid, p.21.

Part One: The Early Years
Chapter 1. The Making of a Maverick
1. H. Amies, *Still Here*, p.5.
2. H. Amies, *Just So Far*, p.21.
3. Ibid, p.23.

Chapter 3. Hardy Spreads his Wings
1. Ibid, p.34.
2. H. Amies, *Still Here*, p.14.
3. Ibid, p.16
4. C. Bryant, *Glamour Boys*, p.55.
5. Ibid, p.52.

Chapter 4. Rumblings of War and a Foot in Couture
1. H. Amies, *Just So Far*, p.52.
2. H. Amies, *The Englishman's Suit*, p.27.
3. Ibid.
4. H. Amies, *Still Here*, p.27.

Part Two: Wartime Service
Chapter 5. A Singular Soldier
1. H. Amies, *Just So Far*, p.72.
2. H. Amies, *Still Here*, p.31.
3. Ibid.

Chapter 6. The Designer Diversifies

1. H. Amies, *Just So Far*, p.73.
2. H. Amies, *Still Here*, p.32.
3. Ibid.
4. *Mail on Sunday*, 16 March 2003 'A Very Peculiar Couple'.
5. H. Amies, *Just So Far*, p.78.
6. H. Vickers, *Malice in Wonderland*, p.28.

Chapter 7. Setting Europe Ablaze

1. P. Howarth, *Undercover*, p.139.
2. H. Amies, *Just So Far*, p.83.

Chapter 8. Serving King and Country

1. Ibid, p.78.
2. J. Summers, *Fashion on the Ration*, p.58.
3. Ibid, p.104.
4. Ibid.
5. A. Huth, *Well-Remembered Friends*, p.445.

Chapter 9. Throwing Himself into the SOE

1. S. Bourne, *Fighting Proud*, p.185.
2. P. Howarth, *Undercover, Stories of The SOE*, p.3.

Chapter 11. Fighting with Pride and Panache

1. J. Summers, *Fashion on the Ration*, p.94.
2. Ibid, p.102.
3. N. Attallah, *Of A Certain Age*, p.14.

Part Three: Business Begins
Chapter 12. Settling into Savile Row

1. Ibid, p.4.
2. G. Spanier, *It Isn't All Mink*, p.218.
3. Ibid.
4. H. Amies, *Still Here*, p.162.
5. H. Amies, *Just So Far*, p.124.

Chapter 13. Establishing the House of Hardy

1. Ibid, p.135.
2. H. Amies, *Still Here*, p.174.
3. G. Spanier, *It Isn't All Mink*, p.219.

Chapter 14. Management and Expansion

1. H. Amies, *Just So Far*, p.165.
2. Ibid, p.129.

Chapter 15. The Queen is Here!

1. H. Amies, *Still Here*, p.84.
2. J. Summers, *Fashion on the Ration*, p.178.
3. H. Amies, *Just So Far*, p.249.
4. S. Bradford, *Elizabeth*, p.165.
5. H. Amies, *Just So Far*, p.241.
6. G. Brandreth, *Philip & Elizabeth*, p.207.
7. A. Glenconner, *Lady In Waiting*, p.62.
8. Ibid, p.69.
9. H. Amies, *Just So Far*, p.256.

Chapter 16. More Than Friends

1. H. Amies, *Still Here*, p.171.
2. Ibid, p.147.

Chapter 17. A Very Special Relationship

1. R. Strong, *Scenes And Apparitions The Roy Strong Diaries 1988–2003*, p.417.
2. G. Brandreth, *Philip & Elizabeth*, p.82.
3. H. Amies, *Still Here*, p.110.
4. M. Pick, *Hardy Amies*, p.163.
5. Ibid, p.181.
6. N. Attallah, *Of A Certain Age*, p.16.

Part Four: People
Chapter 18. Changing Faces

1. H. Amies, *Still Here*, p.78.

Chapter 19. A Sibling Bond

1. Ibid, p.175

Chapter 20. Friends in Foreign Places

1. Ibid, p.126
2. M. Pick, *Hardy Amies*, p.236.

Chapter 21. The Silver Screen and More

1. C. Mosley, The Mitfords: Letters Between Six Sisters, p.316.

Chapter 22. A Living Label

1. H. Amies, *Still Here*, p.67.

Chapter 24. Collaborations

1. Ibid, p.161.
2. M. Pick, *Hardy Amies*, p.282.

Part Five: Coming to a Close

Chapter 25. The House in its Later Years

1. N. Attallah, *Of A Certain Age*, p.9.
2. H. Amies, *ABC of Men's Fashion*, Frontispiece
3. M. Pick, *Hardy Amies*, p.216.
4. R. Strong, *Scenes And Apparitions The Roy Strong Diaries 1988 2003*, p.416.

Chapter 26. The Final Years of Hardy Amies – The Man and The Brand

1. Ibid, p.261.
2. Ibid, p.415.
3. A. Huth, *Well-Remembered Friends*, p.443.
4. H. Amies, *Still Here*, p.130.

Bibliography

Allport, Alan, *Demobbed: Coming Home After World War Two* (Yale University Press, 2009)

Amies, Hardy, *Just So Far* (Collins, 1954)

Amies, Hardy, *Still Here* (Weidenfeld and Nicolson, 1984)

Amies, Hardy, *The ABC of Men's Fashion* (V & A Publishing, 1964)

Amies, Hardy, *The Englishman's Suit* (Quartet Books, 1994)

Attallah, Naim, *Of a Certain Age* (Quartet Books, 1992)

Bolitho, Hector, *A Penguin in the Eyrie: An RAF Diary* (Hutchinson, 1955)

Bourne, Stephen, *Fighting Proud* (Bloomsbury Academic, 2017)

Boyd, Julia, *Travellers in the Third Reich* (Elliott & Thompson Ltd, 2018)

Bradford, Sarah, *Elizabeth* (BCA (William Heinemann), 1996)

Brandreth, Gyles, *Philip and Elizabeth* (Century, 2004)

Brown, Craig, *Ma'am Darling* (Harper Collins, 2017)

Bryant, Chris, *The Glamour Boys* (Bloomsbury, 2020)

Buckton, Henry, *Artists and Authors at War* (Leo Cooper, 1999)

Burke, Carolyn, *Lee Miller – A Life* (Bloomsbury, 2005)

De Courcy, Anne, *1939 – The Last Season* (Thames & Hudson, 1989)

Dennison, Matthew, *The Queen* (Head of Zeus, 2021)

Glenconner, Lady Anne, *Lady in Waiting* (Hodder & Stoughton, 2019)

Hicks, David, *Cotswold Gardens* (Weidenfeld & Nicolson, 1995)

Hoey, Brian, *At Home with the Queen* (Harper Collins, 2002)

Howarth, Patrick, *Undercover* (Routledge & Kegan Paul, 1980)

Howell, Georgina, *Vogue Women* (Pavilion, 2000)

Huth, Angela, *Well-Remembered Friends* (John Murray, 2004)

Levin, Angela, *Camilla: From Outcast to Future Queen Consort* (Simon & Schuster, 2022)

MacMillan, Margaret, *War: How Conflict Shaped Us* (Profile Books, 2021)

McDowell, Colin, *Forties Fashion and the New Look* (Bloomsbury, 1997)

Morrow, Ann, *The Queen* (Granada Publishing 1983)

Mosley, Charlotte, *The Mitfords: Letters Between Six Sisters* (Harper Collins, 2007)

Palmer, Alexandra, *Dior: A New Look. A New Enterprise* (V&A Publishing, 2009)

Purnell, Sonia, *A Woman of No Importance, the Untold Story of Virginia Hall* (Virago, 2019)

Richardson, Lance, *The House of Nutter, the Rebel Tailor of Savile Row* (Penguin, 2018)

Strong, Sir Roy, *Scenes and Apparitions, Diaries 1988 - 2003* (Wiedenfeld & Nicolson, 2016)

Summers, Julie, *Dressed for War* (Simon & Schuster, 2020)

Summers, Julie, *Fashion on the Ration* (Profile Books, 2015)

Vickers, Hugo, *Malice in Wonderland* (Hodder & Stoughton, 2021)

Vogue Magazine, (Conde Nast Publications, London)

Walker, Alexander, *Vivien* (Weidenfeld & Nicolson, 1987)

Glhsonline.org: The Gay and Lesbian History on Stamps

Index